COLLEGE IN CRISIS

COLLEGE IN CRISIS

A Report to the National Commission on the Causes and Prevention of Violence

WILLIAM H. ORRICK, JR.,
DIRECTOR, SAN FRANCISCO STATE COLLEGE
STUDY TEAM

AURORA PUBLISHERS INCORPORATED
Nashville/London
1970

NASHVILLE, TENNESSEE 37219
LIBRARY OF CONGRESS CATALOG CARD NUMBER: 74-114772
STANDARD BOOK NUMBER: 87695-007-1
MANUFACTURED IN THE UNITED STATES OF AMERICA

CONTENTS

PART II

PREFACE

If we were dealing with hunger instead of education, you can imagine what would happen if we had a walled city in which the citizens had all the food they needed while outside there were hordes of starving people. We could not open the gates just a little to admit handfuls of the starving and expect the rest to remain patient outside.

No.

We would have to be prepared to open the gates wide and to admit everyone, or be prepared for a riot. That is the situation now with higher education.

We have opened the doors just a little with special programs that serve hundreds while thousands are clamoring for education. I believe we should open the gates fully, even at an enormous expense, to provide educational opportunity at every level–high schools, adult schools, junior colleges, State colleges and universities–for our entire minority and poor populations. We should mobilize the best brains available, just as we did when the nation attacked the problems of modern science, to solve an educational crisis that means as much to our national welfare as our efforts in outer space.

It is not easy at this point to predict the course of events on our campus or elsewhere. I feel that the danger to the Nation and to higher education has been vastly underestimated by a majority of people. Most of the news and much of the commentary deals with the action rather than the underlying causes of dissent and the methods to correct obvious ills.

If we are to end campus rebellion without destroying the educational institutions, we must redirect our energy. We must look beyond the day-to-day combat to the reasons underlying this deadly attack on higher education. We must learn to deal both with the dedicated revolutionary leaders and the unsolved problems that help them enlist followers. The solution to these problems will take time, brains, and money. This nation is amply endowed with those resources. But we must act promptly and decisively.

S. I. Hayakawa

INTRODUCTION

This report of the San Francisco State College Study Team concerning the San Francisco State College strike was prepared under my direction at the request of the National Commission on the Causes and Prevention of Violence. It is largely the product of three highly trained, exceptionally gifted writers and fact gatherers: James Brann, Michael Parker, and Austin Scott. These men wrote most of the report from information obtained by them from examination of pertinent records, interviews, and on-the-spot observation.

The report draws no conclusions from the tragic events that overtook San Francisco State in the fall and winter of 1968-69. It was conceived and executed, except for the comments in chapter VII entitled "Outlook for the Future," as a history of one of the most distressing episodes in American higher education.

More than 400 individual interviews were made by teams of trained interviewers directed by Messrs. Brann, Parker, and Scott. These interviews included State College trustees, administrators, legislators, law enforcement personnel, community leaders, public officials, faculty members, and students in the San Francisco Bay Area, Los Angeles, and in Sacramento.

Over 1,200 newspaper articles were accumulated and studied (newspaper articles have not been used as sole sources of information in this report except where specifically so indicated); the photographic files of San Francisco's two daily newspapers were reviewed; and many days were spent on the campus viewing the actual physical confrontation.

In this undertaking, the team received the fullest cooperation from the Governor of California, the mayor of San Francisco, the Federal Bureau of Investigation, the San Francisco Police Department, the chancellor of the State college systems, the trustees of the California State colleges, the acting president of San Francisco State College, the academic deans, other faculty members, legislators, public officials, and many student leaders and interested persons in the community.

The report could not have been compiled without the very useful and imaginative work of the Team's administrative officer, Mrs. Janet Brune, and the full-time assistance of researchers Bruce Pollock, Douglas Haydel, Robert Young, and William Zeidler.

Finally, I am grateful to Jack Abbott and the able staff of the Commission, including particularly Messrs. James Campbell, William McDonald, Joseph Laitin, and Ronald Wolk, for their help and valuable counsel.

William H. Orrick, Jr.
Director, San Francisco State College Study Team

May 15, 1969

COLLEGE IN CRISIS

"Words changed their ordinary meanings and were construed in new senses. Reckless daring passed for the courage of a loyal partisan, far-sighted hesitation was the excuse of a coward, moderation was the pretext of the unmanly, the power to see all sides of a question was complete inability to act. Impulsive rashness was held the mark of a man, caution in conspiracy was a specious excuse for avoiding action. A violent attitude was always to be trusted, its opponents were suspect. . . . So civil war gave birth to every kind of iniquity in the Greek world. Simplicity, the chief ingredient in a noble nature, was ridiculed and disappeared, and society was divided into rival camps in which no man trusted his fellow."

—Thucydides, *History of the Peloponnesian War* [discussion of the social revolution at Corcyra], 417 B.C.

PART I

Chapter I

WHY SAN FRANCISCO STATE COLLEGE?

Late in the afternoon of November 5, 1968, a group of black students presented San Francisco State College President Robert R. Smith with a list of 10 "nonnegotiable" demands (the demands are listed in app. 1). The list had already been published in the daily newspapers. Among other things, the black students ordered the college to establish at once a black studies department with 20 full-time faculty members. They insisted that the new department be controlled by its faculty and staff, free from interference by college administrators or the statewide Board of Trustees.

The students also demanded that the college accept all Negroes who apply for admission in the fall of 1969 without regard to the academic qualifications of the applicants. And they insisted that Black Panther minister of education, George Mason Murray, 22, a graduate student, be reinstated as part-time English instructor. Murray had inflamed California's political leadership and the board of trustees with speeches in which he described the American flag as "toilet paper" and said that black students should carry guns on campus to protect themselves from "racist administrators." Under orders from State College Chancellor Glenn S. Dumke, President Smith had reluctantly suspended Murray on November 1.

Unwilling to agree to all of the students' demands, President Smith offered to discuss them with the black students. They refused, insisting on a yes-or-no answer.

On November 6, the black students, their demands unmet, launched a strike against San Francisco State College. A week later, 65 faculty members joined the students on the picket lines.

In the following weeks, San Francisco State College was the scene of violence unmatched in the history of American higher education. The campus became the first to be occupied by police on a continuous basis over several months, and it was only the daily presence of 200 to 600 policemen which kept the college open from the start of the strike on November 6 to the end of the fall semester. Even so, the campus had to be closed on three occasions during late 1968. (A comment on the police is contained in app. 2.)

By the end of the semester on January 31, 1969, there had been 731 arrests on campus; more than 80 students were reported injured as they were arrested, and others were hurt and not arrested. Thirty-two policemen were injured on the campus. Damage to campus buildings exceeded $16,000; there were scores of small fires and a major one in a vice president's office. Eight bombs were planted on campus, and two firebombs were hurled at and into

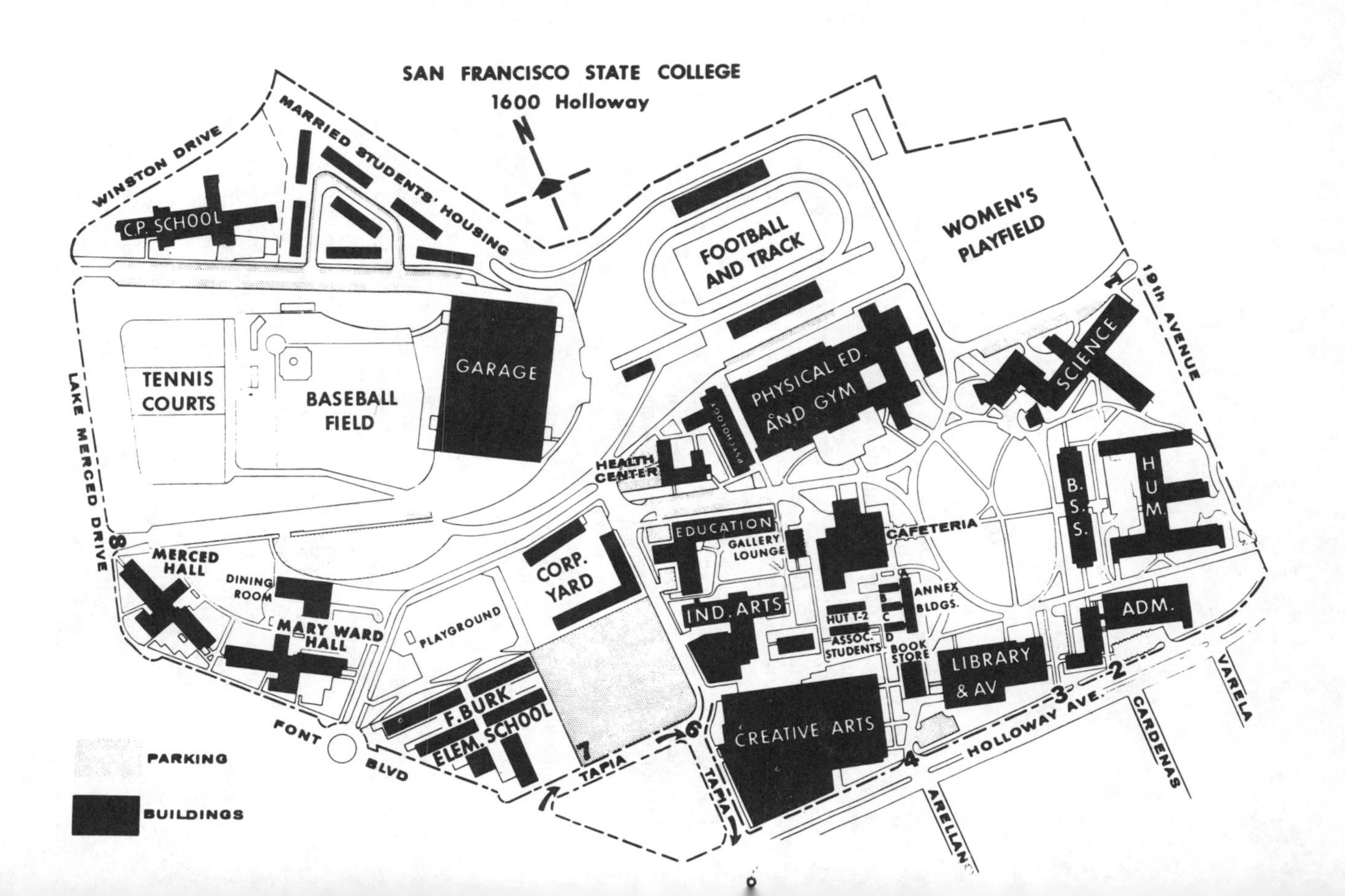
SAN FRANCISCO STATE COLLEGE
1600 Holloway
N
WINSTON DRIVE
MARRIED STUDENTS' HOUSING
C.P. SCHOOL
FOOTBALL AND TRACK
WOMEN'S PLAYFIELD
19th AVENUE
1
SCIENCE
PHYSICAL ED. AND GYM
PSYCHOLOGY
GARAGE
TENNIS COURTS
BASEBALL FIELD
HEALTH CENTER
B. S. S.
H U M.
CAFETERIA
EDUCATION
GALLERY LOUNGE
ANNEX BLDGS.
A
B
C
D
HUT T-2
ASSOC. STUDENTS
BOOK STORE
IND. ARTS
ADM.
LIBRARY & AV
LAKE MERCED DRIVE
8
MERCED HALL
DINING ROOM
MARY WARD HALL
CORP. YARD
PLAYGROUND
F. BURK ELEM. SCHOOL
CREATIVE ARTS
2
3
4
6
7
HOLLOWAY AVE.
VARELA
CARDENAS
ARELLANO
TAPIA
FONT BLVD
PARKING
BUILDINGS

the home of an assistant to the president. In mid-February, a campus guard received head injuries from a bomb that exploded at the entrance to the administration building. Three weeks later, on March 5, 1969, a 19-year-old Negro sophomore in social sciences was partially blinded and maimed when a time bomb—which police said he was installing—exploded in the Creative Arts Building. Ordnance specialists discovered two other bombs, one of them with six sticks of dynamite, in a nearby room.

But why did all this happen at San Francisco State College? San Francisco State was and is one of the most liberal institutions in this country in terms of active student participation in the administration of the affairs of the college. For example, the students controlled a budget on the order of $400,000 per year, established the first experimental college, participated in the administration of the college through student government, and enjoyed more freedom than most other college students. The administration, far from being rigid, was very flexible. Although during the 2 years preceding the strike the San Francisco State campus had been disrupted on numerous occasions by protesting and demonstrating students, these events generally, like those on other campuses, were episodes involving an issue, such as antiwar protest, or a specific campus problem.

Why, then, did the San Francisco State College strike become the first sustained assault on an institution by its students, embroiling, as it did, not only the faculty, administrators, trustees, students, and alumni, but also political leaders of the city and the State, and the off-campus community?

This report addresses itself to answering this question, and in so doing provides insights into some of the causes of the ever-growing campus protests in the United States. It focuses on the underlying reasons for the strike as they emerge from a description of the educational system and the attitudes of those involved. It presents, as objectively as possible, the attitudes of some representatives of the various groups which were embroiled in the controversy.

The first part of the report (chs. I-V) describes the California system of higher education and San Francisco State College, the conditions which obtained there prior to the strike, and the strike. Because the student strike leadership was centered in the Black Student Union, the second part of the report (ch. VI) deals with the black community and some of the reasons underlying the actions of the black student strike leaders. This is followed by a brief comment on the outlook for the future (ch. VII) and appendices containing a list of the demands (app. 1), a comment on the police (app. 2), a list of the trustees of the California State colleges (app. 3), and a summary of the proposed Black Studies Program (app. 4).

We begin with a description of San Francisco State College.

Chapter II

WHAT IS SAN FRANCISCO STATE COLLEGE?

Barron's *Profiles of American Universities and Colleges* describes San Francisco State as follows:

> San Francisco State College, established in 1889, is a publicly-supported liberal arts college occupying a 94-acre campus within San Francisco. It has a faculty of 664 members, 479 of whom hold doctorates. It has a library containing 355,000 volumes and 2,500 periodicals. It serves a student body drawn mainly from California but 6% of the students come from other places.
>
> In addition to its program in the liberal arts, the College offers students who have finished 2 to 4 years of liberal arts work, a complete junior and senior program of training as elementary school teachers. This program is carried on at the Santa Rosa Center. The College also has off-campus centers at Hamilton Field Air Base and at the Presidio of San Francisco for service personnel seeking B.A. degrees. . . .
>
> The College has a plant valued at over $18 million. Its facilities include dormitory accommodations for 400 men and 400 women and institutional apartments for 72 married couples. Among its notable buildings is its Creative Arts Building which has facilities for teaching radio and television, an 1,800-seat auditorium equipped with stereophonic sound and an elevator orchestra pit, a little theatre with a stage capable of containing five wagon sets, and a theater-in-the-round.
>
> The majority of the students are commuters, with only 3% housed in the campus dormitory. About 3% of the students are members of Greek letter organizations but these do not provide housing. Honor students on this campus may become eligible for membership in Sigma Xi, and numerous departmental national honorary groups.
>
> Athletic activities are varsity football, basketball, baseball, track, swimming, water polo, soccer, cross-country, fencing, wrestling, tennis and golf.
>
> Of the entering classes, 18% drop out at the end of the first year and 33% remain to graduate.
>
> Religious organizations are available to students of all major faiths.
>
> The College operates on the semester basis and offers a summer session. It is accredited by the Western Assoc., the American Chemical Society, and the National League for Nursing.
>
> *Programs of Study:* The College confers the degrees of B.A., B.S., B. Voc. Ed., and B.E. Major fields of concentration are Anthropology,

American Studies, Bacteriology, Biology, Botany, Business Administration, Classics, Chemistry, Comparative Education, Comparative Literature, Dramatic Arts, Engineering, Economics, English, Fine Arts, Geography, Government, History, Home Economics, Industrial Arts, Journalism, Language and Area Studies, Literature, Mathematics, Music, Nursing, Philosophy, Psychology, Physics, Romance Languages, Sociology, Speech, Speech Pathology, Social Work, Special Education, Statistics, Elementary Education, Secondary Education, Higher Education, and Zoology. Juniors are permitted to study abroad.

> *Expenses:* There is no tuition for state residents; fees are approximately $120 yearly; out-of-state students pay an additional $720. Room and board are $880.
>
> Aid is limited but loans are available from the federal government, local banks, the College, and private funds. The average amount of aid from loans is $600 and the maximum, combined with campus employment, is $1,500.
>
> *Admissions:* . . . It is to the student's advantage to be able to present advanced placement or honor courses, and it is most important that records be accompanied by recommendations from the high school authorities. Other considerations are personal impressions, extracurricular activities, and leadership potential.

To call San Francisco State a college is misleading for it is much more like a university, with its 18,000 students, 63 types of bachelor's degree, 44 master's degree programs, and doctorates in education.

For several years in the mid-1960's it appeared that San Francisco State's administrators, students, and faculty had discovered the formula for campus peace. Neither the 1964 nor the 1966 disturbances at Berkeley had spread across the Bay to San Francisco State. During the 1966 troubles at Berkeley, San Francisco State students had helped militants at the university prepare press releases, but when asked by a reporter at the time if the revolt might spread to San Francisco State, a student replied: "No. Why should it? We have free speech, and we're treated like adults."

Many of the college's students *are* adults; the average age is 25 years. Moreover, San Francisco State is a trolley-car college, serving thousands of older students who pursue their studies while working full time off campus.

In the fall of 1961, long before the turmoil at Berkeley and long before other campuses worried about student rights, San Francisco State adopted a policy statement for dealing with students. A key paragraph read:

> At San Francisco State College, students are respected as adults and citizens of the community and, as such, have all the rights and responsibilities of adults and citizens to participate in college and community affairs. These rights and responsibilities are to be jealously guarded and fulfilled.

This was no idle promise. The student government at San Francisco State has long had control of large budgets derived from student fees. The money has gone to support athletic programs, student newspapers, theater groups, ghetto tutorial programs, an experimental college, the Black Student Union, or whatever else students chose. The Associated Students of San Francisco

State College, Inc., controlled a budget of $482,771 in 1966-67; the budget totaled $501,096 in 1967-68, and in the current year it is well over $400,000.

When other colleges were preventing students from inviting controversial figures to speak on campus, San Francisco State students heard such persons as Communist theoretician Herbert Aptheker and American Nazi Party leader George Lincoln Rockwell.

The college reflects the city in which it lives. San Francisco is recognized as a national example of urbanity; it is a geographically compact, freeswinging town with a polyglot population including substantial black, Oriental, and Spanish-speaking communities. The college is also cosmopolitan, with students from all minorities and all classes. It is squeezed into an area adequate for an institution a fourth of its size. Although it nestles in the midst of a white middle-class neighborhood, the campus is a few minutes away from three of the city's poorest neighborhoods.

San Francisco State has long been a forerunner in educational innovation and student trends. The Nation's first successful experimental college (where students design courses and teach other students) was founded there in 1965. Today, more than 400 other campuses have similar experimental colleges. The first Black Student Union (BSU) in the country was born at San Francisco State in March 1966, and it evolved from the Negro Students Association, chartered in 1963. The Third World Liberation Front—an amalgamation of Latin-American, Mexican-American, Negro, Asian-American, Chinese, and Filipino student groups—also began there in 1968.

The college moved faster than any other institution in beginning black studies courses and in accepting the ideal of a black studies department. Despite tight budgets and active disapproval of some trustees and politicans, the administration endorsed and encouraged students to develop the experimental college which attracted the attention of foundation and Government officials. This and other student-run, student-financed programs received national publicity a few years ago as examples of what responsible student government could produce.

Thus it is understandable that the position of San Francisco State's administrators in the fall of 1968 was one of puzzlement, frustration, and anger. They had moved faster than any other college or university in beginning black studies courses and in accepting the idea of a black studies department. They had endorsed and given encouragement to the student-founded experimental college and related programs well ahead of other institutions of higher learning. And they had done this in an era of tight budgets and what they regarded as unwarranted interference from the governing Board of Trustees and the State's political leaders.

The students see themselves as noble people fighting battles to uplift the nonwhite races and promote reforms or revolution that will produce a better way of life. Officials who slow down or interfere with this process are branded enemies of the people.

The administrators of San Francisco State College do not, of course, view themselves as enemies of the people. Nor do they consider themselves reactionary gatekeepers of the Establishment. Quite the contrary. They point out (accurately) that the college has been in the forefront of change.

Students across the Nation are now agitating to convert their own institution into the kind of college that San Francisco State was, in large measure, between 1960 and 1966.

Nov. 20, 1968: San Francisco Mayor Alioto attempts to speak to a group of jeering students at San Francisco State College as he leaves the office of College President Robert Smith. AP photograph

Dec. 4: As police move in, an estimated 1,000 strike demonstrators retreat from the San Francisco State campus. The students had been attending a two-hour rally when they were warned to leave or face arrest. The day before, the campus was the scene of a wild melee in which police used nightsticks on the demonstrators, some of whom had thrown stones at the police. AP photograph

Dec. 5: The Reverend Claire Nesmith is grabbed by the lapels by a policeman as Nesmith and others were placed under arrest during demonstrations on the campus. The Reverend Jerry Pedersen (left), a Lutheran minister, was also arrested. AP photograph

Dec. 2: Dr. S. I. Hayakawa, the newly appointed acting president of the College, yanks wires from loudspeakers on top of a sound truck on the campus. Hayakawa ordered classes resumed after four weeks of turmoil and the interruption of classes at San Francisco State. He had just ordered the sound truck off the campus. Students jostled Hayakawa after the incident, but he was not injured. AP photograph

Dec. 2: Dr. Hayakawa tells students that he meant what he said when he ordered loudspeakers and other sound equipment off the San Francisco State campus. He has just pulled the wires from this speaker; repairs could not be made. AP photograph

Dec. 2: Hayakawa faces up to a dissident objector on the picket line at San Francisco State. AP photograph

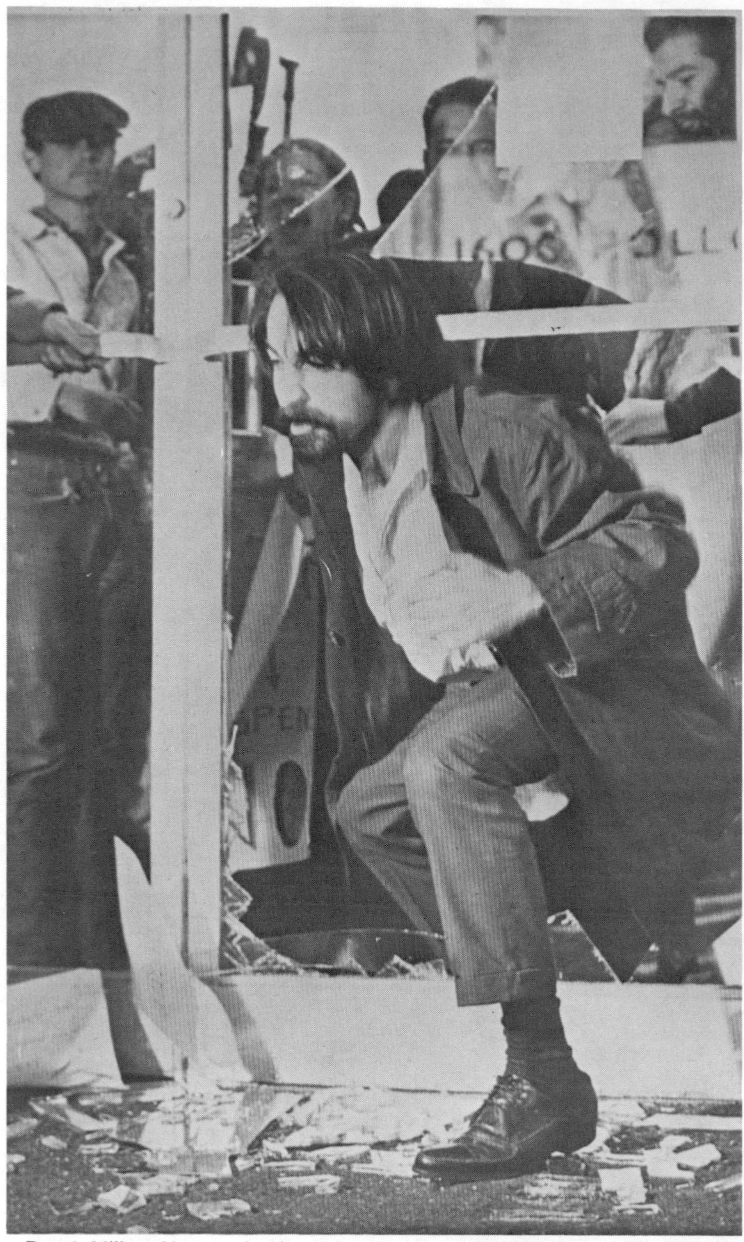

Dec. 6: Militant Negro and white students break into the Administration building. The purpose of the demonstration was to obtain reinstatement of four Negro students who had been suspended. AP photograph

Dec. 9: Dr. Hayakawa inspects the damage in a fire which swept through the office of San Francisco State College Vice President, Glenn Smith. AP photograph

Dec. 9: Mounted police are used for the first time at San Francisco State College. Here they pursue two men who were probably not students. There were a few clashes between demonstrators and police when a rally broke up, with demonstrators breaking windows in the Business Science and the Administration buildings. AP photograph

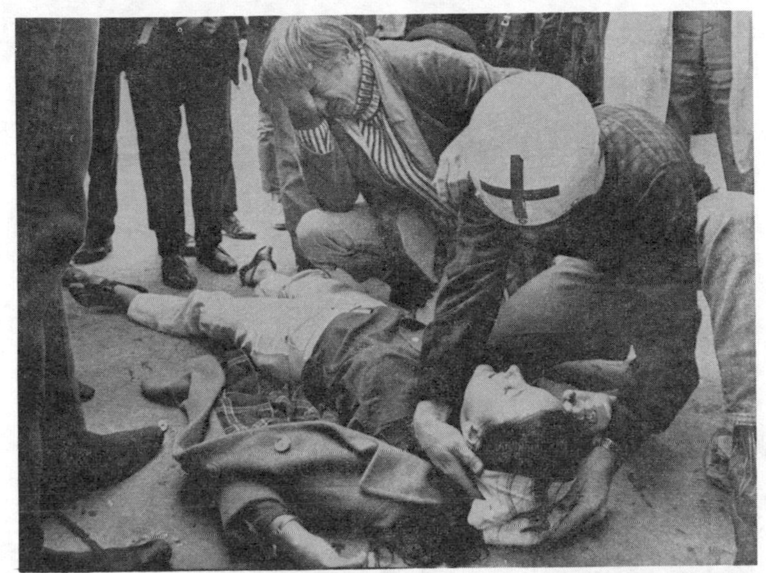

Dec. 11: A young female demonstrator receives first aid from a campus medic after she was downed during a brief flurry between the police and the strike demonstrators. **The girl's companion is on the medic's right. AP photograph**

Jan. 6: Striking teachers, students, and sympathizers man a picket line on the sidewalk at the main entrance to the college, as it opens after a three-week holiday vacation. Third from the left, holding the sign reading "Faculty-Student Unity Will Win!" is Dr. Carlton Goodlett, a Negro community leader. San Francisco State faculty members aligned with the American Federation of Teachers officially struck in support of the striking students. AP photograph

Jan 7: An unidentified picket talks to a police officer who has turned his head away. The woman was marching with the striking teachers and students. AP photograph

Jan. 9: Nesbitt Crutchfield, San Francisco State Black Students Union leader, is arrested on the campus as violence flared on the picket lines. AP photograph

Jan. 24: A student member of the Committee for An Academic Environment, which opposed the student strike at San Francisco State, stands on the shoulders of another student while restoring the flag to the flagpole after it had been cut down by strike demonstrators. AP photograph

Chapter III

THE SYSTEM

In view of its progressive attitude and action, San Francisco State might reasonably have expected to escape the kind of student unrest and turbulence that has swept the nation's campuses in recent years. There were, however, severe stresses within the college and the statewide system—some shared by most of America's colleges and universities, some peculiar to the California State colleges and San Francisco State. Chief among the internal strains were problems of structure and governance—problems which not only contribute to tension on a campus, but which hamper the peaceful resolution of disputes. To understand the tragic sequence of events leading up to the present student strike, it is necessary to understand the structure of San Francisco State and the way in which it is governed.

San Francisco State is part of the 18-college system in California. The colleges were established on an individual basis as "normal schools" for teacher training. In 1920, the legislature placed them under the jurisdiction of the State board of education as a means of developing a statewide system of teachers' colleges. Fifteen years later, they were renamed "State colleges" and broadened to include programs other than teacher training. Until 1961, however, the colleges remained basically independent and separately financed institutions with emphasis on teacher education.

By the late 1950's, higher education in California had become somewhat chaotic. The competition for funds, programs, and prestige among the State colleges, the multibranch university, and the rapidly growing network of junior colleges had become intense. The legislature was besieged with requests from colleges, universities, and junior colleges for more funds and new programs. To remedy this situation and to mobilize the State's resources toward providing low-cost, high-quality education for all, the California Legislature enacted the Donahoe Higher Education Act of 1960—a master plan for higher education in California.

The California master plan was a bold and pioneering venture, hailed (and imitated to varying degrees) by educators across the country. It embodied a curious paradox: The plan epitomized the notion of "democracy's colleges" by providing virtually free education for all of California's youth; it also recommended, however, a classification of students by ability, with the upper 12½ percent eligible for the university, the upper third eligible for the State colleges, and anyone with a high school diploma free to attend junior colleges. Thus, the master plan was designed to distribute educational functions among the university, the State colleges, and the junior colleges. The primary mission of the State colleges was to be undergraduate education.

To govern the State colleges, a Board of Trustees was established, with 16 members appointed for 8-year terms by the Governor, and five ex officio members: the Governor, the Lieutenant Governor, Speaker of the California Assembly, State superintendent of public instruction, and the chancellor of the State college system. (A list of the members of the Board of Trustees is contained in app. III.)

The chancellor of the system and all vice chancellors are appointed by the trustees. Each college is administered by a president, also appointed by the trustees. Although local faculty committees advise the trustees in the selection of a president, they have no statutory power, and the authority rests with the board. The responsibility for appointing faculty lies with the individual college presidents, but, in fact, academic departments hire the faculty, subject to a rarely used veto power of the president. Thus the screening of potential faculty and employees on a personal basis has been left almost entirely to the heads of the various departments on the college campuses. The ultimate authority in personnel matters remains with the trustees, and they have the power to order the transfer or suspension of a professor.

In theory, the master plan promised harmony and efficiency in organization and governance under a rational division of labor among the State's institutions of higher learning and a realistic classification of students by academic ability. In practice, the master plan has contributed to the friction on the campuses of California.

Some of the problems created by the master plan and its administration have had serious impact upon San Francisco State. Chief among these are problems resulting from the lack of the centralization of authority, the lack of parity with the University of California, the lack of financial flexibility, the lack of a faculty voice, and, finally, the faculty-chancellor relationship.

PROBLEMS CREATED BY THE CENTRALIZATION OF AUTHORITY

Bringing the originally separate and independent State colleges together under a single managing executive, the chancellor, was bound to leave some scars. In any organization, the centralization of management authority necessarily means some loss of prerogatives and power for those who operate at the local level.

While the chancellor describes the system as "far more a federation than an empire," there are many who would reverse the emphasis. Perhaps most important is the fact that the chancellor's office serves as staff for the trustees. Like so many other committees and commissions, the Board of Trustees is very largely a prisoner of the information provided by the staff operation. It is the chancellor's office that fundamentally controls the agenda for the trustees' meetings, and the content of the reports they read. In short, the chancellor controls most of the meaningful access to the Board of Trustees.

The mammoth budget of the State college system (the 1969 request to the legislature is $268 million) works its way upward from the individual campuses through the chancellor's office. The colleges no longer can seek support in Sacramento on the basis of local political strength. Because the State colleges use a line-item budget, the power of the chancellor's office extends ultimately to the major decisions regarding personnel and academic program (although not to individual appointments). The resentment normally felt against those who deny budget requests is directed now at the chancellor and the trustees. "We are always the people who have to say no; we are always in a negative position," said one member of the chancellor's staff, "we can never say 'yes, this is how you do something, and here's some money for your new program.' "

The chancellor's staff numbers around 215 persons; it operates on an annual budget of some $3.7 million; it is housed on several floors of a Los Angeles skyscraper. Perhaps out of a desire to maintain the image of federation, rather than empire, the staff has remained relatively small for a $250 million enterprise. According to one campus administrator, however, the combination of a small staff and the tremendous growth of the State college system has created a massive bottleneck at the chancellor's office.

Notwithstanding these difficulties, those who seek increased campus autonomy must deal with the chancellor's argument that only a master plan structure, with its divisions of functions among the university, colleges, and junior colleges, gives the teaching institution a fighting chance to compete for funds with the research-oriented university. Without question, the State college system has received a continued high level of financial support under the central administration. While campus autonomy proponents must concede as much, they argue that it would not, on the other hand, be impossible to give up a degree of decision-making power to the campuses. The idea of increased campus autonomy has some support among the trustees.

PROBLEMS CREATED BY LACK OF PARITY WITH THE UNIVERSITY OF CALIFORNIA

One observer in the University of California's administration said: "There is an Avis (as in 'we're number two') paranoia which permeates the State college system." The "paranoia" does not necessarily result in those who make up the college system "trying harder." More frequently, it is the cause of serious friction between the faculty, the governing trustees, and the chancellor. The faculties would have chafed under the newly imposed central governance in any event. But the inferiority complex of the State college faculties has multiplied many times over the difficulty of transition.

Even the trustees have the feeling they are "number two." It had been recommended in the master plan that trustees be given constitutional status, like regents of the University of California. But that recommendation was rejected by the legislature; the State colleges and their governing board remain creatures of the legislature, theoretically subject to abolition at any time.

When the colleges were brought together under the master-plan legislation, there were ardent advocates of changing the name of the institutions to the California State University, and creating a parallel structure with the University of California system. The drive for a name change continues to this day, and the chancellor is one of its supporters. The name change would be mostly symbolic. But underlying the desire for formal designation as a university are problems that are deep sources of faculty discontent and that prevent effective recruiting and retention of qualified faculty.

Workload is perhaps the most basic of these problems. It became a key issue in the American Federation of Teachers' strike at San Francisco State.

The average workload of a State college teacher is 12 units, higher than the average for the University of California campuses. The AFT wants a reduction in the State college workload to nine. From the teacher's standpoint, the heavier the teaching load, the more time spent in the classroom and in preparation for teaching, the less time there is for research. From a system standpoint, however, teaching load and the budget for faculty salaries are opposite sides of the same coin. A 25-percent reduction in the teaching load must be compensated for by a comparable increase in budget for faculty salaries, an increase in class size, or a reduction in full-time enrollment. The chancellor appreciates the seriousness of the problem. He believes that specialization of the State colleges primarily as teaching institutions will receive genuine acceptance from the faculty only if there is parity of compensation for comparable work.

Another problem is the nature, quality, and extent of the graduate program. Top-quality faculty want the challenge of teaching in a good graduate program and the opportunity to conduct research. But the purpose of the master plan was to specialize the functions of the State colleges primarily as undergraduate teaching institutions. The University of California, as a research-oriented institution, was to conduct most of the doctoral training. The university wants undergraduates, and the college system wants a graduate program, but, in general, responsibilities have so far been worked out along the lines of the master plan. The solution has been a "cooperative" graduate program, under which the Ph.D. degree is granted in the name of the University of California, although the work is done at a State college. It is just one more morsel which feeds the teachers' feelings of second-class status.

The chancellor is clearly on record in favor of moving toward increasing parity with the University of California. He really has no choice, since it is on these issues that the State colleges' recruiting drive falters, and it is for these reasons that the system is experiencing an increasing rate of faculty turnover. In 1968, the system had to recruit almost 3,000 new faculty members; in 1969, the figure may be higher.

In his "Fifth Annual Report to the Governor and the Legislature on Personnel Matters" in January 1968, the chancellor cited the colleges' decreasing ability to recruit qualified faculty. There has been a continued, steady decrease in the proportion of newly recruited full-time faculty who hold the doctorate, generally regarded by the academic profession as the mark of qualification. "Parity" issues–salary, teaching load, and research opportunities–were the reasons most frequently cited among a group of 1,206 prospective faculty for rejecting offers of appointment. There was also evidence of the colleges' increasing inability to retain faculty. The turnover rate climbed steadily from 8.8 percent in 1963-64 to 10.6 percent in 1966-67.

The chancellor's office surveyed faculty salaries in 18 comparable institutions in 1966-67. As a result of a similar survey in 1967-68, the chancellor recommended to the Coordinating Council, the Governor, and the legislature an average salary budget increase of 12.8 percent, a figure which was intended to put the State colleges on a par with most comparable institutions, and to stem the loss of faculty. The chancellor's recommendation was not accepted by the Coordinating Council which, on December 2, 1968, made its own recommendation for a salary increase of only 5.2 percent.

PROBLEMS CREATED BY LACK OF FINANCIAL FLEXIBILITY

The State colleges operate on a line-item system of budgeting, common with public agencies. This system prevented the central administration at one point from spending $281,000 to correct an erroneous reduction in faculty salary checks even though literally millions of dollars remained unexpended in the huge budget. In another instance, administrators were required to scrape up funds from every available pocket in the entire State-college system in order to meet a $300,000 deficit at San Francisco State.

While the Department of Finance is allowing the colleges some increased flexibility, the line-item budgeting method severely limits the ability of the college system and its individual campuses to make program changes with any reasonable degree of speed. Nor does State-college budgeting provide a way to meet emergencies and special needs; the trustees have sought contingency funds, but have been denied. Finally, the State colleges have no independent endowment. All of this should be seen against the background of a budgetary process which consumes 2 years from program development to program funding.

The budget of each individual school and of the State colleges as a whole depends on the estimated full-time enrollment. The task of estimating enrollments for budget purposes begins in January each year, 1½ years prior to the budget year involved. Each school prepares its estimate which it then discusses with the chancellor's office. After revisions are made, the colleges submit their final estimates to the chancellor's office in October. The chancellor then submits the estimates to the Department of Finance and the Office of the Legislative Analyst. The estimates may again be modified before they are included in the Governor's proposed budget.

Following legislative consideration and action, the budget is sent back to the Governor for his approval, which he can exercise with an item veto which permits the rejection of specific budget items. The funds which are finally approved are allocated among the various schools by the chancellor according to the previous estimates.

The line-item budget limits the use of funds to the specific functions and categories for which they have been budgeted. Rigidity has been reduced to some extent in the last few years. The Department of Finance now allows funds to be shifted by the trustees from one campus to another so long as they are used for the same function (e.g., capital expansion, faculty salaries, etc.). If more money is needed for faculty at San Diego State, faculty-budgeted funds from Fresno State can be used; but amounts budgeted for capital expenditures at any campus cannot be used for salaries.

Along with this relatively rigid system of budgeting, the State colleges have no reserve for contingencies. Coupled with a 2-year lag in the budget, this greatly restricts the ability of the colleges and the trustees to deal with unexpected problems.

An example of the difficulties created by the lack of flexibility occurred a few years ago. The chancellor's office had underestimated the amount needed for faculty salaries by 1.8 percent and therefore were forced to withhold an equivalent amount from faculty salary checks. There was a considerable surplus in other areas of the budget, but the Department of Finance would not permit its use. There were promises of relief from the legislature, but the promises were not kept. Since there were no contingency funds and the surplus could not be used, the faculty simply ended up 1.8 percent short.

The scars from this incident remain (if indeed the wounds have ever healed). Feelings run so high that faculty, trustees and administrators all refer to it as "the famous-one-point-eight-percent-incident!" It is prominent among the grievances cited by the statewide academic senate in their review of the faculty-chancellor relationship.

In marked contrast, the University of California receives a lump-sum budget with only few functional categories. Added to this is the fact that the university has accumulated a large reserve fund. These differences give the board of regents of the University of California much greater flexibility. Thus, the study team was told that University of California President Charles Hitch recently was able to obtain $500,000 in a matter of weeks to fund a previously unbudgeted "urban crisis" program.

The financial flexibility of the State colleges has been increasing, but probably not fast enough at a time of rapid social change. It must be repeated that there is a 2-year lag between the time a budget is estimated and when it becomes effective. Thus, funds for new, unbudgeted programs, such as a department of black studies, at a specific campus must be found within the same categories in the budgets of other State colleges, or the campus must reorder its own priorities.

An individual campus *can*, however, reorder priorities if programs such as black studies are of sufficient importance. For example, new positions allocated to San Francisco State in the spring of 1968 for the expansion and improvement of the graduate program were shifted over for the implementation of a new trustee-approved "Educational Opportunity Program." This permitted the college to admit up to 423 students who did not rank in the top third of their high school graduating class. In the current attempt to create a black studies department at San Francisco State, the 11.3 positions which have been allocated for the new department were "donated" by various existing departments within the college.

While the reordering of priorities is possible, it is not easy; departments are understandably reluctant to give up faculty positions and thus to give up courses taught in their departments or increase the teaching load of the remaining faculty. Significantly, one of the issues raised by the AFT in its strike was a demand for the "return" of the 11.3 positions donated to the black studies program.

PROBLEMS CREATED BY THE LACK OF A FACULTY VOICE

Six organizations are competing with one another, vying for influence over the statewide academic senate and the right to be the voice of the 10,000 State college faculty members. As a result, there is no clear and consistent faculty voice. Even the academic senate, whose executive committee attends the trustees' meetings, cannot claim to speak for all the faculty. The organizations range widely in their general philosophical bent from the activist American Federation of Teachers to the moderately conservative American Association of University Professors.

Everyone seems to recognize the need for some clear and consistent, representative faculty voice, but approaches differ sharply. The chancellor and the majority of the trustees would favor the statewide academic senate as the representative organization. The academic senate came into existence largely through the efforts of Chancellor Glenn S. Dumke. And, while "a certain breed of academic politicans" has turned the academic senate into an unruly stepchild, both the chancellor and the trustees continue to favor the senate as the basic instrument of faculty governance. Their reasoning is that the academic senate is a structure in which all faculty are entitled to participate because they are State college teachers. Those who object to this approach argue that the academic senate is a "captive" organization, dependent for funds upon the Board of Trustees, whose annual budget carries an appropriation for the senate.

Sharpening the competition to represent the faculty is the drive for collective bargaining, a development which extends far beyond the California State colleges. There have been garbage collection strikes in Nashville and New York, the "thin flu line" of the police slowdown in New York City, and teachers' strikes in various cities across the country. Even as this report was being prepared, San Francisco faced the threat of a bus and streetcar drivers' strike, and the possibility that such a strike might spread to other municipal employees' unions. There is general dissatisfaction on the part of employees in public and public-related employment, and, in broadest perspective, the drive for collective bargaining among the California State college teachers is a part of that larger development.

The trustees' position is that for two reasons they are unable to bargain collectively. First, they believe there is no way in which they can commit themselves to a binding agreement involving wages, hours, and working conditions because only the legislature can provide the funds to back up such an agreement. Second, they feel they cannot negotiate with a group which represents only a portion of the faculty because California's Brown Act requires them to meet and confer with *any* employee organization to discuss conditions of employment. They argue that it is impossible for them to meet with any group for the purpose of working toward the conclusion of a binding agreement which would, in effect, foreclose other groups from discussing the same issues with the trustees.

The unions contend there is nothing in the law which prevents the trustees from entering into collective bargaining, nor indeed anything which prevents public employees from striking. The trustees succeeded in obtaining a permanent injunction against the AFT strike at San Francisco State on the ground that public employees have no right to strike, but, like injunctions in other public employees' strikes in other cities, it had little effect.

The drive for collective bargaining has aggravated the difficulties at San Francisco State. The American Federation of Teachers represents a definite minority of the faculty. It had already been rejected once by faculty vote at San Francisco State when the current difficulties arose in the fall of 1968. An election was held on the campus in September 1966 to determine whether the faculty desired collective bargaining; they voted 2 to 1 in favor of it. Later, in December 1966, when the representation election was held, the AFT lost heavily to a competing faculty organization, the Association of California State College Professors (ACSCP). It is this background which leads some people, including some of the trustees, to the judgment that the AFT strike at San Francisco State was really an economic matter, and that the union members selfishly used the student discontent to support an organizing drive.

In the long run, unless the problem of collective bargaining is resolved, and until a clear voice for the faculty emerges, there will probably be continued discontent on the part of faculty of varying persuasions who feel disenfranchised or underrepresented on one issue or another. The immediate prospect is for aggressive competition among the six organizations to continue, bringing with it tensions and friction and making faculty-trustee disputes harder to resolve.

PROBLEMS CREATED BY THE FACULTY-CHANCELLOR RELATIONSHIP

Resentment against the chancellor and his staff goes beyond historical patterns and institutional frictions.

Relationships between the chancellor and the faculties have long been strained. Some of the issues contested at San Francisco State are peculiar to that campus alone. Some of the personalities involved at San Francisco State College are unique, and there are long-harbored animosities and reservoirs of ill feeling which remain from Glenn Dumke's tenure as president of the college. But aside from all the personal dislikes and animosities, injured feelings, prestige, and personal grievances, there is no gainsaying the fact that the relationship between the chancellor and the faculty today is little more than an uneasy coexistence. It is a substantial source of friction within the State college system.

When Glenn S. Dumke left the presidency of the college to become vice chancellor of the newly created State college system, he made a speech in which he told faculty and administrators that he would be watching, to make sure that what he had created at the college remained intact. In their view, it was a promise that he would remain a hovering presence, ruling from afar, and indeed that is the way in which many see him today. The resentment surfaced clearly when it became known that Dumke was being considered for appointment as the successor to the first chancellor, Buell Gallagher. San Francisco State faculty members were among the leaders of the opposition to Dumke's appointment. Some of the early critics have persistently opposed Dumke's policies since his appointment. Overall, the situation has come to the point where, as one college administrator put it, the chancellor and the trustees see the San Francisco State faculty as "a bunch of intractable rebels."

On May 24, 1968, the statewide academic senate, citing lack of communication, lack of consultation, lack of delegation, and lack of leadership, called for Glenn Dumke's resignation as chancellor. The academic senate prepared a report, "Review of the Relation Between the Academic Senate, CSC, and Chancellor Glenn S. Dumke from 1962 to the Present," which set forth in detail their complaints against the chancellor; subsequently the senate conducted a statewide referendum of the faculty on the question whether the chancellor should be asked to resign.

Of an estimated 10,000 eligible to vote, 5,931 exercised their right to do so; 3,743 voted "no confidence," while 2,188 supported the chancellor. On a campus-by-campus basis, only one of the 18 colleges voted for the chancellor. While one trustee has suggested that the friction and resentment between the faculty and the chancellor have so impaired the chancellor's effectiveness that he should resign or be removed, the board reaffirmed its support for Dumke following publication of the academic senate poll results.

Chapter IV

CONDITIONS AT SAN FRANCISCO STATE BEFORE THE STRIKE

Faced with serious, virtually insoluble problems of structure and governance, it might be expected that the presidency of San Francisco State College would be a hazardous position. The incredible fact is that the college has had seven presidents since 1960; three in less than 6 months during 1968.[1] Presidential succession, occurring once or twice in a decade under normal circumstances, can cause serious problems of adjustment in a college or university; to have seven presidents in 8 years is tantamount to having no presidential leadership at all. Glenn P. Smith, Vice President for business affairs at San Francisco State, has served all seven presidents.

He told the Study Team:

> There has been a terrible, terrible discontinuity of leadership at the College. You know about the presidential problem. You don't know about the vice-presidential problem, the dean problem, the accounting office problem, and everything else. There are few positions in that college, and this is not an overstatement, at the first, second, third, and fourth levels that haven't turned over two or three or four times in the last decade. The number of people that were there in 1958 that are still there today in their jobs in administration could be numbered on one hand.

Robert R. Smith, who served as president of the college between May and November 1968, served on the presidential selection committee's meeting to consider two of his predecessors: Paul Dodd and John Summerskill. He told his colleagues at that time: "There is no place for a president at San Francisco State College," and he urged them to resolve that problem even before considering candidates for the office.

The presidential problems began with the presidency of Glenn Dumke. His predecessor, J. P. Leonard, had been somewhat autocratic. It was Dumke's intention to give a major share of college governance to the faculty, and he began the process by creating the institutional structure for faculty governance. Dumke, however, was occupied with the formulation of the master plan and was an absentee president much of the time. Paul Dodd followed Dumke, but did not assert the power of the office. John Summerskill came to the college from Cornell. A vigorous and handsome young man with a liberal style of personal leadership, he soon won support of both faculty and dents. But Summerskill dealt with a wide variety of matters personally, rather than delegating them to his staff assistants, and he acquired the reputation of being changeable; the word went out that Summerskill's decisions were frequently reversible. By the time Robert Smith became president in 1968, two developments had progressed to the point that his job was made almost impossible: everyone was by then accustomed to going directly to the president to get a problem solved; and the faculty had occupied the power vacuum left by the lack of presidential leadership in previous years and considered that it had the power to make policy for the college. Any president would probably have found himself in this untenable position—everyone looked to the president for decisions, but the faculty was unwilling to relinquish the power he needed to decide.

Finally, San Francisco State College has suffered from an exceptional lack of workable, operational disciplinary machinery.[2] To some extent, this is a problem common to institutions of higher education. John Summerskill told the Board of Trustees in December 1967:

> I think our whole disciplinary structure, techniques and procedures were built for another era. As someone remarked "this is not the panty-raid era, but of tough determined people."

Faculty grievance and disciplinary machinery is a subject of contention throughout the California State college system, and the matter of a new framework for faculty grievances was a major issue in the AFT strike. San Francisco State's problems go deeper. The faculty disciplinary machinery for San Francisco State had been worked out during the spring of 1968. When the semester ended, it was only paper, and nothing was done to make it operational during the summer months. Thus, when the George Murray case arose, Robert Smith was faced not only with the substance of the matter but also with the problem of putting the disciplinary machinery into working order.

Student disciplinary procedures were in no better condition. There was an appeals panel, which was operational. But a student-faculty court, which John Summerskill had been working out with the students, was not. It was held up over a disagreement whether decisions of the student-faculty court would be final, or whether there would be some appellate review. The students believed that Summerskill had agreed there would be no appeal. Whether he had or not, it was an issue with Robert Smith, who believed there must be some form of appeal. As a result of this disagreement, the student government refused to appoint any members to the panel until the matter of jurisdiction was clarified. In addition, the college had a very loosely defined code of conduct—a set of rules adequate only to deal with more traditional subjects of discipline, such as cheating, theft, and plagiarism, subjects of the "panty-raid era" Summerskill referred to.

Many colleges or universities are not structured to deal adequately with student discipline in the era of confrontation politics. Too many lack the codes of conduct, the investigative machinery, and the means for student defense required by a quasi-judicial disciplinary system. Nor have the thorny problems of concurrent jurisdiction been resolved: (should the college proceed with a hearing, when the student's testimony would be admissible in a criminal proceeding involving the same actions which are the subject of the college disciplinary hearing?). The difficulties at San Francisco State were infinitely compounded by the lack of operational disciplinary machinery capable of proceeding with due process when the crises arose in the fall of 1968.

These, then, were the promises and problems of San Francisco State College in the midsixties—problems complicated by the diverse personalities who attempted to deal with them.

PRESIDENT SUMMERSKILL

When John Summerskill, 41, became president of the college in September 1966, there was still hope that San Francisco State might continue the era of good will that had prevailed since 1960—the problems of structure and governance notwithstanding.

Summerskill was an outstanding clinical psychologist, he had served as a vice president for student affairs at Cornell, and he was a consultant to the Peace Corps. He seemed an ideal choice to preside over the cosmopolitan and aggressive campus and to pursue the cause of reform.

The college he was to lead was the only public college in the nation where students had developed a technique to hire some of their own professors and to get credit for courses taught by other students.

President Summerskill expressed a strong interest in innovation and the success of the experimental college. "I'm for innovation in general education and the undergraduate studies," he said in an interview with the student newspaper on his arrival. "I would like to see experimentation and innovation in teaching methods so we can figure how best to help a person become a different person by the time he leaves college."

In the interview, Summerskill praised the experimental college and gave much of the credit for it to James Nixon, student body president. He would later discover that not all of San Francisco State's students were as constructive as those who built and ran the experimental college. And he would find that while the experimental program helped the college's national image, some of its courses—dealing with sex, revolution, drugs, guerrilla warfare, and socialism—proved a constant irritant to California legislators.

Even when student unrest, particularly over the Vietnam war, began to increase on the campus in the fall of 1966, Summerskill recognized that the campuses mirror the troubles and strains of America's urbanized society. He agreed with his Vice President Glenn Smith who had said earlier:

> It is totally unfair for the public at large and its elected officials to blame the campuses for changing kids—for creating problems—when city governments are wrestling with all the same kinds of problems, for the most part unsuccessfully. It is unfair to think we can be an island of tranquillity and calm when we draw our students from troubled cities in a troubled society. It is not college that makes them that way.

Summerskill's insights, the aspirations, the past successes, however, were not sufficient to withstand the tide of discontent that rolled across the campuses. As 1966 drew to a close, the era of good will and successful student-administration relations at San Francisco State also drew to a close. Revolt was about to replace reform; the struggle for the college was about to begin in earnest.

355-234 O - 69 - 3

END OF AN ERA

San Francisco State's era of good will and successful student-administration relations appeared to come to a close with an SDS-sponsored boycott of the student cafeteria in late 1966. "That marked the end of responsible student government," recalls one administrator. The SDS, long ignored by the mass of students and the student government at San Francisco State, called for a boycott of the student cafeteria, on the issues of poor food, high prices, and overcrowded conditions. The boycott got off to a slow start, and the SDS stationed large male students at the cafeteria door to argue with those who entered.

As support for the issue grew, student government officers were forced to decide where they stood. Those in power at the time would have preferred to ignore the SDS-created issue and continue work with their experimental college and other programs. But political realities intruded, and student government leaders joined the boycott–resulting in the overhaul of the campus foundation that runs the cafeteria.

Throughout the spring of 1967, white radicals kept the pressure on President Summerskill on antiwar issues–often attracting white-moderate support, and the blacks pressed for a black studies program. Some 30 to 40 SDS pickets attempted to disrupt his inauguration in early May by heckling the processional march and shouting at intervals throughout the ceremony: "End class rank," and "military off the campus" and "warmongers."

Students confronted Summerskill in his office several times during the spring. In a brief April 26, 1967, sit-in, Summerskill told the antidraft students that he disliked the war in Vietnam and agreed that the draft system was unfair, but said he did not have the authority to halt submission of student performance and ranking to draft boards. He pointed out that the colleges had been instructed by the chancellor's office to submit such rankings. The students argued that he should defy authority and refuse to submit the rankings. They said that changes are produced only by defying authority.

"That's your politics," answered President Summerskill. "You might be right sometimes, but I don't accept that."

There were several protests against military recruiters that spring–and the combination of these events angered some of San Francisco State's conservative students, who felt they had long been ignored by the student government and the administration. They began to bring pressure from the other side of the spectrum. They put together a coalition and won the student government election against a Negro opponent in the spring of 1967–and they succeeded in getting some cutbacks in hoped-for appropriations for the experimental college and other programs. Even the campus election victory did not give conservative students much influence or voice at the college. Their new president blocked much of his conservative legislature's proposals, and the 1968 election returned the liberal, pro-experimental college "programs" coalition to power.

However, the conservative students were able to add to the headaches of President Summerskill. In May 1967, the new student government charged the Black Students Union with "reverse racism," misuse of student funds, and threats of violence. They visited Max Rafferty, California's superintendent of public instruction and a trustee of the State colleges, and other State officials to describe their charges.

As a result of the student accusations, the Board of Trustees sent a committee to investigate the BSU and related student financial affairs at San Francisco State. The committee found there was not enough evidence to support the charges, but recommended that the college tighten up its student disciplinary procedures and fiscal controls.

The summer issue of *Open Process*, a campus newspaper containing poems and essays on sex, and a photo of a reclining nude, was mailed by conservative students to politicians and trustees. The criticism from Sacramento resulted in a brief suspension of the newspaper, and Summerskill had to devote much time in the early fall of 1967 calming outraged politicians and answering letters from angry citizens.

College presidents were not the only recipients of such letters. The members of the Board of Trustees were receiving an increasing amount of mail expressing displeasure with the situation on the campuses. Much of the campus protest was directed at the Vietnam war, and many people saw the dissent as unpatriotic. Emotions ran high in the autumn months of 1967, as supporters and opponents of the Asian conflict clashed in marches, demonstrations, and name-calling sessions across the country. The campuses mirrored the tensions in the society at large; "the war" and "racism" were the issues. The conflicts and contradictions in American society were inevitably reflected in the student unrest on the California State college campuses.

THE UNEASY AUTUMN OF 1967

San Jose State College is some 50 miles south of San Francisco. During the week of September 18, 1967, the United Black Students for Action issued charges of racial discrimination in housing for students in the area around the college; they also charged discriminatory practices in the conduct of the school's athletic program, fraternities, and enrollment policies. The college's president, Robert D. Clark, immediately began discussions with students and community leaders on the conglomeration of issues involved. As the week progressed, the discussions grew angrier and the situation more explosive. There were numerous threats that fraternity and sorority houses would be burned, and that there would be serious violence at the upcoming weekend football game.

Clark dealt with the situation "first . . . [by acknowledging] that discrimination exists. . . . The simple bald fact . . . that as a civilized, democratic, intellectual community we have tolerated discriminatory behavior against blacks. . . ." To avoid violence, he canceled the football game. State and local agencies were alerted, and local police and sheriff's forces had been mobilized. By Thursday, September 21, Clark had arrived at a plan of action that was endorsed almost unanimously by a vote of the black students. In late October of that year, Clark reported to the Board of Trustees on his response to the threats of violence. The board commended him for his handling of the situation. Clark's words are well worth noting:

> Finally, I should like to comment on the threats of violence. No one who believes in law and order, as I do, wishes to yield to threats of violence. But when a society is deeply disturbed, as ours is, and when it is guilty of grave injustices, as ours is, threats will occur. What, then, does

> one do? The first thing, and the most important, is to move vigorously to ameliorate the injustice. We made that attempt. The second is to protect innocent people by excluding them if possible from areas where violence is likely to occur. That is why we ground an aeroplane or evacuate a building when a bomb threat is reported. That is why we canceled the football game. The third is to take all possible measures to maintain law and order. And that we did. From the first moment of threats we were in communication with the law enforcement agencies. The San Jose Police Department and the Santa Clara Sheriff's office were fully mobilized, with all vacations cancelled. The Governor's office was notified and appropriate state agencies placed on the alert. That these precautions, necessary as they are, have limits to their effectiveness, one devastated city after another in this country can attest.

The Vietnam war was the major cause of student discontent in the fall of 1967. Autumn was the season for business and military on-campus recruiting. A series of demonstrations ensued, as students, and sometimes faculty members, protested the Vietnam war at five of the campuses. Some of the demonstrations were peaceful, but in others there was violence. Antiwar protest was occurring many places across the country. On the California State college campuses, protest took the form of attempts to inhibit recruitment by Dow Chemical Co., the principal manufacturer of napalm, and by the CIA and the Armed Forces. The chancellor's acting dean for student affairs still ranks the war as the No. 1 cause of student unrest.

While antiwar protest dominated the scene, racial issues were beginning to surface. The first signal was the San Jose State College incident in September. The next serious incident occurred at San Francisco State.

On the morning of November 6, 1967, a group of black students entered the office of the *Gater*, a student daily newspaper, and beat and kicked the editor. A *Gater* photographer took spectacular photos of the ensuing melee between blacks and newspaper staffers. The Black Students Union denied having any part in the beating, but the photos in the *Gater* the next morning showed that BSU members comprised the attacking force.

The black students felt the paper had racist overtones. Allegedly, it had printed some "humor" containing racial slurs; the paper's continued reference to Muhammad Ali as "Cassius Clay" was seen as yet another evidence of racism. There was also some question about alleged "rigging" of an election for homecoming queen.

A fire occurred in a dormitory the same morning, further unnerving the campus. No link was established between the fire and the beating of the *Gater* editor, but the juxtaposition of the two frightened many. "In all my years at this school, I've never seen anything like that day," one veteran administrator said.

A few days later, the black students turned themselves in in response to warrants for their arrest. One of them was George Mason Murray, coordinator of the student-run ghetto tutorial program, and a graduate student who held a part-time teaching post in the English department. President Summerskill announced the suspensions of Murray and three others, pending disciplinary action.

By November 30, 1967, as a result of the continuing series of largely antiwar protest incidents, the chancellor felt it necessary to reassure the Board of

Trustees with a "special report" on campus disturbances. Noting that student unrest was a worldwide phenomenon, he said that—

> The basis of much of the current unrest is legitimate student and faculty concern with the problems of this nation and the world. To that extent it is defensible, for such concern is appropriate to the academic community. More and more, however, there is a tendency for this concern to move in dangerous directions to the extent that free discussions and dissent become confused with personal license, violent advocacy, and lawlessness. One dangerous development is that special interest groups consider the campus a pawn in their struggle to capture and control the educational matrix. Another is the growth of the idea that the campus is properly a staging area for revolution and violent social and political change. A third and still more common danger area is for protagonists of an idea to consider it quite proper to prevent opponents from expressing their views.
>
> Academic freedom works both ways. If it means anything at all, it means that the guarantee of free expression for one point of view must be accompanied by a similar guarantee of free expression for opposing views. . . .
>
> The academic community always has been one of the consciences of society. This is one of its most venerable functions. It is a questioner, a worrier, a critic, an idealist. . . . But a thorn is not a lance. A critic is not a thug. . . .
>
> Students and indeed faculty members who countenance physical violence and massive disruption of collegiate functions are seeking to exercise what they refer to as "power." In fact this turns out to be force—not power.

The Board of Trustees responded by passing a moderate resolution on student governance. In the words of the resolution, the board "expected that the leadership of the president, the judgment of the faculty, and the good sense of the students will maintain the college campus as a place of order in balance with freedom."

The board's calm and even mood did not persist for very long. Apparently unrelated, separate incidents of disorder and violence on Wednesday, December 6, 1967, at the Los Angeles and San Francisco campuses brought the trustees into special session on the morning of Saturday, December 9, 1967. President Greenlee of the Los Angeles campus and President John Summerskill of San Francisco State were asked to report to the board on the events of the previous Wednesday.

The December 6 disturbance at San Francisco State revolved around the issue of student discipline. The banned newspaper, *Open Process*, had resumed printing, and it printed another issue that proved offensive to State legislators and many California residents. It featured a poem on masturbation dedicated to the director of the physical education department, and a picture of a male student clad only in a cluster of grapes. President Summerskill said the poem was "offensive" and "insulting," and suspended the newspaper, its editor, and the poet, Jefferson Poland, founder of the Sexual Freedom League. The American Civil Liberties Union threatened to ask for a Federal court injunction to readmit the *Open Process* students, on the ground that the offending publication did not constitute sufficient cause for summary suspension. Summerskill consulted with the chancellor's office and was advised by the general counsel that the ACLU would prevail on the question of summary suspension. He therefore announced the withdrawal of the suspension of the *Open Process* students to 500 demonstrators picketing outside his office. "I acted precipitously," he told the crowd.

The paper remained suspended. This angered the white student supporters of the publication, as did Summerskill's declaration that disciplinary procedures would continue against the students involved, although not on a summary basis. He said the college's board of appeals and review would hear the case and make a disciplinary decision.

Black students in the crowd demanded to know why the president had not also withdrawn the suspensions of the four black students then charged with the *Gater* beatings. Jimmy Garrett then took over the microphone to announce a rally of area black students to be held at San Francisco State December 6, "to express their opinion."

The black students accused President Summerskill of "racism" for withdrawing the suspension of whites, but not blacks. However, by that time, the board of appeals and review had already acted in the *Gater* incident to suspend four black students, put two on probation, and warn three. The cases were different.

(As a result of criminal proceedings, Murray and seven other attackers in the *Gater* incident received 6-month suspended sentences. All were soon readmitted to the college.)

Summerskill later regretted his decision to lift the *Open Process* suspensions. "It turned out," he said "that politically, it probably would have been better to go to court and take a licking from the Civil Liberties Union, but I thought this was a fair thing to do."

The December 6, 1967, demonstration united students with a wide range of grievances. There were the BSU blacks, ghetto high school students, antiwar whites, and people who were angry over the firing of a controversial professor.

According to Summerskill, the protest—

> brought together for the first time various radical elements on the campus with their supporters from a number of Bay Area communities. . . . We have never been confronted by this group of people. . . . Black Student Union people by and large simply do not talk to SDS antiwar people but this time, because suspensions were involved, they were talking and acting in unison. . . .

"School is closed!" chanted the crowd. Several hundred of them surged up the steps to the administration building. The locked glass door (with TV men and photographers on the other side) broke and the crowd poured through. A roving crowd of Negro high school students broke into two other buildings and did minor damage. Summerskill was in his office with two representatives of the San Francisco Police Department. There were 200 police waiting a call in an apartment complex near the campus. President Summerskill and his police advisers decided to close the campus and not risk bringing police on campus to battle the mob. Fist fights broke out between students and nonstudents, and the crowds dispersed after about 3 hours—without rioting.

The scene of the mob breaking through the glass of the administration building incensed television viewers throughout California. The trustees called an emergency meeting 3 days later to chastise President Summerskill for his failure to call police. Several politicians called for his firing.

What viewers saw on their TV screens was apparent chaos, followed by Summerskill's statement that he had decided not to bring the police on campus. The original version of Summerskill's statement had included a reference to his liaison with the police department. The reference was removed at the request of a police department representative. In retrospect, everyone recognized the deletion was a mistake. It was not until the morning of the trustees' meeting in Los Angeles that the whole story was ultimately told, and the hue and cry was ended by a report from San Francisco Police Chief Thomas J. Cahill, concluding that: "Proper procedure was followed taking all circumstances into consideration. The police advised President Summerskill and his decisions have my full approval."

The legislature had begun to investigate Summerskill's handling of the incident, but backed off when the police chief said he agreed with Summerskill.

THE TRUSTEES' INCREASING CONCERN

It was apparent from the chancellor's opening statement on December 9 that rhetoric was escalating, and positions were hardening. The chancellor was clearly under pressure. Once again he sought to reassure the board, and the colleges' critics, that the disruptions involved only a fraction of the system's 190,000 students. He told the board that the State colleges were not the first in the country to experience campus violence and that, on the whole, they remained peaceful and quiet centers of learning. He told the board, "We HAVE met the problem over the past two years, we ARE meeting it now, we WILL meet it in the future."

Some of the words were the same, but the mood was clearly different. The Governor was in attendance. The chancellor assured him that—

> . . . force will be met by superior force on any of these 18 campuses without hesitation; that the day is past when ANY student, professor or administrator will be asked to operate in a climate of fear and intimidation; or when any of our overwhelming majority of serious, responsible students cannot face the school year with an absolute guarantee of uninterrupted, undisturbed study.

Calling the campus security forces "our first line of defense," the chancellor requested an immediate additional appropriation of $100,000 to augment the college system's campus security forces (which then totaled 113, with an additional 40 persons enforcing parking regulations). He also asked approval of the appointment by each campus president of a single responsible individual who would have the primary duty of establishing and maintaining "constant and effective liaison with outside police agencies to assure that these forces are ready to come onto campus at any time with their maximum amount of available force." The chancellor told the board that it "must face the possibility at some campuses of a riot growing into a general insurrection."

The trustees appointed a task force of five to "evaluate" President Summerskill's "stewardship." (Their investigation ultimately resulted in an endorsement of his handling of the December 6 incident.)

The statewide academic senate was furious at the trustees' action and described the December 9 emergency meeting as a "humiliating hearing at which President John Summerskill . . . and other college presidents were in effect tried publicly while the leaders of the Democratic and Republican Parties—attending their first trustee meeting of the year—demonstrated by their very presence how much public higher education has become a political football in California."[3]

The San Francisco State faculty gave President Summerskill a standing ovation at their next meeting, a 245-to-62 vote of confidence, and made an implied threat to strike if he were fired. The faculty also recorded its objection to an emergency resolution passed by the trustees, providing mandatory suspension for students or faculty members guilty of violence on the campus. The faculty meeting was filled with discussion of the "erosion of local control"—a major complaint in the AFT strike a year later.

The board's emergency action had such an inflammatory effect upon college presidents, faculty, and students alike that the board was forced to withdraw from its position a few weeks later. Faced with the strong opposition of the presidents and faculties, the trustees modified the regulations in late January 1968 to return discretion to the college presidents in suspension or dismissal of students, faculty, and employees. The trustees also appointed a subcommittee to study the modified regulations. After consultation with representatives of the faculty, students, and college presidents, the subcommittee recommended that the modified regulations remain in force, and that the board promulgate guidelines for maintaining the educational process on the campuses.

As the December 9 special session moved to a close, the board resolved that it found it "unthinkable to even contemplate looking forward to a continuous conducting of the educational processes on campuses which resemble armed camps."

* * *

The spring of 1968 brought little relief. The Vietnam war and the bombing continued; the antiwar movement was at its peak; there were demonstrations on city streets and college campuses across the country. In California, the State colleges were no exception.

There were other irritants, too—other kinds of campus activity upon which antagonistic segments of the public could focus, and which were sources of conflict between the statewide administration and some local faculty and students. At Long Beach State College the chancellor intervened to close a controversial art exhibit of life-size nudes in poses which were considered pornographic. Students and faculty at the Long Beach campus regarded this as a transgression of academic freedom. A similar outcry arose at Fresno State College when another controversial art exhibit was closed (without the chancellor's intervention).

* * *

PRESIDENT SUMMERSKILL RESIGNS

On February 22, 1968, President Summerskill announced his resignation, effective in September. In his resignation statement, he charged the Reagan administration with "political interference and financial starvation" of the State college system.

"I do not think we will see peace on our campus until we see peace in our cities, peace in Vietnam," he said.

Asked if he felt a firm disciplinarian might replace his, President Summerskill replied, "Discipline has been maintained on our campus. Discipline isn't going to solve the problem that 80 percent of our students are opposed to the Vietnam War."

He complained about what he called "interference" by trustees and politicians with the State college system. "This whole system is going to break down if the trustees and politicians are going to hire and fire professors," he told the *Los Angeles Times*.

He said he was quitting because–

> I couldn't say what I'm saying now as president, but somebody had better start saying something about these problems.
>
> The issue is: are we going to let the educational establishment be taken over essentially by people who are running for political office?

Somewhat more than a month later, the statewide academic senate issued "with great regret" its position paper on "Politics in Higher Education." The academic senate strongly denounced the actions of the trustees, the legislature, and the general interjection of politics into the affairs of the State colleges. The paper, unanimously approved by the academic senate on March 29, 1968, suggested that faculty members might be forced to take "the option of leaving, even though . . . the ultimate victims will be the many California students." The paper also recommended that in hiring professors it be made "perfectly clear what the situation is in the California State colleges and what it may become."

In April 1968, the trustees sought to relieve partially one major source of discontent–inadequate minority enrollment.

The effect of the master plan, with its limitation to the upper one-third of the high school graduating class, had been to reduce minority enrollment at the State-college campuses. The effect of the board's action was to increase from 2 percent to 4 percent the number of students who could be admitted as exceptions to the normal enrollment standard, under a new program which became known as the Educational Opportunity Program (EOP). More than 400 students were eligible for admission to San Francisco State pursuant to the new policy. The Educational Opportunity Programs were developed during the spring of 1968, and as of July, when the chancellor's office issued its first status report on the EOP, it was estimated that for the entire system, roughly 4,000 students were to be admitted to the program in September 1968. The program was underfunded from the beginning, and attempts to obtain the necessary support, from within and outside the system, have been only minimally successful. It does not have the Governor's support. He struck approximately $250,000 of EOP money from a 1968 appropriation by item veto; and his budget for 1969–70 does not include $2,472,000 recommended for EOP by the Board of Trustees.

President Summerskill worked throughout the spring to lay groundwork for a black studies program. On the advice of Jimmy Garrett (and against the wishes of his staff, deans, and a prominent black community spokesman) he brought sociologist Nathan Hare to San Francisco State College from Washington to launch the department.

Demonstrations against military recruiters and campus discontent continued even to the final days before Summerskill left the country.

In late May, Summerskill called in San Francisco police to clear demonstrators who were staging a sit-in and had refused to leave the administration building. It was an SDS-led sit-in with the goal of forcing Air Force ROTC off the campus—and the SDS had persuaded Mexican and Latin students to join them by including demands for admission of Third World students (which the administration had essentially granted) and the hiring of professors acceptable to them.

Twenty-six persons were arrested in the building with no resistance. But a crowd of students had gathered outside and the police felt they were blocking exit of their vans—and moved to clear the students away. Police used clubs, and students threw rocks. Said one witness:

> They tried to move the first van out and they gave a couple of warnings to the crowd to move so they could move.
>
> Then the cops moved in, and they moved real fast.
>
> You know, batons up and real fast, and people started falling down and clubs came out and Terry Hallinan [a San Francisco attorney] ran and got zapped in the head and it was a real sticky scene.

The administration building sit-in resumed for several more days—with amnesty added to the list of demands. Summerskill determined to meet the sit-in by keeping the campus open 24 hours a day. The chancellor's office was prepared at one point to intervene and clear the administration building if Summerskill would not. The chancellor's demand was rejected and after additional discussion, withdrawn.

Summerskill met with leaders of the Third World Liberation Front (TWLF), leaders of the sit-in, and several members of the faculty, and agreed that the college would admit 400 minority students under the Educational Opportunity Program. He further agreed that 9 of the 12 new faculty positions which the college expected to get in the 1968–69 budget would, pursuant to a recommendation of the academic deans, be assigned for support of the special admissions program. And, he agreed to give the TWLF a full and effective voice, according to established college procedures, in recruiting and employing personnel for the additional staff positions allocated for minority programs.

On Thursday, May 23, Summerskill agreed, in a reversal of a press statement he had issued earlier the same day, that he would call a college community referendum May 27–28 on the question of keeping the ROTC on campus.

President Summerskill and his staff disagreed sharply on some of the concessions he made to the students.

He left the campus Thursday night. By Friday morning, it was learned that he did not intend to return prior to his departure for Addis Ababa, Ethiopia, for an indefinite stay (where he is now working on a Ford Foundation-financed project at the university).

Friday afternoon the deans and the executive committee of the academic senate met and reached a general consensus that the administration building should be closed. In the course of closing the building and evacuating those participating in the sit-in, 25 arrests were made.

As the 1967–68 academic year came to a close, the chancellor sent a letter, a "Review of Recent Events," to all State college faculty. He listed six critical problems for the State colleges:

1. Making education relevant to issues of the day—peace, poverty, discrimination, social progress, etc.
2. Making all of higher education accessible to a larger portion of our citizens.
3. Making effective the sharing of decisionmaking more broadly through democratic processes with those affected by the decisions—especially students and faculty.
4. Drawing the large central segment of uncommitted students and faculty into more active participation in the affairs of the academic state.
5. Preventing the manipulation of academic institutions by willful minorities for private or nihilistic ends.
6. Streamlining traditional academic governance so that it can more adequately respond to a dynamic, high pressure, volatile environment.

The chancellor called for salary parity with the University of California, changing the name of the State college to California State University, adjustments in teaching load, an independent Ph.D. program, and increased funds and more budgetary flexibility.

In August 1968, the chancellor's office issued a report summarizing *Dissent, Demonstration and Disruption in the California State Colleges, 1967–68.* Viewing the scene detached from the pressure of any single decision, any particular event or disturbance, the report listed the fundamental causes of campus problems as seen by "most observers":

> (1) War protest, (2) racial discrimination, (3) desire to use the colleges and universities as vehicles for social change, (4) curricular irrelevance, (5) institutional inertia and resistance to change.
>
> If these are indeed the true causes, it is apparent that there is little that the individual president or dean can do with assurance to *guarantee* the peace and tranquility of a particular campus, particularly if it is an urban one. War protest will continue as long as does the war in Vietnam. Racial discrimination can be alleviated but its lessening is dependent more upon desire in the hearts of men, rather than upon legislative concessions and special programs as compensation for its damage. The push to utilize the campus as a staging ground for social reform can be debated but probably cannot be deterred. So closely have large universities, for example, become interwoven with the Federal government in military programs and defense research (e.g. IDA) that higher education in its major centers at least appears to have committed itself so fully to

the political and financial world outside the cloister that this association seems unlikely to be reversed.

* * *

PRESIDENT ROBERT SMITH

Robert R. Smith, former head of the education department and a long-time critic of the trustees, was named to succeed John Summerskill as the president of San Francisco State College. He asked for a 3-year term, "figuring that if I got into it at all and give up what I was doing, I ought to work the cycle through and see if we could put the college in shape so that maybe it would be fit for a president to assume."

The shattered administration was delighted by the choice of Smith as the new president. 'We go into the summer in tatters, and we work and we are tired as hell trying to prepare ourselves for the fall," recalls a vice president.

GEORGE MURRAY

From the beginning, it was a busy fall for San Francisco State's administrators. Their troubles began long before the November 6 deadline. Black Panther George Murray had visited Cuba during the summer. While there, he was critical of the "imperialistic" United States and was quoted as saying that every American soldier knocked out by the Vietcong in Vietnam meant "one aggressor less" to deal with here at home.

When he returned in the fall of 1968 to teach as a part-time instructor in the English department, his reemployment received headlines in San Francisco newspapers. The stories recalled Murray's participation in the *Gater* beating. After a few days of newspaper stories and public comments by San Francisco area figures, the fuss died down. Then, after a respite of nearly a week, the Los Angeles newspapers picked up the story.

Murray's renewed employment set the stage for the first of a series of encounters between the Board of Trustees and the new president of San Francisco State College.

While there was general agreement that Murray's classroom performance was good, the Board of Trustees began to take a different view; and the pressures that were building up did not aid them in maintaining calm detachment. Murray was a Black Panther; he had traveled to Cuba; his reported statements were couched in the exaggerated rhetoric of black militancy. Eldridge Cleaver was speaking throughout the State, and the University of California regents, the Governor, the Berkeley chancellor, and students were waging open warfare over the proposed course, "Social Analysis 139X," in which Cleaver was to lecture. Election fever was in the air. Of direct importance was a bond issue: $250 million for construction for higher education, requiring the voters' approval. (Robert Smith told a September 12 meeting of the college's local advisory board that the failure to pass the bond issue would be disastrous for the State colleges—the whole building program was at stake.) There was also the bitterest U.S. senatorial campaign in recent years—a campaign in which Cleaver and conduct on the campuses became issues.

Vice President Garrity discussed this period with the Study Team:

> Cleaver has captured the press at this time. All we hear in the local papers is Cleaver—here and all around the State. The only place Murray is getting mentioned is in Los Angeles. All of the concern is from Dumke and his people, and we're saying: "There's no trouble here. Forget it."
>
> And we continue this kind of effort and they continue to contend that it is: "terrible, terrible."

According to its chairman, the Board of Trustees did not know of Murray's status as an instructor until publication of a *San Francisco Examiner* story. They were aware that Murray had been disciplined *as a student* for his participation in the *Gater* incident in November 1967. (The suspension was subsequently lifted by President John Summerskill, acting on his own.) But they were shocked to learn that a member of the faculty had been involved in an assault on a student, and that no disciplinary action had been taken.

Following the *Gater* incident in 1967, the English department recommended Murray's suspension from the faculty, and this was approved by the executive committee of the academic senate. But a small group of faculty members succeeded in getting President Summerskill and the academic senate to urge the English department's HRT (hiring, retention, and tenure) committee to reverse its recommendation. The HRT committee did so, but with serious misgivings, and then only on the understanding that Summerskill and the academic senate would institute disciplinary proceedings against Murray. Summerskill, in the words of one administrator, "took full charge of the matter," but charges were never filed. When Murray's contract for reemployment came before the HRT committee, the English department took the view that Summerskill had personally assumed the responsibility for Murray's discipline. Consequently, the department considered only Murray's performance as a teacher. There is agreement among those interviewed by the Study Team that there was no criticism of Murray's teaching; nor was there any indication that he ever used his classroom for political purposes.

On September 19, 1968, the chancellor and Robert Smith met to discuss the reassignment or firing of George Murray. Smith declined to take any action.

On September 26, the trustees voted 8 to 5 to ask President Smith to reassign Murray to a nonteaching position.

The meeting of the board had covered 2 days, September 25 and 26. As the probable nature of the board's action became apparent, faculty and student spokesmen expressed their concern. Leo McClatchy, chairman of the campus' academic senate, said that any hasty action or failure of due process in the Murray case would result in "a drastic faculty reaction, not only on our campus, but all over the State." The announcement of the board's action brought immediate, negative reaction from a variety of faculty spokesmen at the meeting:

> Leo McClatchy, academic senate chairman at San Francisco State, protested that Murray had not been charged with being unqualified for his teaching duties, and had been afforded no opportunity to defend himself.

John Stafford, chairman of the statewide academic senate, said the board's action appeared to be an implied attack by the board on the principle of delegation of authority to the campus. He agreed with McClatchy that there would be faculty reaction.

Richard Peairs, a western regional official of the American Association of University Professors, and that the board's action appeared to be inconsistent with long-standing AAUP standards on college governance, and inconsistent also with the board's own actions in the past.

Bud Hutchinson, executive secretary of the College Council of the American Federation of Teachers, and Ross Koen, of the Association of California State College Professors, objected to the board's dealing with this matter in executive session, and called its action illegitimate.

Robert Phelps, of the California College and University Faculty Association, urged the board to reconsider. He said the board's action would create far more difficult problems and urged the board to recognize due process.

A week went by. President Smith refused to honor the trustees' request that he reassign Murray, noting that Murray had a contract with the college, and that it could not be broken without following established procedures. Smith said that he interpreted the board's "request" as leaving the responsibility for the assignment of personnel to local campus administrators within the framework of established policy.

In announcing on October 1 his refusal to reassign Murray to nonteaching duties, President Smith said his decision was made after consultation with the academic senate, the English department, the college's advisory board, and "other interested persons." President Smith told a press conference that any reassignment of Murray to a nonteaching position "would require charges and an open hearing at which the individual has opportunity to defend himself.

"The public statements and political philosophies of faculty members are not grounds for punitive action."

"This brings us to the real question of public and official attitudes," said Smith. "The Trustees' concern apparently stems from Mr. Murray's actions and statements outside the classroom. The exact basis for their request that I reassign him has not been communicated to me in any written charges and his record at this college does not warrant action at the present time under our rules and procedures."

Smith was playing for time, and a way to deal with Murray within the procedures of the college. His task was made virtually impossible by the lack of an established, operational mechanism for faculty discipline. The machinery was there—but only on paper. There had been some movement toward the creation of appropriate machinery in the spring of 1968, but as the semester ended, so had the effort; over the intervening summer months, nothing was done. When the fall semester began, the machinery for due process was not yet able to function. Thus, Smith sought a way, amidst faculty and student pressure, to deal with the Murray matter.

For the moment, the trustees did not seek to force Smith's hand, although they were growing restive. At least until October 24, the issue was avoided. At the trustees' regular monthly meeting on that day, Chairman Theodore Meriam told the board:

> We have received numerous questions concerning Mr. George Murray, instructor at San Francisco State College. President Smith of San Francisco State has advised us that the College is currently investigating certain conduct of Mr. Murray as reported to campus offices. In my judgment it is inappropriate for this Board to take any action today which, while an investigation is being conducted by proper campus authorities, might interfere with the process of that investigation. We shall anticipate receiving the outcome of this investigation in a report from President Smith at our next Board meeting.

The board believed Smith had made a firm commitment to take action with respect to Murray.

Murray added to the furor by continuing to make inflammatory speeches. On October 24, Murray made a speech at Fresno State College—while the trustees were meeting on campus—which destroyed any hope of further restraint on the part of the statewide administration. He reportedly told 2,000 students: "We are slaves and the only way to become free is to kill all the slavemasters." During the speech, he referred to President Lyndon B. Johnson, Chief Justice Earl Warren, and Governor Ronald Reagan as "slavemasters." Murray said that the country needs "an old-fashioned black-brown-red-yellow-poor white revolution. That's the only way we're going to change things in the U.S.," he said.

"Political power comes from the barrel of a gun," Murray told his audience. "If you want campus autonomy, if the students want to run the college, and the cracker administrators don't go for it, then you control it with the gun."

THE STUDENT UNION

The October 24 meeting of the Board of Trustees produced an action which added further to student discontent. The trustees again rejected—by an 8–8 vote—the design of architect Moshe Safdie for a new $5.8 million student union building. The building would have been built with student funds. Safdie expressed amazement a few weeks earlier when a committee of the trustees had rejected his work as "ugly, impractical and incompatible with the campus architecture." Russell Bass, president of the Associated Students of San Francisco State, presented the trustees with a petition with 6,000 student signatures endorsing the union.

"I live closer to the lives of students than you do and I am not threatening, but I do want to give you a report," said Bass. "The kind of disruptive activity that you are so vehemently opposed to is simply the discontent which has surfaced. The volume of student discontent is far greater than that."

The trustees' rejection of the design exemplified for many of the students all they found objectionable in the rule of the "absentee trustees."

Those who worked on the project feel that the campus badly needs a new student union; there are few places on the crowded campus to gather, talk, or study in anything like an accommodating atmosphere. A great deal of time and effort, and a substantial amount of students' funds, went into a design study for the new union. Safdie's design, based on a combination of modules with sharply angled windows, was unique and controversial. It won an architectural award, but ran into immediate difficulties with the Board of Trustees.

There were questions about the cost estimates and objections to the physical design. The trustees' budget committee gave the project reluctant approval, but the building and grounds committee wanted the design modified for a number of reasons, including safety factors related to the windows. The board had requested the students to bring back a modification of the design. The design was not modified, in part because Safdie objected. The matter was then brought before the full board on October 24, 1968, when, after much debate, the design was rejected. Robert Smith has cited the rejection of the design as one of the main issues on the campus in the fall of 1968.

MURRAY'S SPEECH

On Monday, October 28, Murray, speaking from a cafeteria table at San Francisco State, is reported to have said that black and brown students should carry guns to protect themselves from "racist administrators."

Some newspaper accounts tied Murray's speech to the black students' call for a November 6 strike. And the impression was given that Murray was calling for them to bring guns particularly on that day. Murray disagreed with this version, pointing out that he meant they should carry guns at all times to protect themselves.

In the days immediately following the speech, there was confusion as to what Murray actually said. When Robert Smith and Mayor Alioto sought sufficient grounds to justify a criminal complaint, there was no hard evidence—no recorded version of Murray's statements could be found. The *San Francisco Chronicle* reporter who first broke the story had not been present—he had reported a hearsay account. But the press reports, coming as they did on the heels of Murray's Fresno speech, were enough to force the issue with the statewide administration.

In his talk, Murray had touched on what was to be a central theme of the black philosophy in the turmoil here. He accused the administration of delaying the implementation of a black curriculum:

> The black studies department is no department at all. There are four and one-half million black and brown people in California, and they all pay taxes to pay for the racist departments here, but none of their taxes go to black and brown people.

The reaction to Murray's call for guns on campus was explosive. San Francisco Mayor Alioto asked the district attorney to see if Murray's statement violated any laws. "This is a wild and extremist statement," the mayor told a press conference. 'Such exhortations to violence are part of the reasons for tensions in the city."

The mayor might well have been concerned; it had been a tense week in San Francisco: The Richmond district police station had been bombed; there had been a major fire in a housing project; it was approaching Halloween, traditionally a difficult time for the police force.

On October 31, State College Chancellor Dumke, after consultation "with a number of trustees," ordered President Smith to suspend Murray both as an instructor and as a graduate student for 30 days, pending completion of the investigation of his conduct.

For several days, the college administrators had been pleading with the chancellor's office to let them handle Murray through normal disciplinary procedures.

Smith refused on October 31 to comply with what he called the "unprecedented" order and requested a November 1 meeting with Dumke to discuss the suspension "in the context of the local situation." Such a meeting, said Smith, "would allow the participation of both campus and community officials who will bear the impact of this action."

Smith had sought out Mayor Alioto. After conferring, the two were agreed the city was filled with tension, and any incident which might trigger violence should be avoided.

Both Smith and Alioto knew the tremendous pressure the trustees were under, and realized that some action by the trustees was a certainty. Both hoped that any action would be deferred for a few days. Thus, the mayor and the college president telephoned the trustees, meeting in Los Angeles, to request a delay until Monday, November 4. At the least, they wanted time to build up evidence for a solid case against Murray in any campus disciplinary proceedings, and Alioto wanted time to better prepare local officials and police if trouble did occur. Their request was refused.

The mayor also sought opinions from the district attorney, the U.S. attorney, and the State's attorney general as to whether the facts would support criminal action against Murray. It was the mayor's belief that a criminal charge would be better accepted on the campus and in the community than summary action by the State college system's hierarchy. All three law enforcement agencies gave negative opinions.

On Friday, November 1 (after most students had left for the weekend), Smith carried out the order to suspend Murray. But he issued a statement saying he did so reluctantly:

"I do not believe that this abrupt manner of handling this situation contributes to the solution of a complex problem."

Smith's statement also said:

> My option to resolve the Murray case using college procedures in a manner designed to benefit the San Francisco community, the college and Mr. Murray have been removed by an order to suspend Mr. Murray immediate. . . .

Smith said that the "continuing statewide controversy over the matter has complicated the disciplinary process already under way," but that this process would continue and that Murray would have "adequate opportunity to respond to the charges and defend himself."

President Smith described the events of that week in his interviews with the Study Team:

> I thought that the Murray-Cleaver dispute across the state was about two-thirds tied to the November election. I wasn't about to throw another catalyst into the city when it looked really threatening in the city, so I went to check with the mayor to see what he thought about maintaining stability on the campus. At that time we were having all kinds of turbulence around the high schools in the city, and then Halloween was coming up, and we had turmoil on the campus. The mayor was

convinced that nothing should be done that week regardless of the merits of the case.

And the second thing was that we didn't have the evidence to suspend Murray. What we had were newspaper accounts, and you couldn't get anybody to testify. We did get a tape later. Dumke felt that I had committed myself to the trustees the week before to do something about Murray by the middle of the week, and Wednesday is the middle of the week. So I started getting calls from the chancellor's office and Murray made an additional speech that didn't help things. And so I was trying to deal with that and we couldn't get anybody to make explicit what they had heard except the report in the *Chronicle*.

So in the meantime, I decided I wasn't going to act until the following week for the good of the college, for the community, and because of the politically laden operation. That's when I started getting orders to suspend him.

On October 30, Smith had an appointment with the mayor scheduled for 11 a.m.

Then I got a call [from the chancellor's office] about 9 or 9:30 a.m. saying: "When are you going to move on Murray?"

And I tried to tell them what I was doing about it. They felt in my going to Alioto–I had the impression that they felt it was an effort to drag the Democrats into the situation rather than an effort to see whether we were going to blow up the campus.

So I held out stubbornly until Friday afternoon.

As the Board of Trustees and the chancellor saw it, Smith was being dilatory–he was not honoring his commitments. As Smith's friends among the faculty and college administration saw it, the trustees were forcing him to do something he had already determined to do–to suspend Murray, but forcing it to be done in a way the academic community would surely find unacceptable. As to timing–while Smith and Alioto sensed tension in San Francisco, the trustees sensed rising public dissatisfaction throughout the State, perhaps endangering the bond issue, and generally undermining the public's willingness to finance higher education in California.[4]

References

1. Dr. Glenn S. Dumke, 1957–61; Acting President Dr. Frank Fenton, Nov. 1961–Sept. 1962; Dr. Paul Dodd, 1962–65; Acting President Dr. Stanley Paulson, Dec. 1965–July 1966; Dr. John Summerskill, 1966–May 1968; Dr. Robert Smith, May–Nov. 1968; Dr. S. I. Hayakawa, November 1968–present.
2. In its entire history to the date of the strike, no one has ever been expelled.
3. "Politics in Higher Education," a position paper prepared by the academic senate of the California State colleges, Mar. 28, 1968, AS-157-68/GR (Rev.).
4. Murray was fired in late February 1969; his probation arising from the criminal assault charge brought against him following the *Gater* incident was revoked in mid-February 1969, after he was apprehended in a neighboring community and charged with illegal possession of firearms.

Chapter V

THE STRIKE

On October 31, the Black Students Union made their official announcement of the strike—to begin November 6—and unveiled their demands (releasing them to the press).

In late summer the college administration had learned that the black students had chosen November 6 as the day for some sort of activity to commemorate the beating of the *Gater* editors. The black students explained that "black people in this nation do not have any meaningful holidays," and they felt some should be created. The anniversary of the beating of the *Gater* editor would be a beginning.

The Study Team discovered there is some confusion about whether the student strike was to be a 1-day affair or an attempt at a long-range shutdown of the university. President Smith said that when the 10 demands were presented to him in his office on November 5, the black students announced they intended to strike whether or not he granted their demands. He was unclear whether they meant for a single day or longer.

President Smith issued a tough memorandum to faculty and students warning all that: "We will not condone violence and will take whatever steps are required to meet disruptive or violent action, with responses calculated to insure safety of individuals and property."

* * *

On November 5, a black delegation visited President Smith in his office and formally presented 10 demands to him.

On November 6, the strike began. Roving bands of black students—in teams of 5 and 10—entered classrooms to ask teachers and students why they were not supporting the strike. Some professors and newsmen reported that these teams threatened that tougher groups would be along to enforce the strike. President Smith closed the campus that afternoon—for the day—after announcing that he had reports of several small fires and other destruction, including a typewriter thrown through a window in the Business and Social Sciences Building. President Smith said he was closing the campus to protect "the majority of students and faculty members who are concerned with education." At the steps of the Administration Building, he told 300 white radicals that "this is not the time or place" to discuss strike grievances.

Two days after presentation of the BSU's 10 demands, the Third World Liberation Front added five similar ones. (The five demands are listed in app. I.) The original plan had been to have each of the five member groups of the Third World present its own list, but it was felt this would be confusing, Roger Alvarado, a TWLF leader, explained to the Study Team, so they issued only an additional five. Like the original 10 demands, the additional 5 were also labeled "nonnegotiable."

The demands were chiefly concerned with establishment and control of a black studies department in a School of Ethnic Studies. Many of them were on their way to being granted at the beginning of the strike, or had been granted, in effect. And several were granted during the strike, but the students insisted all 15 were nonnegotiable and had to be fulfilled, including the retention of Murray.

The BSU reasoning is sharply illustrated in their explanation of demand 1—that all black studies courses being taught through various other departments be immediately part of the black studies department and that all the instructors in this department receive full-time pay.

The BSU explanation of this demand:

> The black studies courses are being taught by established departments which also control the function of courses. In order for a brother or sister to teach a course he must go before the assigned department head to receive permission to teach, which clearly shows that the power lies with the departments and the racist administrators, not with the black studies department, chairman, faculty, and staff.

LIFE ON STRIKE

The campus reopened November 7. There was some violence but not as much as the day before. A group of about 500 white and Third World students held a campus rally, then marched on the Administration Building. When the students reached the steps of the Administration Building, they were met by Robert Beery, head of the campus police, who read a statement from President Smith:

> We must warn you that attempts to enter this Administration Building or harm the occupants will result in disciplinary action or arrest.

The students shouted some obscenities, then withdrew. Part of the group marched through the Business and Social Sciences Building and the Humanities Building, banging on doors and yelling, "Rehire Murray," before they dispersed.

There was one arrest. A 28-year-old Nigerian student, enrolled in two drama courses, was arrested for carrying a small bomb. Police said the bomb was about the size and shape of a transistor radio, and was filled with black powder.

Another bomb made of .22-caliber shells wired together in a can exploded in the Education Building. There were no injuries and no arrest in connection with this bomb. There were several fires in wastebaskets, a telephone booth, and in a coach's desk, but all were quickly extinguished.

In the early days of the strike, the striking students assembled picket lines in front of classroom buildings. Later these were moved and consolidated into one large circular picket line at the campus entrance.

A verbal exchange and brief scuffle between two students in front of the Business and Social Sciences Building illustrated the tensions at the troubled campus.

About 9 a.m. on November 7, a glass door of the building was shattered when an unidentified professor opened it hard against a student picket who refused to move.

Half an hour later a student named Leonard Sellers found his way blocked by a picketer as he approached the doors. "Are you telling me I can't go to class?" asked Sellers, a 24-year-old senior in journalism. "I have enough trouble just going to school."

"If you go in, you're a scab," replied the picketer, Kenneth Milz, a 24-year-old graduate student.

"Don't call me a scab," Sellers said, and the two students scuffled briefly. The resulting newspaper photo was published across the Nation. Another student separated the two.

"Go on in, you scab," Milz said.

That infuriated Sellers enough to want to resume the fight, but they were again separated.

"Don't you want to support our demands?" asked Milz.

"No," replied Sellers. "Not all of them. Some of them aren't logical–like the demand that all black students be let in here whether they're qualified or not.

"If they meet the requirements, fine, let them in. But I can't be in favor of letting all black students who want to come onto the campus. It's illogical."

Milz asked Sellers' opinion on the demand that Black Panther George Murray be reinstated as a teacher and graduate student.

"I don't believe that Murray should be allowed to teach here," Sellers replied.

"I was in the journalism department last year when Murray and the others came in and beat up the staff members of the *Gater*.

"I was one of the guys who got clobbered."

Milz, apparently giving up, replied, "Well go on in to class, you scab."

"Why don't I call you a fascist pig honkie?" Sellers said. "Is that an answer to any problems?" And he walked into class.

Friday, November 8, the student militants accelerated their guerrilla tactics. The administration reported that approximately 50 fires were discovered and extinguished on this day. Black raiding parties–some wearing stocking masks–invaded campus offices, overturning desks and smashing equipment. Most of the vandalism was done at noon while a strikers' rally was going on at the center of the campus. Offices were raided in the chemistry, anthropology, and psychology departments. The raid on the office of the chemistry department occurred with a plain-clothes policeman in an adjoining office a few feet away. Five men and two women, all wearing masks, burst into the office and turned over a desk, wrecked a duplicating machine, overturned wastebaskets, scattered files, and broke the glass in the door.

Four Negroes entered the anthropology office and ordered a secretary and two men to leave. One of them cut the wires to the telephone and the electric typewriter, reported the secretary. She said the young girl threw the Ditto machine on the floor and pushed over the coffeemaker. And a radio was thrown out a window.

Asked if she had screamed or protested, the secretary said:

> No, what can you say at a time like that but to say, "please stop."
> It all happened in seconds. And one of the men had wire clippers in his hand. I was worried there might be physical violence.
> After all, it's one thing about machines and another when it's people. But I don't think they meant to hurt anyone.

Commenting on the violence, she said:

> I can't help but feel that in a sense the white man is asking for it. Four hundred years of subtle slavery does weird things to people.
> I don't like violence and I don't like damage, but the blacks are reacting. Most of their demands are right. . . .
> Maybe the violence will accomplish something. It took a great deal of violence in the South and Watts before anybody recognized there were problems there and did anything about them.
> Maybe that's the only way to get people to see.

This sort of hit-and-run action made people uneasy. The administration reported that some secretaries asked to go home early, and many of the students were nervous.

One 22-year-old biochemistry major (male) told a reporter:

> There are a lot of people in my 12:30 class, and every time we heard a noise—even the wind—we looked around expecting a mass of them to come wheeling through the door.
> How can you concentrate on studying?

President Smith announced he was suspending regular student disciplinary procedures. He removed power from the student judicial court and placed it in a special five-member faculty-student committee appointed by himself. President Smith said he was taking the action "because of the series of emergencies on campus, provoking continued disruption of classes and the necessary work of the institution."

After a 3-day Veterans Day weekend, classes resumed on Tuesday, November 12. It was a quiet day. Students held a noon rally on campus. "Classroom education" teams of black students were visiting classrooms, requesting (and getting) 10 to 15 minutes to explain the strike to students. Some of the teams simply described the goals and philosophy of the strike.

At the Psychology Building, police detained and photographed six black students, who they said were disrupting classes.

The student newspaper, the *Daily Gater*, a strong supporter of the strike, said that class attendance was substantially reduced in the departments of economics, English, art, philosophy, and psychology, and down slightly in humanities, chemistry, music, and the school of education. The *Gater* said the strike was 40 to 50 percent successful. The administration has insisted that the *Gater* coverage of the strike has often been unreliable.

Newsmen regularly assigned to the strike estimated that it was 20 to 50 percent successful at times late in the fall semester. However, this did not mean that half the students at the campus supported the strike goals and agreed with the tactics. Many were frightened, or they had no class to attend because their teachers were on strike—or afraid to teach. The most successful rallies of the students drew more than 5,000 persons, but it was difficult to separate the curious from the committed. San Francisco State College had an enrollment of about 900 Negroes in the fall semester. The administration claimed that only 100 to 200 of them supported the BSU and its demands. To many observers it appeared that the percentage of support was much higher. However, there were some Negro students who continued to attend classes through the strike—despite what must have been incredible pressure. Other Third World groups were not nearly so successful in securing adherence to the strike among their peers. Large numbers of Oriental-Americans attended classes regularly. Many students ignored the disruption completely and walked each day through and between picketers and police at the college entrance at 19th Street and Holloway Avenue, completely oblivious to the substance or nature of the dispute.

Students who did attend classes were often subjected to strong verbal abuse as they descended from trolley cars and walked between police and the picket line. Shouts of "Scab, scab" were common.

One result of the disruption was a drop in enrollment for the spring semester which began in February 1969. Enrollment for the fall semester had been approximately 18,000 students. In the spring semester, it was about 16,000.

Strike leaders were claiming in mid-November that their effort was 40 to 50 percent successful. President Smith said a majority of the classes were meeting.

A proposal for arbitration of the strike was made at a noon rally on November 11 by Cyril Roseman, head of the campus urban studies program. He suggested the creation of an arbitration panel with two men appointed by President Smith, two by the BSU, and a fifth to be named by the Community Relations Service of the U.S. Department of Justice. President Smith agreed to the proposal, but the BSU's Ben Stewart rejected this idea. "Our demands are simple," he said. "We don't need any more proposals. . . . It would just be administrators talking to other administrators."

A faculty meeting the next day, attended by approximately half of San Francisco State's 1,300 teachers, voted overwhelmingly by voice vote in favor of a motion censuring Dumke for his action in the Murray case, and calling for his resignation. The faculty postponed consideration of resolutions in support of the strike and in support of President Smith.

STRIKE TURNING POINT

November 13 is considered by most observers and participants (newsmen, college administrators and students) as the turning point of the strike. A major confrontation (incredibly ill timed for all) occurred between the San Francisco Police Department's tactical squad and students—resulting in an almost classic pattern of escalation and the polarization of many previously uncommitted students.

As a result of the violence, the campus was closed. And President Smith's decision to close the campus was criticized, second guessed, and hotly debated by politicians, trustees, and the faculty for the remainder of the fall semester. Ultimately, it was the cause of his resignation.

The day began quietly. Sixty-five members of the American Federation of Teachers had decided to join the student strike—though they had been unable at this time to convince the union local to go out. They had set up a picket line at the campus entrance, 19th Street and Holloway Avenue, and were yelling at passing students, "Don't go to scab classes."

President Robert Smith thought the faculty action was harmful. "I thought the ad hoc operation in November was the first thing on the campus that lengthened the odds of our trying to get a solution at that stage. . . . We had some indications that the black students might have been willing to call the strike off at about that time."

At noon the Black Students Union held a press conference beside the BSU headquarters, a cramped area of the campus dotted with one-story huts used by the student government and student groups such as the BSU and the experimental college.

At the press conference, George Murray told his audience that the strike and its accompanying disruption marked a "very historic" moment. "It's the first time that barriers have been dissolved between classes—between black, brown, yellow and red people," Murray said.

"You can tell every racist pig in the world, including Richard Milhous Nixon, that we're not going to negotiate until the demands are met."

As the press conference was breaking up, a nine-man unit of the San Francisco Police Department tactical squad appeared at the other side of the BSU hut. To students, it appeared that the police were there to intimidate and harass strikers.

The police had come to the area because of a report of a beating of a television cameraman. The cameraman told police that he was photographing two Negroes, "one of them with a suspicious-looking lump in his pocket," when he was jumped from behind by "a big black." The cameraman said he was knocked down and kicked in the back, then he rolled over and filmed the black man running away.

He mentioned the incident to a campus policeman who suggested that he make a report to one of the tactical-squad officers in a nearby building. The cameraman did so and said he thought he could identify his assailant. The police sent two plainclothesmen to accompany the cameraman to the student hut area. As they neared the area, the cameraman decided that he was unable to pick out the black who had attacked him.

At this point, explained tactical squad commander Lt. James Curran, his men lost radio contact with the plainclothesmen. Fearing the plainclothesmen were endangered, the uniformed squad marched to the area. The students knew nothing of this, and felt they were being attacked or at least harassed by police. And the melee was on.

The tactical squad and its reinforcements felt they were surrounded and under attack, and they fought back. It is impossible to re-create precisely how the battle began. To the students it seemed that the tactical squad suddenly appeared and seized and clubbed Nesbitt Crutchfield, a BSU member.

President Smith was eating lunch off campus when the trouble began and was unaware that uniformed police had marched on the students. The police central-command post in Smith's office was equally unaware.

Vice President for Academic Affairs Donald L. Garrity, who was having a sandwich in the president's office at the time, describes the November 13 turmoil as he knows it:

> I've never gone to investigate how the message got from the plainclothesmen to the Tac Squad. . . . The first thing we knew about it was when the officer we worked with—Inspector Ralph Brown, really a first rate guy—said, "Gosh, the Tac Squad is going into the BSU."
>
> And we said, "What?"
>
> And he said, "It's going into the BSU."
>
> At that point, we don't say: "Withdraw the troops." They are there.
>
> We sat and kind of got reports. To this day, I don't think DeVere [Pentony] or Glenn [Smith] or I know exactly what transpired with those two plainclothesmen and that cameraman and how the word got back to move the Tac Squad in. They were in communication with one another. We weren't monitoring it. Brown was as surprised as we were. . . .
>
> You know what that hut situation is like. It is not a very big space, and 50 people is a crowd down there. You come walking a Tac Unit down there and you are all in a nice, cozy little area.
>
> There is the Tac Unit, and black students with all of their feelings about not only the police but the Tac Unit. We have a frightened kind of situation.
>
> They blew it, blew it right then and there. Flat out mistake on the part of the police. With all of the symbolism that's involved for black people and the like, in this movement.
>
> There is a rally going on out in the middle of the campus which is an SDS sort of thing, excoriating everyone, you know.
>
> The Tac Squad comes in and somebody yells, "There's the Tac Squad!"
>
> Hundreds and hundreds of kids run there and they get down there and the Tac Squad sees hundreds of people running in towards them.

They move out toward them. And we have got the wild scene of people yelling and screaming, running this way and then that way. Everybody agitating everybody, and the Tac Squad that is in there being frightened to death, and they lose their cool, and they zap some black guys. Other black guys get mad. And the kids get mad out there. Another unit of the Tac Squad comes in to rescue the Tac Squad unit that is in there.

They get surrounded, and they get panicky and they lose their cool, and by they, I don't mean all of them. Individual officers break by; suddenly being surrounded with students who have broken from around the speakers platform. And I don't mean five or ten, but hundreds. And I don't blame the cops in a sense for being frightened by it, and they lash out and we have a mad swirling scene in which each feeds the other.

> It ends up in both units of the Tac Squad trying to make their way off the campus, but each way they move they run into a group of students who surge upon them, then the students retreat and throw things at them. Maybe one or two guys run out to get the guy who's just hit him on the side of the head with a can or something, and whaps him with a club.
>
> The students see that. They come swinging back with a howl and a roar. We go through that scene. It's bad.

The turmoil was brought to a halt by the intervention of the ad hoc AFT committee which was striking then in support of the students. The faculty members, led by Prof. William Staunton, placed themselves between the students and the police, and the police marched off campus.

President Smith did not think the faculty members were necessarily to be congratulated.

"That afternoon they felt they did a great service by moving in between the police and the students to cut down the violence which I felt they helped generate in the beginning."

It seemed to some observers and many students that the policemen had broken ranks and charged the crowd and were beating people at random. Most observers agree that the campus was a mad swirling scene of frightened students and policemen for nearly half an hour that day.

Eight persons were arrested, seven of them charged with assault or assaulting an officer.

Describing the event, the *San Francisco Chronicle* reported, "There was an almost unbroken chorus of shrieks and screams." And the newspaper reported that the crowd of students had quickly grown from "around 200 to about 2,000."

The students then held a rally at which economics professor William Staunton, a controversial figure and long an activist in California's campus politics, urged that the campus be closed:

> "There are no more classes at San Francisco State," he told the crowd at the rally.
>
> . . . That man [Smith] is a damned fool for trying to work within the system. The trustees must act to restore Murray, guarantee adequate funds for black studies and the Third World people, and make a clear declaration that the faculty will be free to run this college. They must tell us what they intend to do to restore justice on this campus.

He strongly criticized the decision of Chancellor Dumke to require suspension of George Murray. "Any fool should recognize the danger to lives brought on this campus by that action," Staunton said.

John Levin, president of the campus SDS and a member of the Maoist Progressive Labor Party, shouted:

"George Murray was fired for saying students should bring guns on campus to defend themselves. After you saw these pigs walking around with their guns out, can you deny he was right?"

The crowd marched on the administration building and a delegation went inside demanding that Smith come out. They demanded "to know why he called the pigs." President Smith was interrupted as he began his explanation that the police were called to "protect the safety of . . . ."

Shouts of "Whose safety?" drowned him out.

The president began to say, "This is not the way . . .," but again was drowned out by shouts of: "Will you grant the demands?"

He tried to say, "Until we can sit down and talk . . .," but was drowned out and went back into the building.

At 5:25 p.m., President Smith held a press conference to announce that the college would be closed.

"It's clear that as a result of the pattern of confrontation and violence occurring and the turmoil on campus that we don't believe it's possible to carry on the basic instructional program. . . .

"We will keep the campus closed until we can run it on a more rational basis."

He told the reporters that "bringing in police as an effort to keep this campus open has not worked to my satisfaction."

He advised students to remain home and "maintain as best they can their studies."

The president said that the faculty and administration would begin a conference the next day—and soon bring students into it—in an effort to resolve problems at the troubled campus.

On the following day, Thursday, November 14, began the pattern of attempts to resolve the turmoil at San Francisco State College—efforts that were to involve California's leading political figures and which would bring repeatedly to public view the troubles that had long been festering within the system of the California State colleges. The few days after November 13 set the tone for the remainder of the fall semester, which ended January 31, 1969.

The remainder of November and early December was marked by continued clashes between students and police and fierce charges and countercharges about the question of campus autonomy. The question of how far the statewide trustees should intervene as President Smith attempted to settle the campus became a focus of controversy. And the longtime animosity that many faculty members felt toward the trustees and the statewide master plan boiled to the surface.

A CAMPUS CANNOT BE CLOSED

Political reaction to Smith's decision to close the campus was immediate.

Both Governor Reagan and then Assembly Speaker Unruh criticized the decision to close the school. The Governor labeled it "an act of capitulation," and commented that "the campus administration itself contributed in no small measure to the unfortunate events of the past few days." The Governor said he was referring to the fact that President Smith "publicly opposed an order by Chancellor Dumke calling for the removal of a self-professed advocate of violence from the State college faculty."

The Governor said the order to close the college was "an unprecedented act of irresponsibility" and demanded "the campus be reopened to classes with dispatch."

"I want to make it perfectly plain," said Governor Reagan, "that as long as I am Governor, our publicly supported institutions of higher education are going to stay open to provide educations for our young people. The people of this State, the people who pay the bills, want it that way. And that is the way it will be."

The Governor was critical of what he called–

> a small, unrepresentative faction of faculty and student militants determined to substitute violence and coercion for orderly grievance procedures available to all.
>
> Professors are paid to teach, not to lead or encourage violent forays which only result in physical harm to persons and property. If they refuse to honor the trust our citizens have placed in them, they should look for work elsewhere.
>
> And, as I have said before, if students–including members of the BSU and SDS–are unwilling to abide by the rules of the college, they will have to get their educations somewhere else. . . .
>
> It is clear that the administration in its obvious quest for what was considered an easy way out, ignored other options which were available to assure the orderly continuation of the educational process.

Assembly Speaker Unruh sent a telegram to the Governor urging that Reagan get the school reopened:

"You should not sit idly by as Governor and permit San Francisco State College to close its doors. Such a posture would constitute a triumph for anarchy," said Unruh.

"It seems hardly necessary to remind you that the taxpayers of the entire State of California support this institution. They will not tolerate it if you allow riots and rebellion to dictate education policy."

The State College Board of Trustees scheduled a special meeting for the following Monday in Los Angeles.

"I'm in no hurry to reopen the campus," President Smith told a meeting of 800 faculty members.

> We'll make an assessment each night and we'll reopen when we have reasonable stability and we can operate without police forces having to come on campus to put out fires and to protect people.
>
> We have the problems not only of the demands of the black students, but we also have the demands made by other minority students.

The San Francisco State faculty senate voted to ask President Smith to assign 11.3 faculty positions to black studies and for implementation of the program by the spring of 1969. They created an 18-member task force to create an ethnic studies program. They also requested Chancellor Dumke to rescind his order to suspend George Murray.

When told of the faculty action, Chancellor Dumke said he had no intention of reconsidering the suspension of Murray.

Mayor Alioto offered the services of a labor mediator to settle the trouble at San Francisco State. The mayor criticized "Chancellor Dumke and the absentee trustees" for their refusal to agree to his and President Smith's earlier request to delay for 3 days the suspension of George Murray. The mayor disagreed with the decision to close the campus.

President Smith declared on November 15 that he hoped to reopen the campus the following Tuesday, November 19. The decision would hinge on how well issues were resolved in talks between administrators, students, and faculty. And he probably would not know until Monday afternoon if classes could be resumed.

A newly formed student Committee for an Academic Environment held a press conference to demand the recall of the elected officers and legislators in the student government.

Another development on November 15 was the short talk in the faculty meeting by the internationally known semanticist S. I. Hayakawa. "I wish to comment," he said, "on the intellectually slovenly habit, now popular among whites as well as blacks, of denouncing as racist those who oppose or are critical of any Negro tactic or demand.

> If we are to call our college racist, then what term do we have left for the Government of Rhodesia?
>
> Black students are again disrupting the campus. A significant number of whites, including faculty members, condone and even defend this maneuver.
>
> In other words, there are many whites who do not apply to blacks the same standards of morality and behavior that they apply to whites.
>
> This is an attitude of moral condescension that every self-respecting Negro has a right to resent—and does resent.

He was interrupted several times by applause which seemed to come from a majority of the faculty members present.

Hayakawa talked of the need to support President Smith and get classes going again by the following Tuesday.

> No one—no matter how great his need to establish his black consciousness—has the right to break into my classes and tell my students that they are dismissed.
>
> When my classes are dismissed, I shall dismiss them. The conduct of my classes is my responsibility and not anyone else's and I shall continue to fight for the right to continue to do my duty.

He suggested that a faculty-student committee be formed "to keep the peace." And he called for a resolution of support from the faculty authorizing President Smith "to suspend students found creating disorder and to get court orders when necessary to keep disruptive students and nonstudents off the campus."

Smith was searching for a way to normalize the campus. He met in a series of conferences with faculty members and administrators at the college, attempting to identify the basic issues underlying the disturbances and to develop methods of control. Out of these discussions developed Smith's plan gradually to reopen the campus.

On Monday, November 18, the trustees ordered President Smith to reopen the college. He had intended to do this, after a day or two of conferences. Now, he had to go back and face his troubled campus with a direct order from the trustees—who were disliked in the best of times by many students and faculty members.

The trustees' meeting room in Los Angeles was crowded with representatives–students, faculty, and administrators–from San Francisco State. It was a tension-filled meeting that would be discussed angrily by the San Francisco delegation for weeks.

The chancellor urged the immediate reopening of the college and restoration of the basic instructional program, even if it required "maximum security against violence and disruption."

Trustee Chairman Meriam spoke about the trustees' "special obligation to the large majority of students and faculty who want to continue their education." This was a point the trustees returned to repeatedly throughout the troubled months of the fall semester.

On November 18, the question was whether and under what conditions San Francisco State College would be reopened. Seen against the background of the previous 12 months' disturbances, the outcome was never in doubt. It will be recalled that John Summerskill had to justify to the trustees his decision in December 1967 to close the campus for only a few hours. The board members overwhelmingly express the strong feeling that the closing of any one of the 18 campuses is a matter of policy which they must decide. Both the trustees and the chancellor do make a distinction, however, between brief, *tactical* closings of a campus (such as those ordered by Summerskill in December 1967, or by Smith on November 6, 1968) and the "indefinite" closing announced by Robert Smith on November 13, 1968.

There was a consensus at its November 18 meeting that the board could not allow any group to force the closing of a college. Fundamentally, the board rested its position upon the fact that the colleges are tax-supported, public institutions. In the words of one highly respected trustee: "In the final analysis, maintaining the State college system, or any one of the colleges–keeping them open and operational–is a board responsibility. It must be."

Individual trustees told the Study Team they had received stacks of mail from citizens and students urging that the campus be kept open. Some of the letters were from students who were scheduled to graduate soon and had supported themselves while going through college. Such letters unquestionably reinforced the trustees' sincere belief that the school had to be kept open.

The San Francisco State faculty and administration felt, with equal sincerity, that decisions on whether or not it is possible to conduct classes can only be made by people at that campus.

President Smith defended his decision to close the campus, saying "the confrontation was turning from malicious mischief to violence." His plan for reopening consisted of students returning to the campus that day for discussions of the issues, holding a faculty meeting Tuesday morning, and more discussions with students on Tuesday afternoon, all aimed at getting the campus open Wednesday morning. He said he was "trying to develop a wider sense of responsibility among students and faculty so that all the responsibility won't fall on a group of administrators who are suspect already." He said he wanted to open the campus without massive numbers of police.

Chancellor Dumke told the board that he had asked President Smith to reopen the campus immediately. The chancellor said he had made it clear to President Smith that "the demands of some groups at San Francisco State College are far in excess of the resources available to him."

"It is equally clear," said the chancellor, "that the California State Colleges do not possess the kind of instant resources sufficient to meet all demands, however legitimate the underlying aspirations may be. . . . We must all understand that demands alone are not always definable as legitimate needs, and demands backed by violence and threats of violence taint any need or aspiration."

Leo McClatchy, chairman of the San Francisco State academic senate, read a statement:

> We have been thrust into a feeling of reality that we have never experienced before: we have witnessed threats and counter-threats, rocks thrown, heads clubbed—an atmosphere of fear. We cannot operate an institution of higher learning unless we come to terms with the deep causes underlying the dangerous unrest that has come to our campus. . . . The trustees and the public must be assured that the suspension of formal classes was not an act of irresponsibility, but a genuine response to a disturbed state of affairs that made the continuation of formal teaching itself an irresponsible act.
>
> Closing our classes in order to reassess our educational approaches may well be the best educational investment San Francisco State College can make for itself, for the State College system, and for the State of California.

The trustees also heard a plea for protection from William T. Insley, a campus technician, speaking for the 700 nonacademic employees of the college:

> As the sitting ducks in the shooting gallery that President Smith proposes to open . . . a majority of us want to know exactly what is going to be done to ensure our safety when the doors to the gallery are flung open and the guns are passed out to all save us.

The trustees turned to a discussion of the academic merits of black studies and trustee Louis Heilbron expressed fear that it might be used as a forum for "black power propaganda." He was assured by Vice President Garrity that it would be under the same control as other departments.

Edward O. Lee, the only Negro trustee, commented, "I can understand the reluctance of some of the trustees to have black folks consulted because what might be propaganda to one person is education to another."

When President Smith said the faculty might be all black at first, Trustee Charles Luckman called it "a frightening possibility."

"What you're saying," interjected Lee, "is that the faculty might be all black because black people are most likely to be interested in teaching black studies, not by design."

"Like George Murray," said Luckman, to which Lee responded, "What you're really saying is that you don't trust your department, Mr. Luckman."

Governor Reagan, an ex officio trustee, then attempted to place the meeting in what he saw as its proper perspective:

> I don't think that they [the black students] understand the problems or are representative of 90 percent of the responsible Negro community. What we're here to determine is the reopening of that school. If it can be opened in the next 15 minutes it should be opened. The answer to

maintaining safety on the campus is to rid the campus of those who cause disruption.

The trustees then adjourned for lunch and an executive session. When they returned they heard several additional statements. The San Francisco State Alumni Association supported Smith's decision to close the campus and urged that he be given autonomous power to solve the problems of the campus and reopen.

Russell Bass, the college student body president, told them "San Francisco State has been disfunctional for two weeks," and that "as long as the tensions which created the violence and the problems creating that tension are present, a program of education can't go on."

Lowell Clucas, a spokesman for the San Francisco State Committee for an Academic Environment was also asked to make a statement. After he reiterated the committee's position in favor of reopening the campus, trustee Swim offered "congratulations."

Victor Lee, president of the California State College Student Presidents Association, criticized the State college system for tolerating "outside political intervention in its determination of internal affairs which is rightfully that of the students, faculty, and local administration," giving "the chancellor's office the ability to arbitrarily break traditionally established standards of due process relative to the hiring and firing of professors," putting "such a tremendous amount of pressure . . . upon the president of the college by his superiors in an effort to reduce those powers which are rightfully his to that of liaison or errand boy," and permitting "with little review, the existence of a superfluous, outmoded concept of curriculum–that of the general education requirements–while it continues to review with great detail, and reluctance at times, the establishment of minority studies–the most necessary subject matter in society's schools today."

He told the trustees, "If you open that campus by any means necessary, you will simply be no more right than those who say that they will close that campus by any means necessary."

The trustees, however, were determined that San Francisco State should be opened. If there was general agreement on that principle, there was some disagreement as to how it would be implemented. Not all of the trustees were satisfied with the simple resolution which had passed, ordering Smith "to open that college immediately." One trustee sought to modify the language to direct Smith to "begin the process of reopening" the school; another interpreted the board's action to mean that Smith should open the college "as fast as practicable." Ultimately, there was an understanding that the board's policy statement left the exact logistics up to Smith, and that he could wait until Wednesday to reopen the campus.

During discussion of the order to Smith to reopen, the trustees agreed that Smith could hold discussions with the strikers but directed that he not hold formal negotiations or make concessions. The trustees accept as a basic principle that they should not be in the position of negotiating under duress. One trustee, a prominent lawyer, explained the trustees' action on the ground that "No one wants to be forced into a position where, in carrying out a public responsibility, someone substitutes his will for your will."

Robert Smith returned to the troubled San Francisco campus hoping to reopen it through a series of convocations which he believed might result in a better understanding of the underlying issues by all concerned. He announced that classes would resume Wednesday, November 20.

The faculty was distressed with the result of the Trustees' meeting. The Trustees and the Chancellor, because no funds were available, had been unable to furnish needed financial assistance to the college; the faculty chafed under the resolutions which had passed. A faculty meeting gave Smith both cheers and boos, and the faculty voted not to teach. This put Smith in a difficult light with the students. "It demonstrated that I was either unresponsive to the faculty and students or that I was a lackey of the Trustees. Take your choice."

THE CONVOCATIONS

Despite his position that classes should be held, Smith appeared at the November 20 convocation with several of his top administrators.

He also urged students not planning to go to class to attend the convocation, urged students who were attending classes to attend the convocation when they were not in class, called the convocation "the best way" to start reopening the campus.

Although only a few classes met, several strikers expressed dissatisfaction that the classes had not been formally canceled and that some were being held. Nonetheless, they decided to continue the meeting at least for the rest of the day.

Here is how the convocation went on November 20:

Jack Alexis, BSU leader, told the convocation audience:

> We need new rules and regulations, a whole new education, so that we can begin to have education that is relevant to us. Higher education was originally started as education for the elite. Students are saying that we're not part of the elite. Education for the elite is not relevant for us. The role of white radicals is one of destruction, in a positive way. If a structure is decadent, you must destroy it before you can build. The role of black people is to build. That's what black studies is all about. Black studies must be controlled by black people in a large role because it's our thing, it's our baby. Maybe in a couple of years we'll be able to open it up to everybody. Our objectives are to contrive to define and refine the expressions of our community and to contrive to explore ways of integrating the community into our activities.

Leroy Goodwin of the BSU:

> Our major objective is the seizure of power. Power must come to the people and black power will come to black people. As things now stand you must present your program to the pigs in power and they must approve it. Until we have power, everything else is bullshit. The dog believes we want to participate in his political games and that if we demand 10 things all the niggers really want is five. Each day the demands are delayed we will escalate our tactics. If armed struggle is what is needed for us to control our lives and our education, then that is what we will use. Peace and order are bullshit issues.

355-234 O - 69 - 5

> They don't mean anything to us unless we have control of our lives. The pig administration has run down our attempts to win legitimate demands by peaceful means.

Nesbitt Crutchfield of the BSU:

> If you don't deal with the issues you won't deal with anything. That's not a threat; it's a promise.

President Smith:

> I look at this problem from the perspective of a social liberal. Certain styles of action are alien and outside my view of the institution. I agree with the needs but I disagree that it is necessary to revolutionize the entire institution. We need a large amount of autonomy to do what is needed.

Elmer Cooper, dean of student activities, and a Negro:

> The Trustees are worried about a black studies department having an all-black faculty. They didn't mention that there are departments with all-white faculties. These people are scared of giving black people control over their own destinies. Does the college plan to do something about institutional racism or is is just going to fire black power advocates? I haven't seen anybody fired for being a racist.

President Smith:

> Among the mistakes I've made as president is not establishing an interracial group to investigate racism.

Alexis:

> The power is not on this campus. We must educate everyone on the campus so we can go at the people in power. I hope that at the end of this two or three days President Smith will join us in fighting the Trustees.

Joseph White, dean of undergraduate studies, and a Negro:

> The machinery of the college is not set up to deal with black demands, it is set up to deal with white reality. We will never return to normal. You can forget about that. More education has gone since the strike started than in the six years I went to school here.

Throughout the turmoil of the fall semester, traditional faculty governance mechanisms seemed woefully ill equipped to meet the challenges of this novel crisis.

As the strike progressed, the other parties to the problem—especially striking students and the trustees—seemed to regard the faculty and faculty senate meetings, actions and proposals as irrelevant. An observer from the Washington-based American Council on Education describes a portion of a November 19 faculty meeting:

> In all faculty and senate meetings, we were impressed by the obsession with parliamentary procedure, with nitpicking and endless points of

order. [One informant maintained that this was the only weapon left to the moderates.]

As soon as Bob Smith finished speaking, Chairman McClatchy suggested that he would entertain a vote of confidence in the president. At this point, a sequence of events occurred which must be described in detail because it reveals so much of the spirit of SFSC and its faculty.

1. Motion and second for vote of confidence in Smith.

2. Point of order: Such a motion must go to the Committee on Resolutions, which has already established the order of the day, and hence this is out of order.

3. Chair overrules the point of order.

4. Motion [angrily put] and many seconds to overrule the chair.

5. Chair calls for a voice vote. Yeas and nays judged equal.

6. Call for a division.

7. While the yeas begin to stand, microphone seized for a point of order: Nonvoting faculty and students judged to be voting.

8. Chairman says he cannot sort out 1,000 people by sight, asks for suggestions. Suggested that the hall be cleared and that only voting faculty be readmitted. Much groaning. Hall cleared for 15 minute recess.

9. Faculty begin going back in, showing passes to *two* campus police guards.

10. Meantime, side doors and stage doors are thrown open, and students and nonvoters go streaming back down the aisles and even on stage. (I asked the guard why he let obvious BSU members in. Guard: "Listen, one of them told me that I'd better let them in or I'd get my head busted. I ain't about to argue with thirty colored boys, so I let'em in!")

11. Result: Audience in exactly the same state, but now angry and swelled in ranks by militant students attracted to the fray.. From this point on, all voice votes "tainted."

12. Many motions to adjourn, not debatable. All noisily shouted down, sometimes without a formal vote. (Two faculty members walk by me in the doorway, white with anger, explaining to a third, "Mob rule.")

13. Finally, by an overwhelming voice vote, agreement to reconvene next day in general session for a convocation and for open debate between the president and the BSU leadership about "what is possible."

14. Adjournment, followed by a call for a faculty senate meeting in the front of the auditorium. Black students sitting at the front refuse to move, say they will have to be carried out.

15. The senate (about half its members) give up and move to a small conference room in the library building.

In the climate of confusion in the following days, Smith's plan to reopen the campus through a series of convocations faltered. The campus was in limbo—neither open nor closed. Attempts to hold classes were met by striking students, first with protests, and later with disruptions. Much of the time was spent with the faculty denouncing the trustees, and the students denouncing the existing system of education.

The convocations failed, despite urging the support from San Francisco Mayor Alioto. The Governor criticized the holding of the convocations, and the trustees expressed anger that the faculty had not fully returned to work; they considered the convocation just another delaying tactic.

In an exchange November 25, BSU spokesman Jerry Varnado called President Smith a "pig," further reducing chances that the all-college meeting would produce a solution to the strike.

PRESIDENT SMITH RESIGNS

The trustees called Smith to their meeting in Los Angeles on the morning of November 26. During an executive session, Smith was questioned in detail by the board as to when and how he would reopen the campus. His answers did not satisfy them. They felt he was equivocating.

"He would indicate that he would open the campus, but then he would say that if things changed he might not." The trustees wanted the campus reopened; they wanted their policy carried out. "If it took police to do so, then police would have to be used."

Smith felt he simply could not give the trustees a blanket assurance that he could open the campus and keep it open. He felt the "mythology and hysteria" on the campus had grown too great, and the safety of individuals could not be assured. There was as little progress being made in the trustees' session as there was at the convocation. A luncheon recess was called and the morning session ended. As they sat at the table, the discussion continued. Without prelude, Smith interjected into the conversation: "Gentlemen, I will save you a lot of trouble here–I resign!" His resignation statement was brief; he says it contains the best summary of the reasons for his resignation.

November 26, 1968

Memorandum
Robert R. Smith, President
San Francisco State College

REQUEST FOR IMMEDIATE REASSIGNMENT TO OTHER THAN ADMINISTRATIVE DUTIES AT SAN FRANCISCO STATE COLLEGE

I request, as of this date, reassignment from the role of President to duties other than college administration within San Francisco State College. My reasons are:

1. Inability to reconcile effectively the conflicts between the Trustees and Chancellor, the faculty groups on campus, the militant student groups, and political forces of the State. Each has brought such strenuous pressure to bear, sometime concurrently, in efforts to control decisions facing me as college president in severely difficult situations that I believe my effectiveness has been reduced below the point necessary for successfully administering the college in the immediate future.

2. The desperate limitations in financial resources cast against the commitments made in the colleges prior to my assumption of the role of president, June 1, 1968, has been a major factor in my decision. The rigid controls on the available resources is also a crucial factor. Inability to gain relief from financial crisis, evident since June, has contributed much to my decision.
3. I believe any continuation in the role of president beyond this date would merely relieve the various concerned groups of the immediate and urgent necessity to face the many underlying causes which provoke disorder on the campus, and moves the college toward increasingly violent confrontations.

I appreciate more deeply than I can say the professional and moral support I have enjoyed from so many of my colleagues, and others who have worked desperately hard in an effort to resolve major college problems during the past five months.

RRS.ml

Asked by the Study Team to elaborate on that statement, Smith said that his primary problem was that he could not get the trustees and chancellor's office to accept his diagnosis of the problems he was facing and give him the money and the manpower resources needed to deal with them.

"As for the students and their guerrilla warfare pattern of disorders, I felt we had to defeat eventually the tactics being used without defeating all the aspirations that were involved in them–which is a complicated operation."

There are some ironies in Smith's resignation. He has been described to the Study Team as "possibly the most popular man [with the faculty] on the San Francisco State campus." But not even his tremendous popularity was sufficient to hold the college's activist faculty in line. And while his excellent relationship with faculty members gave him a better chance than anyone else to resolve the campus' problems, he was hampered by his poor relationship with the chancellor. At the least it can be said that Smith and the chancellor did not seek each other out during the 5½ months Smith was president of San Francisco State. That this contributed to the difficulty is revealed in the comment of one member of the chancellor's staff that Smith might have avoided resigning "by talking with the chancellor about the decision to close the campus." It is ironic that the question of reopening the campus could not have been worked out, for Smith told the Study Team he had planned to reopen the campus after Thanksgiving and he probably would have required police force to accomplish this, just as his successor did.

Smith's sudden decision surprised everyone. It was about 1 p.m., and the trustees' meeting was scheduled to end at 3 p.m. San Francisco State was without a president in the midst of a serious crisis. Perhaps 100 newspaper and TV reporters were waiting outside, and no one knew Smith had resigned.

ACTING PRESIDENT HAYAKAWA

To replace Smith, the trustees immediately named as acting president S. I. Hayakawa, 62, famous semanticist and part-time professor of English at San Francisco State. Hayakawa had been active in the formation of a group known as the Faculty Renaissance which had tried (with little success) to rally faculty to end the student strike. He had also written several letters to Chancellor Dumke on the subject of the troubled campus during the past year and recently had urged a faculty vote in favor of reopening the campus.

Hayakawa had some definite views on the underlying causes of campus violence. He was not certain that, even in the earlier days, before outright violence surfaced, all that had taken place at the college was either responsible or productive. He told the Study Team:

> Central to the problem of violence on campus is the existence of a large number of alienated young men and women [who] practically take pride in being outside the main stream of the culture, of being against the establishment, against authority, against the administration of the college, the administration of the State of California, the administration in Washington, whether it's a Republican or Democratic administration. How did they get alienated? Well, besides the usual psychologically neurotic reasons for this alienation there is something else that's going on. I think they are taught this alienation by professors. Especially in the Liberal Arts departments. The Humanities, English, Philosophy, sometimes in Social Sciences. There's a kind of cult of alienation among intellectuals, among intellectuals in literary fashion such as you find in the *New York Review of Books* or the *Partisan Review*. They sneer at the world the way it's run by politicians, businessmen, and generals. Knowing that they themselves are so much smarter than politicians, businessmen, or generals they feel there's a dreadful world which they themselves ought to be running instead.
>
> The first great enunciator of this theory was Plato, who believed that philosophers should be kings, and notice that he himself was a philosopher. The contemporary literary critics and philosophers feel the same way.
>
> Supposing your're an alienated intellectual. You're a professor of philosophy or something, you have no power, you have no influence in Sacramento or Washington. But you can influence your students. You use phrases like well, a phrase I just picked up from a professor of English in San Diego the other day, "the illegitimacy of contemporary authority." Now if contemporary authority, of the State government, the Federal government, the San Francisco police, is illegitimate, then you are morally entitled to, in fact, it is your moral duty to oppose that force. It becomes moral duty to oppose that illegitimate authority. The middle-aged professor passes this on to his young students. The young students are more likely to act upon this. The authority of the police is illegitimate, therefore it's proper and moral to throw bricks at them. It's proper and moral to resist the draft, to resist the authority of the government in any way. And anyone who upholds civil authority or military authority is regarded as a tool of the interests, a tool of the military-industrial complex, etc., etc., and because the military-industrial complex is so powerful, so huge, it certainly looks huge if you lump everything together into one abstraction.

All means of bringing it down, fair or unfair, are justifiable. This is why you find among young people today, not simply violence, but completely outrageous forms of behavior.

You see, peaceful marchers protesting courageously racial injustice under the leadership of a Martin Luther King never screamed obscenities. They held up for themselves very, very high and rigid moral standards. And by that they dignified their protest, they dignified their cause. But our protests, especially from the white SDS, is full of obscenities, full of shocking behavior, full of absolute defiance of any values the civilized world insists upon. This is what I find so terribly shocking, and I think it has its intellectual sources, in a kind of disaffection, among, shall I say, the frustrated intellectuals. To paraphrase a famous line, "Hell hath no fury like the intellectuals scorned."

Now, professors tend, therefore, to give A's in their courses to students that are alienated. And as the students get A's they get appointed graduate assistants. Then they soon become professors themselves. And then they pass on this alienation to another generation of students, and college generations of students come fast, after all. And before you know it, you have whole departments which are basically sources of resistance to the culture as a whole.

All this upsets me very, very much. The universities and the colleges should be centers for the dissemination of the values of our culture, and the passing on of those values. But dammit, with enough half-assed Platos in our university departments, they are trying to make of them centers of sedition and destruction.

The trustees were delighted that Hayakawa agreed to accept the position, and they gave him almost immediately the financial and manpower aid that Smith had long requested.

Hayakawa's summary selection became an issue with some faculty members who felt normal selection procedures were bypassed. The chancellor points out that this was an emergency, and there was a necessity for positive action. Even Robert Smith concedes that the trustees "were in a real tough spot . . . when I walked out." Hayakawa remains only an acting president, and the normal presidential selection procedure, operating through a committee of the faculty, continues to search for a permanent president.

Hayakawa's first weeks in office somewhat confused the official policy with regard to keeping the San Francisco campus open. On his first day in office he ordered the campus closed for 1 day prior to the Thanksgiving recess.

(And on December 13, when he ordered the college closed 1 week early for the Christmas holidays, his action was approved by the chancellor, as merely a revision of the college's calendar, and by the trustees' chairman, who said that "The threat of undue physical violence didn't warrant keeping the campus open.")

* * *

By Thanksgiving, it was apparent that the lines of combat had been drawn and the issues of the strike were clear. The pattern changed little through the rest of the semester.

Acting President Hayakawa proved an enigma to observers and to some of the men around him. He seemed to understand well the need to provide access to a good and relevant education for all—and he called for that in a February 3 appearance before Congress. Yet he alienated a wide spectrum of students and faculty, including many who opposed the strike, with a drumfire of get-tough remarks made when he first became acting president. The bitter and bloody campus combat of the first week in December also harmed his image with all but the most conservative portion—which is small at San Francisco State—of his academic community. His stature with the public at large was high. Long puzzled by campus revolts, the American public—and San Francisco businessmen—applauded the tough little professor.

Unfortunately, he antagonized the adult Negro community leaders in a private meeting shortly after he became president. Many of them were upset by the violence used by the young blacks—but supported their demands, and would have welcomed a settlement. They objected to Acting President Hayakawa's "attitude."

His ability to obtain the good will of political leaders and the public at large appeared directly inverse to his lack of success at reaching his campus constituency. But the issues had been drawn before he took office—and perhaps it was beyond the power of any man to please both the trustees and the students.

* * *

Hayakawa held a press conference on November 30 to announce his plans for reopening the college. He said he was declaring a "state of emergency," under which campus disciplinary procedures would be accelerated, but not bypassed. He was openly critical of the previous week's convocations, suggesting that a return to regularly scheduled classes would be more relevant. He was opening the campus primarily "because of the wishes of the vast majority of students who are impatient to continue their education."

Police would be brought onto the campus if necessary to deal with disorder. Hayakawa rejected arguments that police have no place on the campus. The purpose of the police he said, "is to protect dissent and to secure us from those who would interfere with our liberties and endanger our lives."

Hayakawa told the Study Team that he recognized the resentment that may be caused by the presence of police on campus.

"I know," he said. "You just have to let them resent it, that's all. Because if you send them away, then all hell breaks loose. So, you know sometimes you have to ignore people's racial prejudices for example, their racial prejudice against the race of policemen. Just go ahead and do what you have to do."

It soon became apparent that public relations was a strong suit for the new president. In the early days after he assumed control, he appeared to seize upon every opportunity to obtain news coverage and to give broad expression to his point of view on the campus disturbances. One adviser, frustrated by the constant round of television appearances and news conferences, told the Study Team, "I kept trying to interest him in the issues at the college, but he was only interested in public relations."

Another observer thought the new president's emphasis on public relations a shrewd device to build a power base. "He had no constituency on the campus, he moved off campus, through television and speeches, to create one off campus so he could come back with some power."

Not so. It was accident, not design, Hayakawa told the Study Team, that pushed him into an aggressive program of public relations.

> When, on December 2nd, I sort of blew my top and climbed that sound truck and pulled out those wires it just happened that all the media were there. And after that dramatic incident, right to this day, television people, and radio people, and newspaper people are after me constantly because that incident made me a symbolic figure. And so, like any other symbolic figure, you're good copy, you're always news just because you're there.
>
> It wasn't anything planned. That was the luckiest thing that ever happened to me—that sound truck incident. It just suddenly, you know, just placed power in my hands that I don't know how I could have got it if I had wanted it.

Hayakawa rapidly became a national figure. Armbands, floral leis, and a tam o'shanter were all part of the trappings. Within a few weeks, in his own words, he was "a folk hero."

But if he was a hero to the public outside the college, he angered many within the faculty, the student body, and the surrounding community by his actions and statements in early December.

The sound-truck incident received wide news coverage. And he made a statement on Tuesday, December 3, which inflamed students and faculty when, following a day which saw 9 injured and 31 arrested, he said, "This was the most exciting day of my life since my 10th birthday, when I rode a roller coaster for the first time." He also said that he "regretted very much" the day's events.

LIFE ON STRIKE CONTINUES

It had been a regrettable day. While Monday had seen repeated maneuvering and skirmishing between students and police, and while there had been minor property damage, few persons had been injured.

Tuesday, December 3, was different. In the history of the strike, as the students recount it, the day is known as "Bloody Tuesday." Students taunted police, and police struck back at the students. Rocks were thrown at police, and clubs were brought down on students. It was a day which brought charges of unrestrained and unwarranted police action; claims from strikers (notwithstanding the injuries and arrests) of "psychological and political victory"; and a statement from Hayakawa that he was "determined to break up this reign of terror."

December 3 also marked the first time that a number of black community leaders appeared on the campus in support of the students' demands.

Attending a morning rally were Democratic Assemblyman Willie Brown, Berkeley City Councilman Ron Dellums, the Reverend Cecil Williams, and Carlton Goodlett, publisher of the *Sun-Reporter*, a local black newspaper. Earlier in the day they had declared their support for the students' demands, saying that Hayakawa's claim that he knew more about the black community than the black students was incorrect.

"Hayakawa should never have been hired," said Brown. "There ought to be some qualifications for president and I don't think he meets them."

Reverend Williams called on the administration to address itself to the demands. "The sooner they do," he said, "the sooner we're going to get back to having education on this campus instead of the tactical squad."

President Hayakawa met the following morning with most of the black community leaders in what one black reporter in attendance described as an angry, stormy session. The black leaders demanded that police be withdrawn from the campus and classes be suspended so that meetings could be held by all concerned to implement the demands. Hayakawa rejected the proposal and later said:

> Those who call themselves representatives of the black community are in my opinion adding to the problem with their presence on the campus. If black leaders come on tomorrow and cause trouble they will be treated like anyone else who causes trouble.

"Hayakawa says a majority of the white folks want the school open," said State Assemblyman Willie Brown. "He said if we are good little boys and girls, he can get the white folks to support us."

On December 6, President Hayakawa made the peace offer he had promised the day before. It included:

> 1. Establishment of a black studies department to begin operations in the spring semester under the control of Hare and Joseph White, the black dean of undergraduate studies, with 11.3 faculty positions. This had been approved by Chancellor Dumke and the college's council of academic deans.
> 2. The 128 unused slots for special admissions would be used in the spring semester, although not guaranteed for use for minority students.
> 3. Appointment of a Third World associate director of financial aids with "the specific decision-making responsibility in dealing with Third World students."

He added that most of the other demands were being worked on.

"He's offering us tidbits," said Nesbitt Crutchfield of the BSU. "He's trying to divide us." Rev. Cecil Williams said, "The movement is going forward and we want the pigs to know it."

The campus itself was quiet. About 3,500 students, led by black community leaders, held a peaceful rally, marched around the campus twice, then went to the city hall for another rally. There were few police in evidence and there was none of the violence of the past 4 days.

The following week brought fewer injuries and arrests, and less violence—although violence again followed a noon rally on December 12.

Mayor Alioto and George Johns, head of the Central Labor Council, sought to head off the threatened strike by the American Federation of Teachers.

Johns did not want to add to the agonies of the college, but he was under pressure by one of his council's member unions to move for official strike sanction. Johns requested a number of civic leaders to meet with him on December 9 for the purpose of forming a citizens' committee to assist in mediating both the student strike and the potential teachers' strike. In the meantime, he held off the union's request for strike sanction.

The mediation effort, which was to revolve around nationally known negotiators, Ronald Haughton and Samuel Jackson, got a mixed reception. Trustees' Chairman Meriam sent Johns a telegram saying that the trustees would send an observer, but that "It is not appropriate for other agencies . . . no matter how well intentioned, to attempt to intrude in affairs outside their true area of responsibility." Still, Meriam was not willing to "close the door" to eventual trustees' participation, and ultimately the trustees appointed a four-man liaison committee to meet with the teachers' representatives.

The Governor and the chancellor said they didn't think any mediation was needed. The students were negative, too. Roger Alvarado of the TWLF called the mediation effort "a political game" and the participants the mayor's "political lackeys."

Although the union was not yet officially on strike, the AFT put up an informational picket line for the first time on December 11.

The violence of the previous week would have been cause enough for concern even if it affected only the students at the college. There was, however, another factor to be considered. The city's high schools were scheduled to break for Christmas vacation a week earlier than the college. With the rising anger confrontations were causing, there was the possibility of even greater violence if the college remained open.

Hoping to avoid renewed violence, President Hayakawa announced on December 13 that the school would recess 1 week early, and that the entire college calendar for the remainder of the year would be advanced a week to compensate for the time lost.

Student strikers had been planning a "Third World Community Day" on the campus Monday, December 16, for which they would bring in hundreds of high school students and other local supporters to join in their protests. "The safety and welfare of the young people who might be attracted to our campus during this period is of grave concern to the administration and faculty of the college," Hayakawa said.

The AFT strike was also scheduled to begin on Monday.

When President Hayakawa read his announcement over the campus loudspeaker, ending with a "Merry Christmas" he was greeted with jeers.

President Hayakawa visited the academic senate that afternoon. He warned that he would not "try to come to terms with anarchists, hooligans, or yahoos" or "yield to any form of gangsterism."

Working with the academic senate has proved difficult for Hayakawa. He sees it in much the same light as do the chancellor and the trustees—"dominated by dissidents."

They "have tried to frustrate me at every turn, especially in the application of student discipline," he says. Many times, he has found it necessary to ignore the senate, but he has been able to work with the Council of Academic Deans, which represents the schools.

A BRIEF RESPITE

During the Christmas recess, there were several meetings between trustee and AFT representatives, arranged by mediator Ronald Haughton. The talks began optimistically when Chairman Meriam agreed to send Vice Chancellor Mansel Keene and General Counsel Norman Epstein to talk with the teachers. But the discussions did not lead to any resolution of the dispute and the teachers voted officially January 5 to strike.

The teachers' major strike issues included: (1) setting up well-defined procedures and rules for dealing with faculty grievances, leaving the final decision at the campus level; (2) amnesty for all those participating in the student strike; (3) the student strike demands "be resolved and implementation assured"; (4) funds for hiring of more faculty members in order to reduce teaching loads; (5) rescission of the 10 disciplinary rules passed by the trustees November 26; (6) approval of the student union plan done by architect Moshe Safdie for the Associated Students; and (7) an end to efforts to give the administration more control over student funds.

Another development during the Christmas recess was the initiation of a study by the State attorney general's office of alleged misuse of Associated Students' funds.

Acting President Hayakawa had earlier alleged that there had been such misuse, as well as irregularities in the election of student officers, but said the study was launched independently by the attorney general's office. Only two irregularities were publicly mentioned during the vacation. One, a check to the Reverend Cecil Williams for a speech, which he signed back over to the BSU. Reverend Williams said he usually signed honorariums back over to groups whose ideas he supported. The other, expenditure of $150 by BSU leader LeRoy Goodwin for a gun. Goodwin said the money was his salary check.

(In February, however, at the attorney general's request, the superior court ordered the Associated Students' funds placed in receivership. Although student officers opposed the order, the attorney general succeeded in convincing the court that there had been general mismanagement of trust funds and that the continued solvency of the student-run businesses was highly questionable. Expenditures are now restricted to those specifically approved by the attorney general's office.)

Acting President Hayakawa announced tough new rules for the reopening of the college and that as many police as necessary to enforce the rules would be used, although he would try to start out with as few police as possible.

"With only four weeks left in this semester we all have a lot to do if courses are to be successfully completed and credit granted," he said. "In view of the foregoing the period beginning January 6 and extending through January 31 is hereby declared to be a limited activity period. Specifically, rallies, parades, be-ins, hootenannies, hoedowns, shivarees, and all other public events likely to disturb the studious in their reading and reflection are hereby forbidden on the central campus." He said rallies with the use of sound equipment would be permitted on the athletic field, provided they were "conducted and the crowd dispersed in such a way as not to disturb classroom activities." He also banned "unauthorized persons from off the campus" from using the central campus.

"Unlawful picketing in support of strike activity" was banned, but "reasonable information picketing" was to be allowed. Professors would be required to hold their classes on campus, not off, as had been permitted during November and December.

MORE LIFE ON STRIKE

The reopening was peaceful. There were 2,000 teachers and students on a picket line at the 19th and Holloway entrance and at entrances to some of the major classroom buildings. Class attendance appeared to be below normal, although it was impossible to make an exact estimate.

The Labor Council gave official sanction for the AFT strike, "with the clear understanding that we do not regard student problems as labor strike issues." The strike sanction also meant that deliveries, garbage collection, and other work on campus by union employees would stop.

At his press conference on Monday, January 6, Acting President Hayakawa said of the AFT strike, "A militant minority of the faculty has hitchhiked onto the militant, violence-ridden student strike for a vicious power grab."

Earlier he had met with the Labor Council. He told them that San Francisco State was "a working man's school" and that it would "be unfortunate if the working people of San Francisco closed it down."

He said he was considering hiring volunteer teachers to fill the jobs of AFT strikers and that 50 people had already volunteered to teach.

California law provides that a teacher who is absent from his classes for 5 days without authorization is considered to have automatically resigned. While there was much discussion of this provision, it proved almost impossible to apply to the San Francisco State strike when 22 of the 57 department chairmen refused to supply information on faculty attendance. Ultimately, some faculty paychecks were cut. But in the resolution of the strike, Hayakawa agreed to seek reinstatement for all of the AFT strikers who had "resigned" under the law.

Of little use also was the injunction the trustees obtained against the strike. While both temporary and permanent orders enjoined all faculty strike activity, including picketing, and although the orders were served on picketing faculty members, no attempt was made to enforce them. The combined student-teacher strike served to cut class attendance. The administration and the AFT made conflicting claims; the administration said attendance was 68 percent; the AFT, 20 percent. The truth, according to reporters who surveyed classes, was somewhere in between.

Picketing continued throughout the remainder of the semester. On some days the pattern of confrontation was repeated, with police dodging rocks, bottles, and bricks, and demonstrators dodging clubs and horses. Other days were relatively peaceful.

On January 23, an estimated 800 persons converged on the speaker's platform from picket lines all over the campus. Their purpose was to hold a rally to strengthen lagging morale among the strikers, to reassert student (not AFT) control over the strike, and to test Hayakawa's ban on rallies.

Only three persons had spoken when a college spokesman and then a police lieutenant ordered them to disperse. The warnings were drowned out with chants of "Power to the People" and "Strike, Strike." About 200 police began massing on the campus. The students pulled into a tight group, their usual tactic when confronted by police on the central campus, and continued the rally. After the second call to disperse, the police charged, driving about half the crowd away and forming a tight cordon around the rest. Those inside the police cordon were told they were under arrest. There was some pushing and shoving between the outer edge of the crowd and the police cordon. The police and their captives stood in a bone-chilling wind for 3 hours as police vans shuttled back and forth, taking demonstrators to jail. Once inside the vans, the demonstrators chanted strike slogans and banged on the van walls.

Those inside the cordon chanted strike slogans and "552-8211," the number to call for bail. Several strike leaders made speeches. At about 1 p.m. another group massed in front of the library. They began throwing billiard balls and 4-foot 2 by 2 boards at the windows, forcing policemen standing in front of the door into the building. The police then locked the doors and cleared the library while other police drove the crowd out to 19th and Holloway where they dispersed. The arrest total was 457, including many strike leaders and black studies chairman Nathan Hare.

In contrast to the violence which marked the confrontations and arrests of early December, the mass arrest on January 23 was carried out by a relatively small number of police officers, and almost without injury. Tactics had improved.

Acting President Hayakawa called the rally "an act of desperation" by "hard core radicals and militants."

The AFT protested to Mayor Alioto the use of police "to arrest the persons attending the rally at which there was no violence or threat of violence."

Alioto rejected their protest.

The strikers announced another "mass mobilization" for January 30. Judge Edward O'Day issued an order restraining them from gathering in large groups and Hayakawa announced that anyone already arrested on the campus since November 6 and arrested again would be immediately given an interim suspension.

On Thursday, January 30, seeing the large numbers of police on campus, the strikers decided not to hold a rally because they felt the campus situation was "a trap." At about 3 p.m. the strikers announced they were "declaring a tactical victory."

On January 31, 1969, the fall semester came to an end.

ATTEMPTS TO BARGAIN

There were various efforts since the student strike began on November 6 to move the controversies away from confrontation, with its potential for violence, and toward a bargained resolution of the issues. Some efforts never got off the ground; others met with what must be described at this time as only moderate success.

One early proposal for arbitration was made on November 11 by Cyril Roseman, director of the urban studies program at San Francisco State. It was rejected by the BSU.

On November 14, Mayor Alioto offered the services of an arbitrator, but that offer, too, was rejected.

Other offers to arbitrate over the next 2 weeks were also turned down despite the mayor's announcement that he had a commitment from the legislature to send a joint committee to hear the demands of the militant students, and some indications that the trustees might send representatives.

The trustees' resolution of November 18 that there be no negotiation, arbitration, or concession of student grievances until order had been restored made it difficult for any form of arbitration or mediation to get underway, although President Robert Smith was proceeding with his plan to open the school by airing the issues through discussions at the "convocations"; but the convocations were short lived, ending when militant students denounced them as a waste of time, since the demands were nonnegotiable.

Bargaining efforts centered around the Committee of Concerned Citizens, brought together by George Johns, executive secretary of the Central Labor Council–with the active support of Mayor Alioto.

The American Federation of Teachers Local No. 1352 had asked the Labor Council to sanction an official strike at San Francisco State College. On December 4, Johns invited community leaders to meet with the council on December 9 because "only this kind of massive community involvement" could resolve the dispute. Invitations were sent to Reagan, Alioto, Dumke, Meriam, Hayakawa, local political leaders, and various other leaders in the community. Johns called in Ronald Haughton, a distinguished mediator of national reputation, teaching at Wayne State University in Detroit. At the December 9 meeting it was decided to form a representative committee to attempt to mediate the differences between college administrators and teachers and, in the process, tackle the entire State college dispute. The Labor Council then announced it would hold the teachers' request to strike in abeyance while attempts to mediate were in progress. Johns announced that he would, however, grant strike sanction if college authorities did not enter into "meaningful mediation and negotiations."

The Concerned Citizens Committee was initially composed of 21 members including labor leaders, businessmen, and clergymen. The committee was without staff and without funds.

There was mixed reaction to the formation of the committee. Hayakawa announced he would join in the mediation as far as "legal limits" would allow. On December 10, 1968, Board Chairman Meriam sent a telegram to George Johns which stated in part:

> I must point out, and clearly, that the overall problem is a problem of higher education in this State and that the Board of Trustees by Law is the governing body, and that the members of the Board are the representatives of the people of California. It is not appropriate for other agencies, either official or unofficial, and no matter how well intended, to attempt to intrude in an authoritative manner in affairs outside of their true area of responsibility.

This telegram, however, was followed by a phone call from Meriam to Johns saying that the telegram "was not intended as a repudiation of the efforts of your group."

Meriam told the press that the telegram was not meant to "close the door" on the possibility that the trustees might play a direct role in the mediation. But Meriam continued that–

> as head of the board I have to observe the policy set by the trustees late last month—that there will be no negotiations or mediation while the campus of San Francisco State is still in a condition of strife. At an appropriate time, the trustees will be ready to consult with the persons who are experts in the field of higher education.

Where Meriam's reaction was cautiously ambiguous, Governor Reagan's was not. He said that no mediation was needed; a statement in which the chancellor later concurred.

The Citizens Committee met for the first time on December 11, and Bishop Mark Hurley was selected chairman of the committee, which was to meet weekly or more often if needed. It was decided that the committee must retain neutrality to fulfill its role of setting up machinery for meaningful negotiations in an unbiased atmosphere. Ronald Haughton announced at the meeting that he did not want to be financed by any party which could affect his neutrality. He therefore consulted with Samuel Jackson, the director of the Center for Dispute Settlement of the American Arbitration Association in Washington, D.C., and it was agreed that the center would administer the operation. Haughton attended the meetings of the Citizens Committee regularly and worked in close contact with Bishop Hurley during the next 2 months.

The Citizens Committee ran into problems immediately after its formation, and even before it had begun to act, receiving criticism from Governor Reagan and Board Chairman Meriam. The announcement of the committee by Mayor Alioto and references to it in the press as "the Mayor's Committee" served to alienate the Governor's Republican administration. Militant students greeted it with a predictably adverse reaction, as they do anything connected with the mayor's office which is often synonymous with "Establishment" and "police."

The committee viewed its success as dependent upon its own noncontroversial image and therefore enlarged itself from 21 to 39 members, bringing in students and additional community leaders. The result was a rather unwieldy 39-member, racially mixed but predominantly white committee, which the students viewed as "Do-Gooders-of-the-Establishment"; the chancellor and the trustees viewed it as ineffectual; and the Reagan administration viewed it as an arm of Democratic Mayor Alioto.

Two positive steps were taken by the committee which might have reduced the violence. At the January 2 meeting, the committee voted to authorize Hurley to urge Hayakawa and city officials to open the campus on January 6 without visible evidence of police, which was done. The second resolution was adopted at the January 15 meeting when Hurley was given the power to talk to city officials about the practice of police arresting students on the picket line on *old* warrants, a practice which often produced violence. These arrests were clearly distinguished from arrests at the time of overt violence.

The committee occasionally "observed" the San Francisco State campus. William Becker, who served as secretary to the committee, is also a permanent member of the staff of the city's Human Rights Commission. As such, Becker was frequently on the campus as an observer; the mayor had requested staff and members of the Human Rights Commission to be present on the campus to observe police actions.

At a number of meetings the effect of the news media on the level of violence was discussed but no resolution could be agreed upon. The committee also discussed the question of amnesty but again failed to take a position. On January 28, Hurley announced that he was considering the committee's making its own recommendations for solving the campus dispute "to get the situation off dead center. There isn't," he said, "nearly enough free flow of information and willingness of all sides to talk."

On December 12, Meriam appointed Trustees Heilbron, Thacher, Ruffo, and Wente to a four-man trustee liaison committee to discuss faculty differences. However, Meriam cautioned that, pursuant to the Board of Trustees resolution of November 18, there would be no major consultations between college officials and local leaders on student and teacher grievances. Because the AFT was threatening to strike December 16 with or without sanction, George Johns exhorted the trustees to meet with union officials or suffer the blame for further disruption.

Reversing his ground somewhat, Meriam reported on December 15 that two representatives from the chancellor's office would meet with striking teachers to hear their grievances. The two, Dr. Mansel Keene, assistant chancellor for faculty and staff affairs, and Norman Epstein, chief counsel for the trustees, were instructed by Meriam to comply with board policy and State law. Therefore, there could only be "discussions" rather than negotiations.

Keene and Epstein began informal meetings with union leaders on December 19 with Ronald Haughton in attendance. Because of board policy, the trustees' representatives had to pretend that Haughton was not present, but Haughton found that he had little difficulty in talking with the representatives. Formal discussions between representatives of the trustees and the AFT opened on December 27 and continued through into January in an attempt to avert the scheduled walkout of teachers on January 6. Tied by the board policy not to negotiate, there was no way to end the stalemate, and on January 5 the AFT voted to begin its strike the next day.

Talks with Keene and Epstein were broken off, but discussions with the four-man trustee liaison committee continued. However, at one point during the discussions the liaison committee could not even make recommendations and at another time it was under orders not to stay in the same room with George Johns for over 15 minutes.

On January 8, the State attorney general, acting on behalf of Acting President Hayakawa, obtained a temporary restraining order enjoining the faculty strike. Hayakawa claimed that the teachers' picketing "contributed to the tensions on this campus and threatens to bring about a renewal of violence and disorder."

A few minutes after the court order was issued, Meriam abruptly canceled another meeting that had been scheduled between Johns and the four trustees, despite Meriam's previous assurance that he would honor union requests for discussions at any time. The following day, Meriam conceded that the Governor had asked him to call off the sessions, but Meriam added that other trustees felt the same way. Meriam stated that "it was my feeling we were moving into actual negotiations and board policy clearly states that there was not to be any negotiations." Reagan blamed Johns for the cancellation because Johns continually referred to the talks as "negotiations" rather than "discussions." Reagan added that if "negotiations" aimed at the settling of the strike reached the State college board of trustees, "frankly, I would vote against such negotiations." Later, Johns stated termination of the meeting

355-234 O - 69 - 6

was disastrous. "If we had had that meeting, we would have undoubtedly settled the strike. . . . We were just about there."

On January 21, the trustees instructed its staff to continue dealing with the teachers' union. The faculty strike remained very close to settlement for a long time, with the prime remaining issue to be resolved that of the faculty grievance procedure. Haughton, feeling himself unable to contribute to resolution of this final point, returned to Detroit.

A resolution of the faculty strike was finally reached, late in February. The AFT teachers voted to return to work (although the margin was extremely narrow). The agreement included a new grievance procedure and some movement toward an easing of the 12-unit workload. When the agreement was first announced, it was opposed by the Governor, who said the trustees' liaison committee had not been authorized to reach such an agreement. Nonetheless, the Board of Trustees approved the settlement recommended by the liaison committee.

At the December 18 meeting of the Citizens Committee, Bishop Hurley announced that he had called in Samuel Jackson of the American Arbitration Association, primarily to assist Haughton in dealing with the student demands. The appointment of Jackson, a Republican, helped to mollify the Reagan administration.

Over the next 2 weeks, Haughton and Jackson met with all parties involved. However, on December 31, the Third World Liberation Front announced that they would refuse to talk further with Haughton and Jackson, whom they labeled as "lackeys and buffoons." The TWLF announced that henceforth they would meet with the trustees or their representatives, but no one else.

At the January 2 meeting of the Citizens Committee, Hurley announced that an informal invitation which had been extended to him, to meet with the Central Committee of the TWLF, had been withdrawn, and that meetings between the TWLF, Jackson, and William Chester, vice chairman of the Citizens Committee, had been canceled. It was also announced that a meeting had been arranged through Louis Heilbron between the trustees and the TWLF Central Committee for the next day. Heilbron admitted that this was a "relaxation" of the November 18 trustees' resolution. However, at the January 8 meeting of the Citizens Committee, Hurley announced that the students had decided not to meet with the trustees on January 3, despite their earlier announcement.

During this period Jackson had been working secretly with Hayakawa and some blacks, both students and faculty, through Roger Blount, a member of the Black Students Union. Blount thought if he could reach an agreement he could get the BSU to accept it. Jackson and Hurley were trying to get the administration's response to the students' demands down on paper. Formulas for agreement were being developed on such issues as the status of George Murray, the enrollment of more minority students (using unfilled EOP quotas of other State colleges), and amnesty problems. However, newsmen learned of these meetings and on January 11 the *Chronicle* carried the story of the secret meetings in a headline article. As a result of this exposé Blount was denounced by the BSU and all negotiations ceased.

Insiders say, in retrospect, that it was always doubtful that Blount could muster the necessary support within the BSU for any proposal the discussions might have produced. It is likewise unclear whether Hayakawa could have persuaded the Board of Trustees to accept such a proposal, had everything been agreed to. However, all hopes of an early settlement dissolved when the meetings became publicly known.

At the January 21 meeting of the Citizens Committee, Bishop Hurley reported that he and Jackson were continuing to work with the college administration on formal statements of the college's position on the various student demands. At the January 28 meeting it was announced that Samuel Jackson was returning to Washington to assume a post in the Nixon administration, and that he would be replaced by Derrick Bell, a Los Angeles attorney.

At approximately the same time as the formation of the Concerned Citizens Committee, Jack Morrison, a San Francisco supervisor, organized a group called the Save Our College Committee. Most of its members were personal friends of Morrison and many were from the San Francisco Conference on Religion, Race, and Social Concern. The chief interest of the committee at its formation was to get the police off the campus, as the committee felt the police were exacerbating, rather than alleviating, the situation.

The San Francisco State Alumni Association has played a relatively small role in the recent events. After the violence in December 1967, the president of the alumni association called together a group of community leaders who issued a press release supporting President Summerskill's handling of the disturbance. However, this group never convened again and it was felt that its purpose had been superseded by the Concerned Citizens Committee. Since the George Murray incident, the alumni association has issued a few press releases, which favor keeping the campus open though they have been unclear what force should be applied to achieve this goal. It has taken no side in the controversy but is now in the process of sending out a questionnaire to alumni to assess sentiment so that a position might be taken.

The alumni association has tried to contact the BSU but, like the Citizens Committee, the alumni are distrusted by the militant students. The association gave some money to both the militant BSU and the conservative Committee for Academic Environment so that they could send representatives to a trustees' meeting in Los Angeles and present their positions to the Board of Trustees. On December 6, 1968, the association held a panel discussion on the issues. Participating in the panel were Tony Miranda and Roger Alvarado of the Third World Liberation Front and Prof. Edward Duerr, a campus affairs coordinator under Hayakawa. Representatives of the BSU were invited but failed to attend.

Nor was any significant role in the San Francisco State crisis played by the San Francisco State Advisory Board. Each State college has such a board composed of 7 to 13 members appointed by the trustees. According to State laws, the board "shall consult and advise with the president of the college with respect to the improvement and development of the college." However, the board has no power to fulfill this duty. It is without staff or funds. Its main function is to help raise funds for presidential inaugurations at the college (and thus it is kept quite busy at San Francisco State) and for special projects. The board met infrequently under Summerskill and Smith.

At the January 21 meeting of the Citizens Committee it was resolved that Hurley and Johns would discuss the need for the advisory board to become involved in urging State officials to take action to resolve the dispute.

The chancellor's staff realized the ineffectiveness of the advisory boards and on December 16, 1968, recommended a revised statement of the role of the advisory boards. Recommendations include directives to the presidents of the colleges to keep the boards better informed and to the boards to provide for more of a liaison between the colleges and the surrounding communities. Most importantly, the trustees' committee recognized that the advisory boards could not perform any expanded role without adequate informational, clerical and staff service which will require budgetary support.

THE STRIKE ENDS

Acting President Hayakawa and the BSU reached a settlement, announced by Hayakawa at a March 21 news conference.

According to the newspaper accounts the administration granted the major demands of the striking students for a minority curriculum and for the admission of more minority students. The administration agreed to set up a School of Ethnic Studies, part of which will be the Black Studies Department, it being understood that the admission policies at the School of Ethnic Studies and the staffing shall be non-discriminatory. The administration declined to continue the employment of Nathan Hare or to rehire George Murray.

With respect to enrolling more non-white students who do not meet the admission requirements, the administration agreed to try to get the law changed so that the college can waive the usual admission requirements for 10% of the yearly applicants rather than the present 4%. In addition, the administration pledged to actively recruit non-white students, and this fall there will be 4,750 non-white students out of the total enrollment of 17,700.

PART II

Chapter VI

THE BLACK COMMUNITY AND THE REASONS UNDERLYING THE ACTIONS OF THE BLACK STUDENT STRIKE LEADERS

The first part of this report dealt with a description of San Francisco State College, its place in the California State college system, some of the problems created by the system, and a general description of some of the important events leading up to and which occurred during the strike. The reasons for the strike, however, cannot be fully understood without examining the attitudes of the student strike leaders and the conditions which created those attitudes. The student strike leaders at San Francisco State were not white members of Students for a Democratic Society nor is there any hard evidence that they are part of any national or international conspiracy. The student strike leaders were, for the most part, members of the Black Students Union who would not permit white students either to lead or participate in their councils. The Third World Liberation Front leaders played a secondary role in the strike. Accordingly, it is appropriate to examine in some detail the attitudes of the BSU leaders and the conditions creating these attitudes.

THE CHANGED ATTITUDES OF THE BLACK COMMUNITY LEADERS

When the President's Commission on Civil Disorders issued its report a year ago, a number of black activists hooted at its conclusion that the United States was tending toward two societies, one black and one white, separate and unequal.

You're behind the times, they said. The Nation is already separate and unequal, and has been since the early days of slavery. The question is, What are the people in power going to do about it?

Black and Third World student leaders heading the strike at San Francisco State College have carried that conclusion one step farther. Many who just a few years ago debated what the Nation should do to reunite the two Americas no longer discuss that. Despite a flood of good words, they say, white America—the group in power—has proved by its actions that it will do as little as it can get away with. Therefore, they argue, the issue has become one of seizing power: Power that minority groups need to deal with their long-neglected problems themselves, and power to show white America that it can no longer get away with doing as little as has been done in the past.

This adds up to one of the first attempts at a truly radical reorganization of a major American institution, and the tactics used by both sides will probably be refined for use by antagonists in other parts of the Nation. Contained within this drive to reorganize are ways of looking at the communities one lives in that are fundamentally different from the modern American norm. They are feelings of obligation toward one's people, and, turning to the politics of confrontation, constantly confronting the power structure, to keep it off balance, to wear it down until it reacts with such fury that it horrifies its own supporters and recruits support for the other side. People who "knew them when" at San Francisco State College say many of the student strike leaders did not always feel this way. They see these feelings generated over the past few years by a very complicated chain of events, but a chain whose links fall primarily into two categories–the unsatisfactory resolution of America's centuries-old racial struggle, and the unsatisfactory methods of coping with a much newer problem, urban life.

The student leaders' position is not necessarily separatist. Many individuals who accept it argue that, in the long run, nothing will be solved unless there is a coalition of third world groups with whites who see the same needs. It is, however, an excellent indication of just how separate the United States has become, for the students who lead the strike are clearly looking at quite a different society from the one seen by most of the administrators and politicians they say they are fighting. Many have been far more active in their own communities than the average student, and their view of the two Americas has been shaped not suddenly but over a period of time by what they and their friends have gone through. One can paint in broad outlines the topics that crop up again and again in conversation. We are the wealthiest nation in history, but children of minority groups are still more likely to be crippled in body and mind by the struggle to live and become someone. Despite 5 years of urban riots, a clear indication that something is wrong, the Nation has shifted only enough to let a few of the most highly qualified minority group individuals move up. It has done almost nothing about the vast majority still trapped in the slum-bred poverty and ignorance that has been America's heritage for them. And if there is any doubt about the Nation's real intention to avoid acting, one need only look at school desegregation. The Supreme Court declared it illegal 15 years ago, more than a reasonable amount of time to crack down on the recalcitrants. But the efforts made to date add up to almost nothing when viewed against what remains to be done. And the students are keenly aware that many people of their parents' generation fought the same battles they see themselves fighting. It their tactics worked, they say, why do we have to go through this all over again. We have trusted white America long enough. She has betrayed our trust for the last time. If she will not act, we must.

Investigation turned up no reason to suspect these feelings will go quietly away, or be allayed with more promises. Adults who do not subscribe to all these views but who work closely with black youngsters in particular are fond of pointing out that, whether they like it or not, a new breed of young people is emerging from the Nation's ghettos. They are far more aware than their parents were of what the Nation has actually done, as opposed to what it has said. They like to discuss "myths" and "contradictions" like the phrase "liberty and justice for all" in the pledge of allegiance to the flag. And they do so derisively. They have begun a movement back toward the different language, different customs, different traditions that evolved over hundreds of years of separate ghetto existence while white Americans were looking the other way. And they are far more inclined to attack what they see as a scheming, dishonest system on some front than their parents were.

"They began to see that there were continuous activities by the white community to shut them out of the major society," wrote black student leader James Garrett in 1967. "Their response to these activities has been the seeking of their own methods of change and growth. Finally, as a people, they began to adopt new standards." And this movement, as Garrett pointed out, has "the deepest of implications for American society."

"The spin-off from San Francisco State," said black Berkeley city councilman Ron Dellums, "will have implications for high schools, junior colleges, junior high schools, elementary schools as well as other colleges throughout the state and outside the state, if it is handled properly."

These views are found over a wide spectrum of black and Third World people, but particularly among the young activists whose interests tend toward activities like community organizing. They can result in fights against urban redevelopment, individual politicians, community power groups, the police, the draft, or any other issue the activists see as threatening. When the activists are also legitimately students at an urban college, however, the attack zeroes in on the educational system. Many persons interviewed pointed out that the United States talks of education as the great equalizer. Get a good education, the society says, and when you come out you will be able to cope with life's problems. The student leaders saw, however, that not only is it more difficult for minority students to get a good education—but even those who make it through are not equipped by their schooling to solve the discrimination problems they have always faced.

The student leaders "felt very strongly about a program that—as they would put it—would be relevant in regards to the educational process by which they could go back to the ghettoes and work with people," said The Rev. A. Cecil Williams, a black minister who has worked closely with them.

> They had tried everything that the white man taught them, and we [adult black leaders over 30] had tried it, and it didn't work. And we were now saying in fact that there are new moods and new tempos and new vibrations that we understand which are not understood in the academic community, and if they're going to be workable they must become a part of the educational process.

At San Francisco State, two key concepts are found in Garrett's remark. The first, "Their response to these activities. . . ." We are not initiating violence, the student leaders say, we are responding to it. Particularly to a kind of violence that whites have dealt minority groups for centuries.

"Is not the status quo as violent as any Watts or Newark or Detroit?" asked Georgia legislator Julian Bond, at a black student meeting a year ago, bringing his audience cheering to its feet. "Is it not violent to condemn to death twice the proportion of black babies as white babies in their first year?

Is it not violent to send twice the proportion of black men as white men to Vietnam every year?"

The second key concept is "... seeking of their own methods of change and growth." In one sense it is futile to ask whether violence is a good way to demand things simply because many of the student leaders accept it as a legitimate tactic, as valuable when properly used as the threat to withhold an appropriation from a Congressman's hometown if he does not vote right. Authorities, they feel, are capable of putting off decisions indefinitely until they suddenly face the threat of having something torn down. Besides, they argue, the United States is not really opposed to violence, despite what it says, or violence would not be used so indiscriminately in Vietnam. If the country were really opposed to violence, it would not allow police forces at home to behave as they did in Chicago during the Democratic convention, and in the ghettos since the end of the civil war. There are guidelines for its use, just as politicians and businessmen have rules to decide when they can get what they want by cajoling, and when they have to threaten. For example, many believe it makes no sense to terrorize by planting bombs where people might get hurt, because it destroys so much support that the tactics become self-defeating. But individuals differ on the guidelines.

The leaders appear determined not to be guided any longer by white society's view of what is or is not acceptable.

Significantly, the leaders' underlying principles that drastic change is needed to make education relevant to minority students have won wide support from black community spokesmen, and substantial backing from elements of the teachers, the administration, and the student body in general. This has tended to be obscured by news accounts that focus on the tactics used, instead of what the students feel are the underlying issues.

A July 22, 1968, preliminary report on the college from the office of the Chancellor of the California State College System notes:

> What has taken place this past year ... is considered far more serious and far more meaningful. Serious because there appears to be so little understanding of the nature of student protest by so many people, in and out of authority. Meaningful because the demonstrations that have occurred may well represent the first flowering of social revolution as Europe and South America have known it for some years.

The report lists the "fundamental causes" of campus unrest as war protest, racial discrimination, desire to use colleges and universities as vehicles for social change, curricular irrelevance, and institutional inertia and resistance to social change. Its authors conclude:

"The push to utilize the campus as a staging ground for social reform can be debated but probably cannot be deterred."

And Robert Smith, president of San Francisco State College for 7 months in 1968, noted in an interview:

> ... the basic struggle on the campus ... is not necessarily the hard core activists. The struggle is with the other 25-45 percent of the students and faculty, and their loyalty, and this is where we were losing, and by disorderly decision making processes we were either losing or we weren't gaining ground.

The student strike leaders at San Francisco State College differ sharply from the stereotype of the average college student. Many have spent several years exercising an unusual amount of responsibility and authority over their own college careers, and there is a long history leading up to the frustration they now say they feel. The following history of both the Black Students Union and the Third World Liberation Front indicates the attempts they made to get what they considered relevant education in the college. Their actions on strike cannot be understood outside of this history, for they are in the truest sense products of America.

MINORITY ENROLLMENT

In one sense, San Francisco State is a victim of California's attempt to set up a three-track higher education system, where the best students would go to the University of California, the next best to the State colleges, with the junior colleges reserved for anyone else. The dean of students' office said no registration statistics were kept by race before 1968, but administration and student strike leaders agree that until last fall, the proportion of minority students was steadily and visibly decreasing.

Donald Garrity, vice president for academic affairs, said that, when he came to San Francisco State College in 1956, "I saw more black faces in a college classroom than I had ever seen in my life. I never walked into a classroom that had less than 10 percent . . . I often had 20 percent, and that was pretty startling in 1956 in a college classroom."

No one is sure when the proportion began to drop. One administrative assistant said she could see the numbers decline after admissions standards were tightened in 1965. In that year the college added performance on a Standard Achievement Test (SAT) to admission requirements that had been just a high school average in the top third of the graduating class.

"This very systematically excluded a lot of students who had inferior high school educations," she said. "They might have done well in their own schools, but their SAT scores would pull them down."

This drop was quite visible to minority students attending San Francisco State College at the time, and quickly became a sore point. Every Black Student Union member interviewed by the Commission brought it up spontaneously when asked why black students grew frustrated with the college administration. So did most of the black community leaders. So did the campus ministry, which issued a late 1968 statement reading:

> The need for educational opportunities and special programs for minority groups is pressing. At present approximately 4 percent of the student body of San Francisco State are black students. Four years ago they accounted for 10 percent of the student body.

Not everyone in authority, however, was as acutely tuned to this change in enrollment.

"Now we are talking about 1966," said Garrity, "and I like a lot of other persons still saw 10-15-20 percent black faces, when in fact it was 4-5 percent black faces. . . . I was still kind of laboring under the notion that nothing had happened. San Francisco State had been the place of many doors—was a place almost anyone could get in . . . by 1965-66 we weren't that college at all. We were taking off a higher percentage group. The ghetto lad didn't have a chance to get to San Francisco State."

Nevertheless, by the 1966-67 school year, there was so much concern that a series of open meetings was called by President John Summerskill to explore the problems of black students.

"This series grew out of our concern over the drop, over the past five years, of the percentage of black students which make up the student body," notes a report prepared last year for the Council of Academic Deans. The report then goes on to hint at a feeling which was growing even then, and which was to erupt as a major force behind the student strike:

"Within these discussions, one of the major causes for this drop was established: the feeling among many students, not only black, that much of the work required for a college degree is irrelevant. The black students felt that this was a failure of the American middle class."

One of the things to eventually come from those meetings was a special admissions program for the 1968-69 term creating vacancies for 427 Third World students. The administration did not fill all the promised slots, and the breaking of that promise was also a major factor in the strike. But even with that program in operation, the college's official ethnic survey for the fall 1968 semester shows 75.9 percent white students, 5.3 percent black, 2.3 percent Mexican-American, 7.9 percent Oriental, 0.5 percent Indian, 1 percent Filipino, 7.1 percent answered either other, or nothing.

Statistics for the previous year were 83.9 percent white, 4.2 percent black, 1.0 percent Mexican-American, 8.6 percent Oriental, 0.5 percent American Indian. There was no Filipino category that year.

Student strike leaders often compare these statistics with the minority group population of San Francisco–well over 50 percent–in their efforts to prove racist admissions policies.

Governor Ronald Reagan's view is that students not qualified to enter San Francisco State College ought to go to one of the junior colleges, which were designed for just that purpose.

The feeling among the strike leaders, however, is that the education in those 2-year schools is not as good, and that even if it were, admissions policies designed primarily for the culture of middle-class whites would screen out minority students when the time came to transfer to a 4-year school. Eleven of the Black Student Union Central Committee members alone transferred to San Francisco State College from junior colleges, several under a special Black Student Union program that permitted transfers whose grades would normally be unacceptable.

The students got considerable support from black community leaders in their arguments that San Francisco State College, given its urban location, ought to serve the community and be open to anyone who wanted an education there. For one thing, they argued, San Francisco State College gives its students more resources to work with.

"The principle that they started out with was a sound one," said black Berkeley City Councilman Ron Dellums, commenting on the junior colleges, "except that it excludes certain factors. At the junior college level there is an assumption made. The assumption is that you are going to get a lower caliber of students. However, they haven't built in the necessary resources to do anything about that."

Two things resulted from this concern over admissions that were to have enormous effects upon the later campus turmoil. One, due to many other factors as well, was a much sharper awareness developed by San Francisco State College's then largely middle-class black student leaders of the educational problems of blacks who had not had their advantages. The other was a conscious and partially successful attempt by the school to increase the percentage of minority students who might not otherwise qualify.

The effect was to help cement a bond between black college student and black community that made its weight felt later in several of the original 10 nonnegotiable demands.

BIRTH OF THE BSU

San Francisco State's Black Students Union has an ancient history as these organizations go. Ancient and unusual in the amount of political experience it gave its members both in the college and in the larger community. While most college BSU's date from a year or so ago, the one at San Francisco State College can trace its history back to September 19, 1963, when a group of Negro students petitioned the student government to form a Negro Students Association (NSA).

The college's student government, run then and now largely by whites, was unique at that time in the amount of money it controlled, and the freedom it had to use that money, derived from student fees. It could charter and fund a variety of student organizations, which then fought each other in and out of the student legislature for funds, and ran their own programs. College records show the NSA was approved by the student government on January 30, 1964.

This new organization came to the campus at a time of nationwide polarization over the issue of race. The Birmingham, Ala., church bombing that killed four little girls was still fresh in student memories.

One of the few black faculty members around at that time remembers most of the black students as primarily middle class, but "upset, going out of their minds" over the question of civil rights and racial discrimination. Many, along with many whites, had been part of the sit-ins and freedom marches in the South, or would head for Mississippi for the Student Nonviolent Coordinating Committee's 1964 Mississippi summer project. And in addition to the civil-rights turmoil on the national scene, a lot of things were happening locally. Students remember that black community spokesmen who addressed campus audiences made "quite an impact on some of these kids." especially some whose impassioned rhetoric aimed generally at the idea that blacks needed to take education seriously and to develop their own economic institutions.

DeVere Pentony, now dean of the School of Behavioral and Social Sciences, recalled:

> I had Peace Corps training programs in 1963. I used to bring on for the Peace Corps training group some of the black militants to give Peace Corps candidates who were going abroad, many of whom had never seen a ghetto, never had a black relationship, some sense of what their America was really like. . . .
>
> I had a student . . . who was very much in tune with what was going on in the ghetto and the intellectual movements there. And it was that

> group that inaugurated the magazine *Black Dialogue*. And we had kind of the beginnings of all of this at San Francisco State. And these guys were moving out through the whole country saying black is good, black nationalism is good . . . we were getting a lot of black kids who were saying black is beautiful, black is what we are, don't straighten your hair, and all that. This was 1963-64.

Even at that time, said Pentony, these young blacks were divided over the question of integration. "Integration isn't our scene," some of them said. "It is OK somewhere in the distant future, but black is beautiful. Very strong on Negro rights, but divided on integration. They started reading black history and all this kind of thing and that was important to them. This is the way you get dignity. We come up to the North and we hear freedom and we don't find freedom. We don't find any of these things that are important. The people are trying to integrate us but they don't really want us."

According to its constitution, the NSA was to "engage in projects which the membership considers to be in the interest of the Negro community; to engage in the study of Negro history and life; to foster the growth and dissemination of Negro cultural contributions." Students there at the time remember that it seemed to go through four different phases over its first couple of years: First, after deciding student government officers were not acting in their best interests, an unsuccessful attempt to form a coalition with a conservative slate of candidates in return for more funds, then a try at working out an alliance with a liberal-radical slate shaken by the attempt to link up with conservatives, then a period of work in the black community, primarily campaigning against urban renewal in black slums, and finally a sort of African arts and culture phase.

A three-quarters vote of all members present changed the name "Negro Students Association" to "Black Students Union" in March 1966. In the meantime, while some activist blacks had been seeing what they could do with the NSA, activist whites with a few blacks had been putting together a variety of other student funded and controlled programs which eventually, in the form of the tutorial program and the experimental college, would play a major role in the direction taken by the BSU.

In February 1966, a black student transferred from East Los Angeles City College to San Francisco State College. His name was James Garrett, he was 24 years old, and was to become the single most important figure in creating the BSU that exists today, even though he left in spring 1967.

Garrett had been a SNCC organizer in Watts, and before then a SNCC field worker in the South.

"The reason I came to the campus was to try to do some organizing," Garrett told the Commission in an interview. "I wasn't interested in going to school for any other reason than to organize the students."

Nevertheless, he was a good student, rolling up well over a B average, college records show, in courses described by one administrator as including "a little bit of everything."

"Garrett was also blessed with a fantastic brain," recalls one black community leader who knew him. "Garrett, if it had been available to him, would have been at Oxford College. A student without effort, he could write, he could organize, he had personality, he could speak, he was just a phenomenal fellow. He could get people to follow him, and he could still dance and party with everybody. . . ."

Vice President Garrity, a frequent target of the BSU, described Garrett as—

> an extraordinarily bright and able guy, as bright and able as they come, committed to the cause of black people. And a guy who was very much ahead of the time. He did, I guess, really have a real charisma about him, although he did not emerge on the campus. He was invisible as a charismatic leader for a little while. This was on the general campus, but with the BSU he was magic. He had it there. . . .
>
> He got his few guys to associate closely with him, and develop the cadre with them, and from a rather loosely formed organization, Jimmy managed to transform that organization into one which said "to hell with it—we'll be black, dammit, because black is beautiful."

An informed white member of the Associated Students legislature remembers his role as follows:

> Garrett taught a course at the Experimental College, attended their staff meetings. This was after Watts when the rhetoric of burning scared people. One of the things he did was hold informal seminars on the commons in the afternoon, talked real militant.
>
> In May of 1966 he really started moving. . . . He had made a power analysis of the college, identified the group who were in control of the Associated Students, decided that the Associated Students of San Francisco State was part of the same power structure that blacks had to confront all over, then moved in on the tutorial program . . . as a white thing doing real damage to blacks . . . George Murray and Garrett then took over the tutorial program, about the late summer of 1966. . . . This was the first real mobilization of the BSU.
>
> That summer Garrett was elected chairman of the BSU. . . . Garrett led the BSU in a series of funds demands. At this time most of the liberal-radical coalition that dominated student government for 6 years was going through this "Gosh, am I a white racist after all?" thing. The blacks would come in with pretty inflated demands, and there were some wild [verbal] battles. Lots of rhetoric, lots of packing the rooms with more blacks than whites, inexplicit threats. We learned how to have meetings while people pared their fingernails with their switchblades.

(Garrett denied any switchblade knives were ever used, pointing out that they are illegal in San Francisco.)

The white liberals, most of whom felt themselves personally committed to the black cause, agonized over what to do, the legislator said, and finally "we decided to hang tough."

While this did nothing to decrease the intensity of the tactics the BSU was developing, it did, he felt, create considerable mutual respect. The BSU came up with "a very good education program" to be funded, he said, and turned out to be willing, even after particularly violent battles over funds, to take a program back and revise it if the legislature decided it was unacceptable.

It was not an easy decision for the whites to make, however. On the one hand, they were afraid there might be physical violence, although "the battles never came, in that sense." On the other, many felt that monitoring how the BSU spent student funds had real racist overtones of the kind they were criticizing in the rest of society. "We insisted we would not turn over blanket funds to BSU," said the legislator. "We said the money is available, but you've got to do a program of some quality."

"The best thing about fighting with Garrett was he knew what his self-interest was," the white said. "It was possible to build coalitions based on self-interest, or fight it out on who was best prepared. It was a period of a lot of respect, I think mutual."

An interview with Garrett confirmed the basic direction of the white legislator's testimony.

"We had the only solid, concrete program, cultural program, on the campus," Garrett recalled. "What we had done, we had not only taught children how to read, we had . . . given them such a base of understanding that when they went back they had enough confidence to read what they wanted to read. . . . None of the programs were revolutionary programs, although they were designed to build black consciousness."

But, Garrett said, blacks felt the legislature was really saying the programs "couldn't be good because black people ran it . . . so we took the position that we were going to have what we wanted to have. . . ."

> Question: You say that you didn't use tactics of intimidation?
>
> Garrett: "Sure, but we didn't use any switchblade knives. . . . I'm not saying nobody ever got jumped on, but nobody ever got jumped on at a meeting."

Garrett's organizing techniques are one of the keys to understanding the student strike, because many of them are still being used.

"I wasn't interested in building the strongest BSU in the world," he said, "but I was interested in building the strongest black people. So they can build their own institutions."

"I knew that you had to organize black students around issues that are close to them," Garrett said. "Separate issues that you have to organize around, cultural things as well as political. They are two separate cultures.

> So I went up there and groups were broken down into several different groups. One group was the Nationalists, who mostly dominated cultural aspects, who mostly dominated the Negro Students Association. There were the sororities and fraternities, there were the integrationists, the men who went out with white girls, girls who went out with white men . . . and then there were just students who were trying to be what white students are all around the country, just try to go to school to be a good white person. . . .
>
> Starting in February through the beginning of March, I started moving through all these different groups, because I could do it, because I was not known.

Garrett said he personally undertook to make a more militant organization out of the BSU.

> I didn't want the chairmanship. I just wanted to pull the organization together, so I worked to do that. I tried to pull all these different forces together . . . and they began to settle down to work projects, dif-

> ferent kinds of projects, like how to cut out racism in different areas on campus. Finding out what classes were racist. What teachers were racists. We began to set up, well, we call it internal education programs, where we would meet at my house or someone else's house and we would talk about ourselves, seeking identity. . . . A lot of folks didn't even know they were black. A lot of people just thought they were Americans. Didn't feel themselves that they were black people. We discussed that a great deal. . . .
>
> At the same time a couple of people in the organization besides myself were beginning to see . . . that the school itself is racist, at the same time people were saying that it was real absurd that when they began to seek out things in the community which was not far, about four miles away from the school, they began to see things in the community, in the Fillmore area, Hunters Point area, which made what they were learning wholly irrelevant. So we would . . . argue about whether or not we should do something about it, should we burn the city down, whatever should we do? So people were arguing on all kinds of levels.

Garrett's discussion of getting Negroes to realize they are not just Americans is another example of the separate nations, mentioned by the riot commission. For Garrett was just one of a number of young black activists struggling to define this concept at that time, although most of the others were nowhere near the San Francisco State College campus.

The same dialog was going on in earnest that summer of 1966 in the Student Nonviolent Coordinating Committee, where blacks were beginning to push whites out of positions of power, and some whites were beginning to leave voluntarily, arguing that by spending their summers working in the South they not only increased reprisals against local Negroes when they packed up and went home in the fall, but they also prevented Negro children from seeing that black people like themselves could be just as talented as whites.

That summer was also the one where Stokely Carmichael gave young black activists the Nation over a rallying cry when he shouted "Black Power" on a march through Mississippi. By autumn, newsmen who covered civil rights could hear the question being debated from the street-corner soapboxes of Harlem to the largely white experimental college organized by decidedly middle-class students at Stanford University. But because most of it took place in black neighborhoods at meetings like those Garrett would hold, probably the greatest single number of white adults who learned it was going on were the parents of white college students whose sons and daughters would come to them for advice on debates going on at school.

Garrett described his principal goal as "building a strong base on the campus around the issue of taking power, because . . . I felt then and think now that an organized minority controls the world, and that we should organize."

He said he spent the summer of 1966 taking some San Francisco State College students into the South–Mississippi, Alabama, and Georgia–"to let them see what was happening . . . and it changed everybody who went down there." When he came back, he wrote a philosophy and goals for the BSU which "laid out a perspective. "We worked hard trying to be white folks and found out we couldn't, and we had lost interest in that. Now our goals are revolutionary and we had a cultural program. . . ."

STUDENT ACTIVISTS–THE SAN FRANCISCO STATE TRADITION

While Garrett struggled to shape the BSU into a cohesive instrument of power, white activists, helped by a few blacks and Third World students, were working to develop two other programs equally radical in concept. Both were to become important tools for the BSU in its drive to expand black consciousness, but they did not start out with that in mind.

One was a ghetto tutorial program born partly from the frustrations of disillusioned liberal whites who had begun to see that there was as much wrong on the civil-rights front at home as there was in the South.

The other, the experimental college, was an attempt to develop courses dealing with problems the students felt important, but problems not recognized as legitimate areas of academic study.

"These programs . . . were designed by students, led by students," wrote Pentony in a September 19, 1967, report to the college's Council of Academic Deans, thereby getting information firsthand, and not just from textbooks. And the strong feelings of independence this fostered were helped along by the experimental college's emphasis turning students on to educating themselves.

Administrators who worked with the programs in 1965-67, when they were getting firmly established, remember it as a time of trial and error amid great excitement, of mutual respect and communication, of conflict and turmoil. The students' decision to develop and run the programs gave them at once more responsibility, more authority, and more insight into what the "experts" were doing wrong than students at other universities. And some of the "experts" were their professors.

"They have complaints about the way they are being taught and want some courses overhauled," said Glenn Smith in 1966. "The students are questioning the very nature of teaching, and it may be a good thing."

Certainly it gave both black and white students a much stronger base for challenging in later years systems of education and decisionmaking with which they disagreed. They had, after all, proved that they could successfully develop and program much of their own education. One example of the kind of challenge to come later from white students is the introductory letter to the 1968-69 student directory. It reads:

> Brothers and Sisters:
>
> What you see on the front page of this directory is our proposed College Union, a building designed for and by students and entirely paid for by them. It has been vetoed by the Trustees three times already, not on practical grounds, but because it is an expression of *our* culture and *our* aspirations [emphasis in original].
>
> Since you are here to learn, let this be a lesson: why do twenty-five Trustees, who in no way relate to the everyday learning environment of our campus, have the right to veto a project that is entirely paid for by students? From there you might go on to ask why the Trustees have the power of total fiat over our campus, when we, faculty and students, produce the entirety of the work, academic or otherwise, that occurs here?
>
> Once you have begun arriving at answers to these questions, hopefully the true value of this directory will emerge. It is an organizing

tool, a way for us to come together and identify ourselves, our purposes and our rights. Only by coming together can we make this college function in a truly democratic manner—and make it responsive to the needs of all people.

Liberty, Fraternity, Equality.

Russell Bass, *President,*
Associated Students SFSC
Alberto Duro, *Vice President,*
Associated Students SFSC

An example of the challenge issued by nonwhites is the student strike.

There is a general feeling among the school's administration that the civil-rights movement in the South, with its explosive confrontations either witnessed firsthand or brought into student homes in prophetic black and white on television, was crucial in shaping the thrust of both black and white radicals at that time. Students who had gone South only to be told, "Why don't you work in your own communities?" came back with "some glimmering of decisions that would face them," said one administrator active in those early programs.

These were mostly "white, middle-class kids," the speaker continued. It was their first real confrontation with authority, and "they were so shocked by what they saw—people being beaten and FBI guys standing around saying they couldn't do anything," that many came back determined to make the educational system deal with the problems that had defeated them.

"After you've walked around a picket line in front of a store trying to integrate it, your feet get tired or something," said Roger Alvarado, one of the early directors of the tutorial program. "It seems as if the problem is a little more basic than Integrating Mel's drive-in or Cadillac Row."

Not all students active in developing new programs had been South, but activists talk among themselves, and in one administrator's opinion, "the ethos was important . . . kids talk to each other and experiences rub off." The speaker described the process this way:

> The first community project of our students began about 1964. It was the idea of five men, four whites and a black, who had been busted for the sit-ins on San Francisco's auto row. They ended up in a jail cell with each other, and they talked about the things that needed to be done. They decided something was wrong with the schools. So they came back and started setting up a program to teach in the community. . . . It taught reading and writing to elementary school kids.

That was the start of the Fillmore tutorial program, which began in a small Baptist Church on Divisadero Street with about $20 in Associated Students funds, and expanded to 22 centers involving more than 500 college students just before the student strike. It might never have become crucial to the BSU had it not concentrated on teaching black children. But as it went about its task, it became clear that two different things were going on. The whites were concerned with educating black children, while blacks in the BSU were concerned about that and something else besides.

"At first many of the church people were distrustful," wrote Guy Sandler, the program's first coordinator, in September 1964.

355-234 O - 69 - 7

> They were distrustful of secularization and of condescending advice from do-gooders out of what they had seen to be predominantly white, predominantly indifferent college community. They were wary that it would happen as it had before, that outsiders would come to tell them how to do for themselves and how to solve their problems when these outsiders in fact knew little of the situation in the ghetto and had tasted none of the problems.
>
> But it was eventually possible to convince people in the Fillmore that those who were working for the tutorial were asking for an opportunity to learn as much as to teach. . . . It was necessary to talk at great length and to gain the confidence of the people in the Fillmore.

An opportunity to learn as much as to teach. Two years later, in both black SNCC circles throughout the South and at San Francisco State, black activists would begin complaining that when whites learned in such circumstances, it was always at the expense of the blacks they said they were trying to help, and that if whites wanted to learn, they should do so by trying to organize their own communities and stop racism at its source. The argument simply points up once again the different concerns that were beginning to separate the world of black activists from the world of whites.

The whites would come away "frustrated at the length of time it took them to relate to a black person," recalled Alvarado. Those who kept trying, though, gradually became aware of a whole cluster of problems that do not normally intrude on the academic student's consciousness. They would get involved in family programs. A child just would not seem to be able to concentrate, and it might take the tutor several weeks to establish enough confidence for the youngster to explain that he was hungry every morning, or that he had broken his glasses the month before. So the tutor would visit the mother, only to find out that this was the fourth time in 2 months the child had broken his glasses, and the welfare worker had been so nasty and threatening the last time she asked for extra money for a new pair that she had been afraid to ask again.

Or perhaps the child had picked up a nagging fear from a mother who was almost beside herself because she was being forced out by urban renewal and had no place to go.

"They started hitting the education and social sciences schools with the realization that the academic disciplines were not providing them with the answers to the problems they saw," said a college administrator. "They didn't want to talk about redevelopment with only a 20 percent displacement factor. . . ." And despite the fact that the lack of books with pictures of non-white children was considered a major problem, "the school of education said a child is a child is a child, and no punks with jail records could tell them about kids."

Some students concerned with these problems, combined with others, went to work creating the experimental college, designed in part to offer academic credit for some courses that did answer problems the students were facing.

Blacks in the BSU, however, were moving along lines much more conscious of their own separate identity, and doing so in an increasingly organized way.

Even in 1964, when the Negro Students Association was just getting started, some black students were warning prospective tutors that "People have come here before to help. They got what they wanted out of the ghetto and then they left," or:

"Some whites, most all of them, have never stopped to feel the daily burning which a Negro has inside of him. You'll have to have that kind of empathy for the feelings of these kids if you want to give anything to them at all. . . . You'd better be ready to find preconceptions and prejudices in yourself which you never thought you had."

"Some black kids were working with the program because they were concerned about what was happening between the tutors and the kids," recalled a former student active in the BSU at that time.

> There were some very destructive things going on—like kids becoming very dependent on white tutors, and they [the tutors] reinforced this, and then when the whites had to leave, they left, and there the kid was, hanging.
>
> I saw this come out in some very destructive ways. Like John, a nine-year-old, who I saw take food and . . . throw it at the face of a white, acting out against the whites his reaction to rejection.
>
> This was brought to the attention of the BSU. We felt compelled to take some steps toward increasing the number of black tutors in the community. Some of the kids were telling the tutors they were more beautiful because they had long straight hair, and the tutors would reinforce this.

But when the BSU tried to recruit more blacks for the tutorial, they found that "the orientation of the black tutors we were sending was no different from that of the whites."

To reeducate these students along more black-oriented lines, "so they would not perpetuate the mistakes of the past," the BSU began using the just-organized experimental college's Black Arts and Culture series as a political tool.

"Through the experimental college we hoped to reeducate black students who were identifying with the white community," the former student said. "Through the experimental college we would then talk about the needs of the black community. That was the initial interaction with the community."

One of the tools they used was a book by Carter Goodwin Woodson, *The Mis-Education of the Negro,* copyrighted in 1933 and now out of print. It takes the position that Negroes had been educated to perpetuate the power structure, rather than to develop skills and a community.

"The fight was not that the program should become black," the student said. "But that blacks should teach black kids, Orientals should teach Orientals, Spanish should teach Spanish."

Alvarado remembers most of the students running the tutorial program as whites from "very heavy religious backgrounds, Jewish, Quaker, Catholic. All were involved in the civil rights movement, civil liberties, things like that." Most, he said, "felt pretty guilty, too," about what America had done to blacks.

The effect on the people involved was gradual, he recalled, It was not until the summer of 1966 that Garrett first began to move in on the tutorial program, "the idea being that white people working with black children makes it that much more difficult for black kids to get positive images of themselves.

If white people were concerned about what racism was doing to black people, they should confront their own attitudes.

> For about three months the tutorial program was in an unstable condition . . . like two sets of meetings every week, one to deal with operating the program, and one encounter meeting. They were interracial, and outa sight, man. They [the whites] really got frightened about what they were beginning to realize about themselves. The blacks pushed this off on them at first, but later they began to debate it themselves.

By the fall of 1966, Alvarado himself had become convinced the blacks were right. He adopted the position, however, that if blacks were going to comprise most of the tutorial staff, then they should control the program. He met with Garrett over the summer, worked out some accommodations, and when the fall term started turned over the reigns of the program to three coordinators, two of them black. The BSU had established its first major base of operations, and, by 1967, Ben Stewart, the present BSU Chairman, could write:

> We entered this project with the position that since 85 percent of the children tutored are black, then the tutors should be predominantly black and in fact control the tutorial project. This relationship has developed to the point where in May 1966, 90 percent of the tutorial program was white, now two-thirds of the leadership is black.

BSU, A GOING THING

Under Chairman James Garrett, the BSU continued to move, both on and off campus. By 1967, a revised constitution called for setting up tutorial centers, establishing a "lecture tour for Bay Area high school and junior colleges to give insight and to encourage the black students to continue their education," and setting up a statewide news media to inform black students of news programs and services pertinent to them.

"A large part of our thrust for 1967 will be the move to more closely associate ourselves with black community to aid in organizing our people around the issues which directly affect their lives," Garrett wrote in a statement of philosophy and goals. "We must also associate ourselves with the organizations which most directly relate to the needs of black people."

The new constitution also established on- and off-campus coordinators. The on-campus coordinator was to help with lecture tours, tutorial programs, and to "involve the black professional community in the Bay Area as sponsors in club-oriented, academically motivated fund raising programs for black high school and college students." Off campus, the job called for helping set up black-student-initiated touring lecture series, and developing a Bay Area federation of black students.

Like its old NSA counterpart, the new constitution contained a nonrestrictive clause. But where the old one had simply forbidden membership restrictions based on race, religion, creed, or political affiliation, the new one added that any student "will be considered a member . . . if he identifies with the concept of blackness."

There was one other interesting similarity. The 1963 NSA constitution set up a syllabus committee "designated as one of the permanent committees only as it takes to incorporate into the curriculum of San Francisco State College a course in American Negro History."

Language in the 1967 document was almost identical, except that the words "American Negro History" were changed to "Black History."

By June 1967, activities had expanded to the point where the BSU felt the need for year-round funding, and drafted a proposal for the San Francisco State College Foundation for summer funds. Garrett's covering letter read in part:

> . . . In September 1966, because of expanding community interest in the affairs of the black students on this campus and a deepening awareness of the needs of the community by black students, the BSU saw the need to broaden its programs. . . . These programs consist mainly of (1) Internal education project in which black students learned about their history and values as a People. There is intensive examination of African, Afro-Latin and Afro-Asian Cultures as it relates to Black people in this country. (2) High School Black Culture Programs. This program came out of a concern expressed to BSU by Dr. Laurel Glass of the San Francisco Board of Education and the Honorable Terry Francois, San Francisco Supervisor, about the lack of interest in high schools by minority students. With this concern in mind, we have been working with people of high school age attempting to instill in them a sense of pride and dignity. One result of this work has been the development of Negro history and culture groups at three high schools in the area. (3) On-campus education and cultural programs. These programs are designed to educate and entertain the students of SFSC using black music, poetry, drama, and dance as a medium. . . . (4) BSU Theater Project. This project which began last semester as the Black Communications Project has performed all over California in all communities. . . .

The language in Garrett's letter does not begin to describe the intense political dialog going on within the BSU at that time. Blacks like Garrett, who saw the world in sharply political terms, ready to reach down and smother any individuals who were not aware of its weak points and prepared to fight back, were constantly trying to convince less-aware blacks, sometimes described as those who "tried hard to be good white people," that they had to wake up, pay less attention to all the nice-sounding phrases the various levels of American society put out, and much more attention to what it was actually doing.

The message was roughly: If you believe the promises that white people in power make, then you're a fool, because history shows they usually find a way to avoid keeping them, and we can prove it.

History taught by the BSU carefully documented this charge, bringing up examples ranging from the U.S. Supreme Court's *Plessy* vs. *Ferguson*, post-Reconstruction decision that separate but equal was legal, to the fact that many signers of the Declaration of Independence owned slaves, and the theory that President Abraham Lincoln issued the Emancipation Proclamation not because he believed slavery to be wrong, but because it was in the economic interests of the North at the time.

They would also point out that most black students did not learn facts like these in their elementary and high school history classes, and argued that their exclusion had to be part of a deliberate plan by a racist power structure, because otherwise the facts could not have been so well suppressed over so many decades.

One conclusion to be drawn from this approach—and a conclusion some BSU members often talked about—was that education in this country is designed to perpetuate the myths that the power structure wants perpetuated, and therefore is detrimental to black people who seek the truth.

While this was going on, the BSU continued to develop new programs, including a special admissions program for black students that brought in about 30 during 1967 who would not normally have qualified for San Franciso State College (SFSC) because of grades. Some showed dramatic improvement in their grades after coming to SFSC, and some wound up on the BSU Central Committee, their decisionmaking body.

At the same time, new political tactics were being developed, political not in the narrow sense of party and electoral politics white society normally thinks of, but in the sense that almost any action can be looked at as a political move in that it helps or hurts your movement toward some ultimate goal. In this sense, the student strike is a political weapon.

Some white students remember that blacks would take a tape recorder to meetings with faculty and administration, so that later, if an official tried to argue that he had not said something, the record could be brought out and played for him.

Tape recorders were brought to news conferences, where the black spokesman would point to them before the assembled newsmen and announce, "I don't want to see something in the papers tomorrow I didn't say." They had learned the way in which newsmen often take only sketchy notes of what is said and later fill in inaccurate details by faulty memory.

"We say here is the documentation," Garrett noted. "We take it to the black students and we say here's the documentation, what do you think we ought to do? . . . We bring the documentation with us, and say man, you know you've done this, this, this, and this, and you can see for yourself that it is racism, so why don't you cut that out?"

"We'd take people to the president's office, to the dean of students' office, so they could sit and listen to white folks discuss their lives, discuss black folks' lives, and they could learn from that."

Activities like these served—in fact were designed—to "heighten consciousness," to do what Stokely Carmichael calls "sharpen the contradictions," between the way the Nation treats whites, and the way it treats blacks, and in so doing to create a strong sense in the black student of why he cannot consider himself just an American who "happens" to be black.

Not all of the BSU ideas on how to heighten consciousness were original, although many were. The most active students also traveled, talking to other black activists in various parts of the country, and they read a lot. Malcolm X, Stokely Carmichael, Frantz Fanon, Che Guevara, and Chairman Ho Chi Minh were among the writers and strategists' techniques and attitudes most frequently borrowed.

There was also communication with staff members from the Congress of Racial Equality, SNCC, the more radical elements of the National Association for the Advancement of Colored People, the National Urban League, and a new organization springing up in nearby Oakland, just across the Bay, called the Black Panthers.

Communication along these lines was natural, because all these individuals and groups were facing the same basic problem: how to organize a country's disenfranchised nonwhites into a force that could put a stop to their own exploitation by whites. No overall agreement was approached or even attempted. There were too many differences of strategies, tactics, and the people being worked with. But from this dialog–carried on in large part beneath the level of consciousness of the white community–new tactics and ideas emerged, to be tried out both on the SFSC campus and elsewhere.

It should be pointed out here that it was not necessary in most cases to try to hide these activities from the white world. Black activists had learned long ago that whites simply did not care to pay as detailed attention to the black world as they gave to their own, and this was another example of the two separate worlds that kept developing.

To those who paid detailed attention to the black community, examples were so numerous and easily seen that they created a lot of hostility toward whites, particularly toward the news media, which were seen as the filter through which information had to pass to get into the white world.

Blacks were angered, for example, that newsmen came into Mississippi in the summer of 1964 with the influx of white northern volunteers, stayed while the whites were there, then packed up and left when the whites left. The struggle had not begun with the whites' arrival, they argued, and it certainly did not end when the whites went home. But the newsmen acted as if it had. They did not seem to care whether white southerners carried out reprisals against blacks during the winter, when all the white volunteers were back in school. And there was considerable argument a year later over whether the country would have been as agitated over the murders of three young civil-rights workers in Philadelphia, Miss.–James Chaney, Andrew Goodman, and Michael Schwerner–had not Goodman and Schwerner been whites from the North.

Blacks learned that newsmen did not know their way around the black sections of their cities, that they had no clear idea of the dynamics going on in those neighborhoods, that they were less likely to send reporters to a discussion on race relations held among blacks in the black community than they were if the discussion were held among whites downtown, and that they tended to look for people who could "speak for" Negroes as a whole, and call them "Negro leaders," instead of recognizing the enormous variety of opinion among blacks as to where they were going, and how they could help progress along.

Feeding on tactics and ideas like those just outlined, with lots of lively debate, the BSU was slowly shaped into the organization it is today. Other concerns went into building it, too.

"When I went to their meetings before the strike," said one black woman student, "they were very concerned with their membership. The BSU and the Black Sisters Union specifically–that was a function of another power struggle, the girls felt they were being left out in the cold and they tried to figure a way to get out of their secretarial positions.

"But they were also concerned–and so were the boys for that matter–with representing the entire black community on campus. And they were worried because their image was, they said, only of girls who were naturals and were politically radical. And they had to reach the girls in the dormitories or the girls who were uninvolved. And they were trying to figure out how to do this . . . they were aware of this and they felt that it was a fault."

A central committee representing a broad spectrum of activists was in charge of the BSU when the fall 1968 semester began, its officers elected by the BSU membership.

"You have the revolutionary vanguard, the separatists, nationalist philosophy, the militant reformists, and all of them coming together, and in each faction's mind a way to resolve the problem in different ways," commented an observer. Chairman Benny Stewart and on-campus coordinator Jerry Varnado are generally considered the most revolutionary in tactics and philosophy, while administrators and faculty who have worked with or confronted the BSU say financial coordinator Nesbitt Crutchfield, tutorial director Thomas Williams, and Jack Alexis, head of the Center for Educational Innovation, are considered not necessarily less militant, but very aware of all sides of issues and easier for whites to communicate with.

Policy results from often lively debates, but campus officials and most black community leaders interviewed believe power in the central committee has shifted a good deal toward the more revolutionary types since the strike began, partly because of the pressures of running a day-to-day series of confrontations with campus authorities and police, and partly because of the response to what they consider legitimate demands by police and California political officials. Not all BSU members agree, for example, that the demands should be nonnegotiable, although since they lost the vote on that point they agreed to go along with the majority. But they do object to being broadly compared to Nazis by Acting President S. I. Hayakawa, who they feel is guilty along with many others of not making distinctions between the various groups within the BSU, or even between the BSU and some of the white radicals who have been smashing windows and throwing rocks at the police.

It was difficult for Commission investigators to talk to BSU Central Committee members because they voted, after debating a request for a group interview, not to cooperate with any arm of the Federal Government. Some, however, had given interviews before the ban was voted, while others were willing to discuss the organization's history, but not its current workings.

There was also a great deal of resentment expressed about investigations being carried on at the same time by the State attorney general and the U.S. Justice Department, pointing up once again the differences between the BSU's view of the world, and that taken by the average white American.

THE NEW NONWHITE STUDENT LEADER

The BSU's off-campus center is not a particularly easy place to find, even when you have the correct address. First you have to find the center of the "Fillmore," a narrow, low-income, mixed-minority group neighborhood of Victorian-style wooden buildings stretching north over a series of hills from Market along Fillmore Street. The address is on Ellis, but Ellis Street stops at one of the sparkling concrete urban-renewal projects neighborhood groups have raised so much protest over, and you have to snake your way around to a battered, three-story structure in the slummiest, blackest part of the Fillmore, where rotting buildings are rapidly being abandoned in the face of the advancing urban renewal. There, hand-crayoned signs direct visitors to the downstair meeting halls or the upstair tutorial office. One door of the BSU center has been smashed away from its padlocked hasp, and propped shut from the inside with a battered old table. Weatherbeaten plywood panels cover smashed windows. It is the kind of neighborhood where, in larger cities, whites instinctively lock their car doors as they drive through.

Middle-aged and elderly black men lounge around the signposts and building corners throughout the day, some drunk, others just idle. Toward the middle of the afternoon, one of the city's largest interracial prostitution operations swings into action, supplying a variety of girls to stroll the sidewalks in microminiskirts or tight bell-bottomed pants until well past dawn on some corners, volunteering a variety of services to anyone who does not look like a plainclothesed cop.

One block from the BSU office, on Fillmore, between Eddy and Ellis, the San Francisco office of the Black Panther Party serves as a gathering place for the younger blacks into the "militant look"—big, bushy Afro hairdo's for both men and women, black leather jackets for the men, boots for the women. Someone is usually manning a table out front where a variety of Panther literature, ranging from "antipig" stickers to Chairman Mao pins printed in Chinese, is for sale beneath windows plastered with recent issues of "The Black Panther, Black Community News Service."

"Get out of here, man!" a young, white hippie was told recently as he stepped hesitantly down the street, obviously under the influence of drugs, toward a group of Panthers and BSU members talking in the doorway. "If you want to trip, go trip someplace else!"

The hippie kept coming, protesting that he just wanted to talk, and a couple of the black guys spoke with him gently for a moment, then ushered him back in the direction he had come from.

"You should have busted him one, man," said one of the Panthers. "I would have."

Violence, all around. From the obvious—the feeling that the hippie should have been flattened on the sidewalk—to the subtle—the attitudes black children pick up as they romp in the nearby streets, listening to the shouting and the cursing and bumping into drunks and streetwalkers. As sociologists have often pointed out, this is the kind of neighborhood where those who wish to get along well in the streets learn to fight their own battles. Violence is no stranger to these blocks, and to hundreds of others in San Francisco's minority neighborhoods. Many of the BSU and Third World central committee members live, or spend considerable time, in this neighborhood or others like it, and the language and attitudes they bring from there to the campus reflect this violence that is a basic part of ghetto life in every city in the United States.

San Francisco's crime statistics reflect this basic ghetto violence. Among nine police districts, the one that includes the Fillmore ranked generally highest in 1966, 1967, and 1968 in homicides, robberies, aggravated assaults, larcenies, and burglaries. It lost top ranking only to the district that includes Haight-Ashbury, another slum, on forcible rapes, and to that district and the one that includes Hunter's Point, the third major Negro slum in the city, in auto thefts. Over the past 3 years, the police district that includes the Fillmore reported slightly better than one-sixth of all the city's crime in those categories.

The Panthers have plastered the neighborhood with hundreds of the new urban art-form posters preaching their message in various ways, but always making their main point that guns are essential–usually by putting the picture of a rifle on every poster, including those that announce rallies. A fairly common one features ink drawings of five ferociously charging men–two blacks, a Mexican-American, an Indian, and an Oriental–carrying a variety of prominently held weapons that include a fiery torch, a hand grenade, automatic rifles, a dagger and–for the Indian–a bow and arrows. It bears the legend:

"We are advocates of the abolition of war . . . we do not want war. But war can only be abolished through war and in order to get rid of the gun it is necessary to take up the gun." It is signed "Chairman Mao."

Occasional photos of the late Rev. Martin Luther King, Jr., are lost amid the jumble of posters of Eldridge Cleaver, Stokely Carmichael, LeRoi Jones, Malcolm X, and a variety of other black radicals in heroic, weapon-bearing poses. H. Rap Brown holds aloft a burning match without comment on one poster, while another proclaims Carmichael, "Prime Minister of colonized Afro-America."

Even a dozen blocks from the Panther office, the posters are common.

"A rule of thumb of revolutionary politics is that no matter how oppressive the ruling class may be, no matter how impossible the fact of making REVOLUTION may seem, the means of making that REVOLUTION are always near at hand," one reads. Another is much shorter: "The spirit of the people will be stronger than the pig's technology." And on the white-painted walls of the burned-out Pilgrim Rest Missionary Baptist Church, someone has repeatedly stenciled in black letters: "The Revolution is Coming–Tom Paine."

On the southwest corner of Turk and Fillmore, an old supermarket has been taken over by the State. Its plateglass windows proudly proclaim in big gold letters, "State of California Service Center, Ronald Reagan, Governor." On its side wall are three prominent posters. The first, an Eldridge Cleaver campaign tract left over from his Peace and Freedom Party presidential candidacy, reads: "Our purpose in entering the political arena is to send the jackass back to the farm and the elephant back to the zoo."

The second shows Kathleen Cleaver holding a pump shotgun at waist level, aimed just past the viewer's shoulder. Its caption: "Shoot your shot." The third is a photo of the late Panther, Bobby Hutton, with the caption, "MURDERED BY OAKLAND PIGS." Sometimes it is displayed in conjunction with another showing three uniformed Panthers waving their flag in front of Oakland's Civic Plaza. "The sky's the limit if you kill Huey Newton," it reads.

A half-dozen blocks to the south, the Third World Liberation Front uses donated space in a church as a legal defense office. These streets are not known at all well by many of San Francisco's middle-class whites, but their mood, and the mood of similar Spanish-speaking areas of "The Mission" and the side streets of Chinatown, has been a powerful influence on nonwhite student leaders, both in the methods they use to express themselves and in what they have to say. Couple this with the other influences already mentioned that shape young minds, and the result is an overall change of mood that has awed even close observers.

"The black community radically changed in 1964," said California Assemblyman Willie Brown, the first black ever to be elected minority whip.

> In 1960 it was crazy to picket, and in 1965 Watts comes along. There are a whole lot of blacks that commenced to justify Watts, and at that point some kind of tuned out. And then there is all of this commitment to blackness. And there is black this and black that. And our separatism, and that is a whole new concept. Any guy who thinks . . . that he still knows the black community without tuning in to the new attitude is just off base and he is a disservice to the whole process of communications.

Almost everyone the Study Team interviewed who has been close to the development of the BSU and TWLF over the past few years mentioned a number of incidents happening in and around San Francisco which they believed powerfully affected the mood of the nonwhite student leaders. They included–

The Black Panthers.–The role this gun-carrying self-defense group played over the years since its 1966 founding is complicated. There has been more individual mixing among friends in the two groups than formal organizational contact. Panther Minister of Education George Murray plays a key role in the BSU–his reinstatement as an SFSC instructor is one of the 10 demands. And the weekly Panther newspaper, billed as the *Black Community News Service*, often prints items on various black student unions. It ran lists of the SFSC demands, and frequently runs this item:

> "IMPORTANT" BLACK STUDENT UNIONS
>
> The BLACK STUDENT UNIONS have formed a statewide Union of BSU's, and are in the process of organizing on a national level. We call upon ALL BLACK STUDENTS to unite.
>
> If your BLACK STUDENTS UNION hasn't become a member of this UNION of BLACK STUDENTS UNIONS send a letter or telegram giving information about your BSU and the conditions that exist within your area. Become a part of a united movement of BSU's and stop moving on an individual basis. Together we will become the most effective organization on this earth; divided we are weak.
>
> Send your letter to: BLACK STUDENTS UNION
NATIONAL HEADQUARTERS
3106 SHATTUCK ST.
BERKELEY, CALIFORNIA

Relations between the groups have not always been friendly. Although Chairman Bobby Seale and Minister of Defense Huey P. Newton had been students at Merritt College in nearby Oakland, the Panthers first looked on the BSU as "cop-outs," middle-class college kids trying to be white and unwilling to do what was necessary to survive.

"We have had good relationships with the black student unions at local high schools," Minister of Information Eldridge Cleaver is quoted as saying in an interview in the January 20 *The Nation*.

> Indeed some of them have changed their name to Black Panther student unions. The situation on the college campuses has been different. Before forming the Black Panther Party, Bobby Seale and Huey Newton tried to do some organizing at the Soul Students group at Merritt. They discovered that there are problems with starting a revolutionary movement among blacks at the college level because almost all black college students are from the black bourgeoisie.
>
> The black middle class are the most alienated from their roots; when the idea of black consciousness began to develop they had the furthest to go. . . .
>
> The black students now in high school find it much easier to relate to the revolutionary ideas than do the black college students. When they get to college they will wash away this regressive phenomenon.

Publicly, relations were good by the time of the strike. BSU leaders had long ago begun using the Panther rhetoric of "pigs" and "dogs" for police, and Seale spoke at at least one BSU on-campus news conference.

The most visible contribution the Panthers have made to the revolutionary climate has been the creation of martyrs to the cause, particularly Newton, Cleaver, and Bobby Hutton.

Newton's murder trial and manslaughter conviction was avidly followed by blacks of all ages throughout the Bay Area. Here was a young black activist who drew considerable sympathy for several reasons.

Bits of testimony and happenings at the trial, including testimony from police that they had lists of all known Panther vehicles and would follow one when spotted, spelled clear harassment as far as many were concerned, and they said so.

In addition, a court stenographer left a keyword out of testimony reread to the jury during deliberations, an error that was not caught until the next day, and is a factor in Newton's appeal. Then there was Newton's style, that of a young warrior being persecuted for trying to put an end to persecution.

"There was a general feeling in many circles that the verdict was a compromise," said sociologist St. Clair Drake, "that Huey was innocent, but that the racist power structure had to stand behind their police. A general feeling that Huey hadn't been done right by."

People were still talking about the Newton trial when controversy flared over a course Cleaver was scheduled to teach for credit at the University of California in Berkeley. Gov. Ronald Reagan and Superintendent of Public Instruction Dr. Maxwell Rafferty jumped into that one, finally succeeding in getting Cleaver limited to one appearance with no course credit allowed. But in the process they convinced many students that the University of California administration had no power to run its own campus, if it tried to cross the State's top politician, an idea reinforced at SFSC by the subsequent suspension of English instructor George Murray.

These contributed to two ideas that later showed up in the student strike. One, that blacks would not be allowed to have teachers they considered relevant, was translated into a demand for autonomy. The other, that the administration had no real power, became visible as a refusal to talk with anyone below the level of State-college trustees.

General antipathy toward police was continuously fed. Not only by police admissions about their relations with the Panthers, but by the kind of abuse and brutality that continually go on throughout low-income areas that blacks have complained about for decades. The most notorious of these was the case of Police Sgt. Michael O'Brien, accused of terrorizing neighborhood residents with racial slurs and orders to line up against a wall, hands over heads, before finally killing a young black man. There is a strong feeling in the black community that O'Brien would never have been brought to trial had it not been for the roar of community protest that followed. Posters proclaiming "Wanted, Pig O'Brien, for MURDER," went up in the Fillmore. His trial was still in process at the time this report was compiled.[1]

Feelings among black activists ran extremely high on these issues, quite independent of whatever impact they had on the white community. Throughout this period, of course, the activists were also conscious of things going on in the larger society—the assassinations of Dr. Martin Luther King, Jr., and Robert F. Kennedy, the riots that followed the King assassination, the failure of the Poor People's campaign, President Nixon's wooing of the South and his emphasis on law and order—read crackdown on blacks for the benefit of whites—during his campaign, the behavior of the police in Chicago, and the war in Vietnam.

"If you doubt that the American flag is a lie," said George Murray in a late-1968 speech at Fresno State College, "how in the world is it in 1968 you can have some racist politicians, three, running around the United States dastardly and criminally saying that the issues confronting all the people in the United States, the main issue, is the issue of crime in the streets. . . .

"And when politicians say that they are not talking about Chicanos; they are not talking about descendants of African slaves; they are not talking about Chinese . . . they are merely talking about white people, and only a certain segment of the white population, that is the segment that they can whip up into a fever of mass hysteria."

Items of particular interest to blacks had a way of traveling across the country even when whites may not have paid much attention to them. Late in 1968, Washington, D.C.'s black community was incensed when a white policeman shot and killed a Negro he said had first refused to stop jaywalking, and then had turned to fight the officer. While some Washington blacks were talking about imposing gun restrictions on the police to stop what they considered clear cases of "overkill," the item found its way into Murray's Fresno speech in this form:

> . . . Like the brother in Washington, D.C., two weeks ago who was murdered by a white police because he refused to accept a ticket for jaywalking. . . . The brother was about six blocks [actually seventeen blocks] from the so-called White House when he was shot down like a dog in the street. And Lyndon Baines Johnson, that racist cracker, was in the White House at the same time that the brother was murdered six blocks from there, talking about, "the issue in America today is one of crime in the street." So you get people . . . deceiving the general populace . . . with fabrications of lies, sheets and sheets

of lies, merely to manipulate everybody . . . to the extent that you'll die for some nonfreedom in Vietnam.

Vietnam is a topic that comes up often in BSU rhetoric. One of the posters seen frequently in the Fillmore shows an Associated Press photograph of a Vietnamese woman being questioned by a South Vietnamese officer while an American soldier, the caption says, holds a gun at her head. The gun muzzle is pressed tight against her distraught face, and the soldier identified as American has grabbed a hank of hair with his other hand, and is pulling it so hard that little ridges of skin have formed around the gun muzzle, where the flesh is being pressed so tight it cannot move. "Today the Vietnamese," an overline on the picture reads, "tomorrow the blacks." The poster is signed "Associated Students of San Francisco State College, Black Students Union."

"These things build each other," said a black administrator. "Students particularly tend to blame schools for what society at large hasn't done . . . they become more impatient. Things are seen as part of a continuing duplicity."

All of this had a twofold effect on the BSU. It further convinced the most revolutionary that they had no alternatives left. But more important, it helped drive the activist students out of the isolated academic lives college students normally lead, into their communities. And this was another key difference between the way Americans normally think of college students, and the way these students saw themselves.

COMMUNITY INVOLVEMENT

> We see ourselves being basically servants of the community. That is to say, we go to a college campus and we learn academic skills and we see ourselves as returning back to that community to enhance the progress of that community rather than to exploit or misuse it as the traditional Third World lackey, Uncle Tom bootlicker students have done in the past. Also another thing: we see ourselves as educating our communities to the fact that education is not going to make them free. You notice that when the racist dog pig comes down into our community, he's coming with shotguns, AR-15's, kicking and stomping babies, knocking children out of the way like mad savages, like Michael O'Brien who killed a black man and got away free . . . What's happening is that basically they [college authorities] don't want to heighten those contradictions because they know we will return to our community and they want us to perpetuate the same old bullshit lie that if you get an education somehow you will become a human being and you will become free from police brutality. . . . We will return to our communities and by our struggle we will achieve liberation for all our people.

The speaker is Ben Stewart, BSU chairman for 1968-69, speaking in a campus newspaper interview. His language is designed for his goals, and his point is crucial. The BSU is trying to carve a new role for the black college student, to return to the black community some of the skills that blacks on the way up have taken from it in the past. This is a point well understood by San Francisco's black community spokesmen:

> The BSU as an organization is operating on the principle that the college for the black student is not an ivory tower but a place where he gets some kind of preparation to come back to these ghetto communities and try to take what skills he has developed and relate those to the relevant needs of the people in these communities from which these kids are coming.

The speaker this time is Hannibal Williams, the only black minister in the campus ministry association, and a community organizer in the western addition. "The kids are beautiful and they are to be admired for this. The traditional Uncle Tom, Sam, shoe-shining type Negro that we have had in the past has rushed to the university to get himself a white education. Then he has rushed pellmell from the black community in the same manner that white people have been fleeing to the suburbs, and we think this is the most reprehensible of creatures because he denies his own birthright. It's his brothers and sisters and mothers and fathers from whom he is running."

Williams is a member of WACO, Western Addition Community Organization. It's a relatively new community group formed to help coordinate the fight against San Francisco's hotly contested urban-renewal plan that pushed out low-income blacks to make room for middle-class housing.

The Black Students Union is a dues-paying member of WACO, and Williams thinks some of its leaders got valuable experience "in organizing here in the community, working with community people to help us organize community organizations."

Tactics used by the BSU members then were forerunners of those used during the student strike. After trying and failing through all the accepted methods to have the project ground rules changed so that more poor people would be able to move back in, WACO and several BSU members planted themselves in front of the earthmoving machines already grading the site.

"We got to the point," he said, "where it was obvious that they were going to bulldoze over our feelings, over our rights, over our protestations. They were going to bulldoze over everything that we believe makes us human. They were going to strip us of our self-respect; and it was at that point that we decided that humanity and self-respect was more valuable than life as a sub-human species and we stood in front of the bulldozer and said 'this project is shut down, and it will only be opened over our dead bodies.' "

The result, Williams said, was a total reorganization of part of the project putting far more black construction workers on the job, and shifting the percentage of low-income apartments from 20 to 57.2.

"Now mind you," he noted, "that was only achieved after we had exhausted the process of begging the white man and shining his shoes and kissing his butt and not getting anything for our trouble but political doubletalk. If there's any one single lesson that we learned from this process it is that there is only one alternate kind of power and that's the power of physical confrontation. The white man uses all the other kinds of power to deprive people of the legitimate goals that they are trying to achieve and until there is some exhibition of physical force, we get nowhere in our community because they make monkeys out of us when we have these verbal exchanges with them. . . ."

Williams' last comment raises another issue that most radical activists like to talk about. They say whites have structured society so that non-whites are always at a disadvantage. They create the field of law, for example, to guarantee justice, then make administering that field so complicated that only highly educated people can operate in it, then refuse to give large numbers of minority people the basic grammar and high school education that would let them go on to understand the profession that's supposed to get them justice.

Or they confuse uneducated people with political doubletalk. Williams again, on WACO's work:

> We had hundreds of people go with us to plead with the Board of Supervisors. We went to the mayor's office and practically shined his shoes while we said, "please . . . listen to us. This is what we want. . . ."
>
> The answer has inevitably been no, and the way a politician says no is he tries to say it so confusingly as to make you believe that is not what he is saying. But inevitably you end up in the frustrating position of finding out that in fact what he has said when you have stripped it of all the verbal shibboleths . . . he has said "No. Your condition is what it is. We can't do anything about it. Come back and see us next year when the legal climate has changed, and maybe in 1999 we can get some laws passed, but right now I'm sorry. I appreciate your discomfort. I extend to you all of my sympathies, and my office is open to you at any time."

WACO is not the only off-campus organization in which BSU members have been involved. The role of SNCC has already been mentioned, as has the tutorial program. The BSU set up an information center in the Fillmore. One central committee member, Terry Collins, ran a black draft-counseling center in the Fillmore for a couple of years. Several helped on Assemblyman Brown's campaign. Chinese- and Spanish-speaking members of the Third World Liberation Front have been involved with a variety of community groups in their neighborhoods. So that these activists come to SFSC with much more experience than students are normally given credit for. And it is not surprising that they would bring to the campus refinements of the tactics they have been trying elsewhere.

Also important to this point is the fact that SFSC, primarily an urban, part-time college that offers the chance for people to either return to college for degrees they had no chance to get after high school, or work for degrees while holding a full-time job, attracts students older than the average.

Administrators say the median age is 25 at their school, a normal course load is 12 units per semester, instead of the more usual 15. And taking 6 years to finish is so common it is not even remarked about. The BSU and Third World leaders follow this pattern. James Garrett was 24 when he transferred in as an undergraduate. Terry Collins is 33, according to school records. Others range from 24 to 30. Roger Alvarado, first admitted as a freshman in the fall of 1961, is a good example of the ways the outside events described up to now can affect personalities. Now heavily bearded with shoulder-length hair, Alvarado is a leading member of the Latin American Student Organization. But when he first arrived, this product of Irish and South American parents said he did not think in ethnic terms at all. College records list one of his very first extracurricular activities as a singing cadet in Air Force ROTC.

The common experiences of this group set them apart from traditional college students, but there were no indications that the number who think along these lines will do anything but increase in the near future. And to leaders of the black community outside the college, the important thing to look at is what these students have learned from their experiences that makes them so different from black college students of their parents' generation.

What young people see, Goodlett thinks, is a society "wealthy beyond comparison concentrating on gadgets, material possessions, but being insensitive to the needs of millions of people who are becoming more and more articulate as the have-nots."

Perhaps more important, they have watched very carefully to see what things produce movement in the society.

> In San Francisco, my generation for about 17 years we negotiated, or tried to negotiate, with the hotel management association [to integrate hotel help]. We never could get jobs. . . .
>
> It's been demonstrated to this younger generation that the only time you can get on the wave length so that the white power structure pays any attention is when you threaten its god, private property. So confrontation has become an attention getting mechanism because not only can you get the man's attention, you can clear a situation where a conflict can be negotiated.
>
> . . . The TWLF's in this country are saying to the power structure and to their supporters in the adult segment of their respective communities that violence in the national struggle for liberation is probably justifiable, especially when you are dealing with an opponent who feels that any response to nonviolent petition is a sign of weakness. And if violence is to be our lot then I say that the insensitive establishment that caused Martin Luther King to die with a broken heart are the provocateurs of violence and we are in the whirlwind of a 15-year period of not responding to nonviolent petition.

"I admit I am very excited about black students," said the Reverend A. Cecil Williams, "because I see some dynamic, superior black students that excite me very much. And their mood, and the commitment they have in regards to this. The fact that they are able to articulate, the fact that they understand . . . they certainly are convinced that they can in fact change society. Now that's very important. . . . We are not ashamed of ourselves. We have pride going on, we have unity going on. There are vibrations going on in the black community like we have never seen in our lives."

Berkeley City Councilman Ron Dellums said he thinks this new mood is both spreading from places where it is already established, and at the same time taking hold spontaneously elsewhere in the Nation, "the chemistry being the insensitivity of a lot of the institutions of higher learning. The black students now are a different caliber of student, not only intellectually capable, but politically sensitive, made politically

355-234 O - 69 - 8

sensitive by the Carmichaels, the Rap Browns, Huey Newtons, Eldridge Cleavers, Ron Karengas."

"There is now an all-pervasive feeling of community among black people," said Hannibal Williams. "Even the bourgeois Negro who has traditionally in the past believed that some day he will grow up to be a white man has finally come to understand that he will never grow up not to be the child of his parents. The spirit that exists in the black community today is one which the status quo is still unable to understand, basically because it does not want to understand, and does not want to assimilate or accept a fact which is disagreeable to it and its status quo condition."

"Schools haven't realized that the students are as serious as they are now," a black administrator added.

THIRD WORLD LIBERATION FRONT

> Look, most of the nonblack Third World people were involved in what we loosely call the movement. Some for as long as five years, mostly working with the black community, or with white volunteers in the black community. About the time that black consciousness became a pretty solid concept . . . a lot of black literature was circulated and dug by everyone concerned. Those of us in the Third World who were not black, we had to turn around and orient our thinking to what was happening in our own communities.

Roger Alvarado was describing the process by which he and nonblack minority group people around him grew to the kind of self-consciousness that resulted in the Third World Liberation Front (TWLF). Not all took their cue from activity in the black community as he did, but most talked of their belief in the need to restructure American society so that it is more responsive to the needs of their ethnic groups.

Born little more than a year ago, TWLF has had a rapid rise to prominence. It began in the winter of 1967-68 with discussions between blacks, Mexican-Americans and Asian Americans, and was formalized during the spring semester. It was formed as a unified political arm to push for the educational needs of Third World students. The Black Students Union is a member of TWLF, so that technically the strike is TWLF led. Actually the other five student organizations active in TWLF did not join the BSU-called strike until its second or third day, and the BSU has continued to play a dominating role in strike strategy.

The BSU, the Latin American Students Organization (LASO), the Mexican-American Student Confederation (MASC), the Intercollegiate Chinese for Social Action (ICSA), the Philippine American Collegiate Endeavor (PACE), and the Asian American Political Alliance (AAPA) are the six groups that now make up TWLF. A 12-member central committee composed of two delegates elected from each ethnic group sets policy, and in the past individual groups have been free to withdraw from TWLF activities they disagree with, or carry on projects alone.

TWLF staged its first major action in May of 1968, demonstrating for a week to support a series of demands that included 400 special admissions for Third World students in the fall of 1968, retention of Dr. Juan Martinez, an activist Mexican-American professor, and financial assistance to guarantee that any students admitted under the special program would not have to drop out because they needed money.

They won that fight, although the college filled only a little more than half of the special admissions slots for reasons that are in dispute but center around a shortage of the necessary funds. That demand was then carried over into the five that TWLF tacked on to the end of the 10 BSU demands at the beginning of the November 6 strike.

Each of the six member groups has its own community action and campus programs in addition to being TWLF members, and Alvarado describes them all as "program oriented," which he defined in a way that sheds some light on what goes through the minds of some activist students:

> Look, man, there are two kinds of directions that you can move in as an organizer. There are concrete issues. You can bring out problems by creating issues around which the people can rally. That's issue orientation. There's program orientation. You define a problem, organize, and begin to exhaust various mechanisms set up to deal with them. After you've done that, put together a composite program that has some kind of functionalism to it and won't exhaust all your resources or your personality, you move that program as an alternative to what is creating the problem.
>
> You get results of two different kinds . . . issue orientation is a flash kind of thing. You've got to bring people together quickly, move them quickly, clearly explain the issues and everything. People won't stay with the issue.
>
> The program approach takes a much longer period of time. Time to become knowledgeable to the people, a lot of work running down the alternatives, then as you go more alternatives become clear, and there are more personal positions. The people you're trying to get to accept the program begin to react to the program, begin to resist it. It threatens him. It tells him that everything he has been concerned about in terms of his job has been responsible for what is wrong. Also, when you exhaust the program approach, you eventually wind up with the system has got no place else to go—and you've got your issue, you've got your confrontation.

When he says the system eventually has no place else to go, he means it is not going to give any ground. "We did a tremendous amount of homework" on a proposal for minorities studies, he said, "laid out sketches, curriculum, instruction, all laid out to meet special needs of the groups involved. Then we began going around to different offices trying to institute some of these courses within the curriculum. What we got was incredible. Even people who thought that the course was a good idea would say, 'Well, you should have had this in six months ago because that's when a decision was made.' You get a real crossfire of information. You go to someone's office, they tell you to go elsewhere. You go there, this cat explains how this function is really a little different from what that cat said, so he can only do this much for you, you got to go somewhere else . . . it's the way the institution is laid out, man. Anyone can do whatever he wants to as long as he doesn't make any changes in the institution.

I don't think it's a question of individuals or anything, just the basic structure of this institution. It's not structured to meet the needs of the people."

The best way to find out why these students decided they needed a political arm to push their causes is just to listen to them talk. First, another member of LASO:

> I spoke Spanish until I was five years old. When I went to kindergarten I wasn't allowed to speak Spanish, I had to speak English, and so I was forced to forget Spanish. This is what I call a cultural depression which is systematic and final.
>
> Throughout school I was never once introduced to a piece of Latin-American writing. I was never once shown a piece of art from either the Indian culture or from the real Spanish Colonial period in regards to art from the aspect of a Latin American person . . . [teachers would say] here we have the missions; here is an example of the Spanish Colonial art. In no way have we gone into how that art and architecture reflected the society of the Spaniards or the condition of the Indian and how their labor went into the building of the missions. . . .
>
> See, the educational system is no accident . . . it's not simply a matter of not including what our culture is about, what our history is about, what our economics are about, what our politics are about. It's a process of mis-education. It has a purpose . . . . One is to teach us not how to change our community, or even live in it, but how to escape it by denying that we are a part of it. . . .
>
> The condition of black people, brown people, yellow people, and red people is essentially that we are all oppressed systematically as individuals and as a people by the society . . . people have been told that black people have certain needs which aren't being met. They aren't being told that there are more Mexican-Americans in penal institutions than in institutions of higher education. They are not being told that the average number of years of formal education of a Chinese American is 1.7 in this city.

This particular student taught a creative writing class in the experimental college, concentrating on approaches he did not feel similar classes at SFSC provided.

> First of all, what I did in class was have people bring in examples of literature by authors of their own ethnic origin. . . . What they would have to do was to go out and look for it. Black people could look to LeRoi Jones, Eldridge Cleaver; Latin-American and Mexican-American people had to dig around a little bit; Jorge Gonzales, Joaquin. The Filipino people had to really dig in and they brought in some beautiful things. There was one by a Philippine writer in 1932. He was in the South, and he walked into a bar, and they said you have to get out, and he asked why. He was told that he was black, and he said, "no, I'm not, I'm a Filipino." And they answered "Oh, that's all right then."

The list goes on and on in the same vein. A 30-year-old Chinese student who tried forgetting about his people's problems for a while but was pulled back by a job with a poverty agency said:

> The Chinese they teach here is Mandarin Chinese, spoken by 90 percent of the people in Red China and Nationalist China. But the province where people migrate to here from is Canton. They speak Cantonese. Ninety-seven percent of all Chinese persons in the United States who speak Chinese speak Cantonese. The written language is the same, but the dialects are different. We need Cantonese so we have a tool to go back to our communities to help our people.

And from another Latin American, born in Argentina, who came to this country 4 years ago at the age of 23:

> We have informal links . . . like Juvenile Hall. I went there as a translator just for one kid, and ended up as a translator for five kids. If I wasn't there they would have gone through everything without understanding, without anyone. All our people end up in the Army in Vietnam because they don't know they have a right to go to school. The whole channeling of ghetto kids to vocational schools, training them for jobs that will be obsolete in 10 years. We have people with skills working as janitors because they were unable to close the language gap.

American schools have not traditionally considered it their business to try to solve community problems like these. TWLF is saying they ought to. Asked his idea of the ideal educational system, a Latin American replied:

> Let me take that in the perspective of a Latin American. It would have in it the realities of how they came to exist in this society. That is it would include in it the realities of the condition of our people. . . .
>
> For example, if we had a course in the economics of the Mission District, if we wanted to talk about the 42-year-old, we would get a 42-year-old Puerto Rican or Mexican to teach that, because he knows it. He lives it. It is his life. We are not talking about getting someone who studied a book which is an abstract of that book, so you are twice removed from the reality.
>
> What we are talking about in essence is really revolutionizing the whole concept of education. By that I mean that we are talking about dealing with reality, by living reality, by being in contact with reality, rather than by studying it.
>
> Question—What kind of people would you like to be turning out 10 years from now?
>
> Answer—"First of all, people who are aware of the context from which they come. They are not stripped of their culture but are enriched.
>
> "Second, people who will go into the various professional realms of society keeping in mind and addressing themselves to their people so that if a person is a lawyer, and say his interest is corporate law, he doesn't work for General Motors but works for his own people, say in setting up a cooperative. And if we had a medical man, he doesn't relate to, say, a Montgomery Street office but addresses himself to need in the Mission District."
>
> Question—You are talking about a sense of community responsibility.

Answer—"Right."

"What we are trying to do," said ICSA Chairman, Mason Wong, "is expose the contradictions of this society to our communities . . . separate fact from fiction. The fiction is that the Chinese have never suffered as much as, say, the black or brown communities in this country . . . rather, the Chinese community has the same basic problems as all other nonwhite communities. The only thing different that it has is some neon lights and a few tourist restaurants, which is all that white people want to know about our community. Yet these restaurants are staffed by illiterate Chinese who work 14 hours a day 6 days a week for starvation wages. The only way to survive in our community is to exploit each other, hence the myth of the successful Chinese businessman. This exploitation is perpetuated at the expense of Chinese immigrants who can only find work in the sweat shops, laundries and restaurants of Chinatown. . . .

WHITE SUPPORT GROUPS

College administrators, sympathetic black community spokesmen, and the Third World student leaders all agree that whites, moderate and radical, have played a large role in visibly supporting the strike and its picket lines, but a negligible one in terms of planning strategy.

There are times when the picket line at the main college entrance is entirely white, and during the days of police-student clashes on the commons in the fall and winter, far more whites than blacks or other minorities could be seen throwing rocks, and shouting insults at police.

Strategy decisions, however, are made by the TWLF Central Committee, which includes no whites. The two most radical white groups on campus, Students for a Democratic Society and the Progressive Labor Party, have had considerable disagreement with minority students in the past over strategy. The BSU did not support an SDS-TWLF sit-in in the administration building in the spring of 1967. "We thought it was irrelevant," said Garrett, "and we didn't think the white students should lead anything." BSU leaders often criticize the tactics of SDS-led demonstrations at other colleges.

"You should not underestimate what you're fighting for," Stokely Carmichael told a Third World meeting on the campus in November.

> . . . Because you're now beginning to challenge real attitudes. Who has the right to hire and to fire. Not even the white student movement in the height of its movement at Columbia was able to do this. Because they held the buildings for a few days, then they gave up, but they had no clear victories . . .
>
> You read about Mark Rudd [SDS leader at Columbia]. Yeah, he's sho 'nuff bad. But he ain't got nothing to show for his badness. And I don't think we can afford that, because we're not in the same position as the white students. They have the luxury of being militant or radical or revolutionary. For us, it is a necessity. We have no other out.

Echoes of this philosophy crop up time and time again in BSU statements, including warnings that seizing college buildings is pointless. Carmichael grasped another element of BSU strategy when he told his audience, "When you fight you depend only upon yourselves, nobody else. . . . You look to make allies among those people who suffer like you do. That's black people, and then that's people of color outside this circle. But you look upon yourself."

The BSU also views SDS as having relatively fixed ideas about class struggles and student power that have little to do with what they see as the key issue, racism. Also, the theory goes, SDS can afford to put on splashy demonstrations over relatively minor issues, like cafeteria food, because individual members can disappear back into white society anytime they want to, perhaps to become corporation lawyers, while blacks are always marked and lashed out against because of their color.

SDS went through quite an internal debate before officially deciding to take a secondary strategic role. They may have had no choice, for the BSU had clearly let it be known anyone was welcome to participate in the strike as long as they did not try to confuse the issues or horn in on the leadership. A pamphlet titled "On Strike, Shut it Down" put out by white supporters described the SDS position this way:

> SDS put forth the position that the main issues of the strike were racism and the class nature of the university. Others felt that we were fighting a battle for campus autonomy and that racism was too amorphous for the white student body to relate to it. Still others felt that "white demands" [i.e., demands for student power] had to be attached in order to win support for the strike. These ideas were discussed in the mass meetings and it was maintained that racism was not a vague issue, but one that could be seen as a tool of the ruling class that affects all oppressed people–including white students.

The SDS-PLP role in tactics is something else. Contrary to popular opinion, TWLF does not appear to have maintained any sort of control over people who decide they want to smash windows or throw things at police. The overwhelming majority of students arrested in the various confrontations have been white, and during melees in the central campus far more whites than Third World students are usually visible. "The word is," said one student, "that if you want to throw rocks or plant bombs, that's OK, as long as you don't try to change the issues or make new demands."

There was evidence of a shifting spectrum of support among unorganized whites, with many of those interviewed indicating that either they supported some of the demands, although they continued to go to classes, or that they occasionally helped out on a picket line.

Issues also tended to shift somewhat in the midst of confrontations, with considerable numbers of moderate whites apparently willing to risk arrest to watch, or object to, police in action on the campus at the same time they were attending class and not observing the picket lines.

It was obvious to observers of the large confrontations, also, that many, if not a majority, of the whites gathered during confrontations in the commons would consider themselves curious onlookers, despite Acting President Hayakawa's warning that no such animal exists.

FRUSTRATIONS ON THE RISE

By all accounts, 1967 was an unfortunate year at San Francisco State. Both students and faculty got caught up in what former student body president Jim Nixon called "an incredibly frustrating eight months."

White radicals were at loose ends because their drives to get massive confrontations with the "oppressive class structure," meaning the administration, just didn't seem to grow into a sustained student movement. White liberals were upset because in the spring they lost control of the student government and its $400,000 budget to a conservative group of candidates, but the conservatives found they could not push their programs through because the head of their ticket, Associated Students president Phil Garlington, proved unexpectedly liberal, especially with his veto power. The result was a series of knockdown, dragged-out arguments over the funding of student programs that stalled programs and frayed the tempers of several groups including the BSU, while Third World students were trying to figure out what they could put together to attack the issues bothering them. President John Summerskill was under fire from the trustees for not cracking down hard enough on unruly black and white activists, while the activists were getting more and more unruly. Summerskill made a lot of promises, they explained, but just did not seem to be able to get things done.

From this boiling caldron of frustration eventually emerged the TWLF strike, with all of its violence. It is clear that for all of the off-campus issues that angered minority students, the frustrations they encountered on campus gave them ample opportunity to practice tactics that would burst into violence in the fall of 1968. And the tactics seem to have been developed first in reaction to obstacles at the student level, then leveled against the administration, and finally at the college as a whole.

These tactics took two primary forms: confrontation with a kind of verbal violence whites were not used to, including shouts, obscenities, derogatory name calling, accusations of racism, and implied threats; and implied physical violence—packing meetings.

A good deal of this was carefully planned both for its impact on the whites being confronted, and on potential black leaders the BSU was trying to radicalize. It is part of the technique of heightening the contradictions that Carmichael talked about, and the verbal part is far more common in black ghettos than white America might suppose. Some of the small black nationalist groups in Harlem have been using similar rhetoric for years in an attempt to win converts. It regularly appears in the Chicago-based Black Muslim newspaper *Muhammad Speaks*. Heavyweight Champion Muhammad Ali used bits of it in the bantering that so irritated some of the white sportswriters covering him. Carmichael and Rap Brown use it when they continually insult whites, as do the Panthers with their animal terminology for police and government officials.

The verbal use can have several effects. First, it shows other blacks that they can get away with a broader range of behavior than they thought. Second, it confuses the white opponent, often making it easier to end his opposition. Or it can provoke him into such strong reprisals that his behavior then proves to other blacks that the terminology was none too strong in the first place, he is a pig or a dog, or something unprintable. There are also more subtle uses, as explained by a member of TWLF:

Look, we have almost like different ways of thinking. It's a different world . . . it's coming to that. I talked last week with SMART [Student Majority Against Revolutionary Tactics], with the Committee for an Academic Environment, down at the TV station. I also talked with some teachers opposed to the strike. One of the things that became really clear was whole definitions of words. We didn't mean the same things. We would use political activity, say. We meant something different from them. We use it having much more direct relation to our lives, like the strike is political activity. For them, it's, like, voting.

One of the functions of rhetoric is that it serves to develop a commonality of thinking, so there's not as much individual pressure. The rhetoric is one that serves to bind the people together in their thoughts. The problem with it is it's not dialogue, it doesn't serve to communicate. Like, language works in a context, and we don't have that context down yet, not just in terms of how we're gonna move, but what we're gonna move for.

From a black public official comes this analysis of the more sophisticated tactics carried out in 1968 against the college administration just after Robert Smith accepted the presidency:

Smith came in ice cold. And it was a learning process for Smith, incidentally. The black students set up a series of meetings with Smith to educate Smith. This was July, August, September. Fabulous meetings. You can't believe the things that were said in those meetings. They'd open the meetings and they had everybody strategically placed. They wouldn't let the administrators sit with each other. They had a black cat between them. They were really just diabolic in their concept.

They would open the meeting, and they would always play Smith off against Garrity, because it was their view that Smith was a figurehead and that Garrity really represented the trustees. So they would ask Smith for his opinion on a proposal and then they would say "Dr. Smith, we . . . ," they wouldn't call him Dr. Smith, incidentally. It was part of the therapy that they refer to him as dog Smith. "Dog Smith, you don't really have any power. That other dog named Garrity is the one who really has the power. We would like to be with you, dog Smith, but you just don't have the power." It was really a therapy session.

And then about halfway through the session they would tear up some paper and put it in an ashtray and shove it down the table and say you people don't understand anything except fire. Really, really quite rank.

Smith developed the same degree of tolerance that Summerskill had. He knew that was all play acting. He had the sophistication to not become offended by that kind of stuff, and as a result the other administrators out there were simply following his leadership. They would have liked to have told them to go to hell and get up and walk out, but Smith was smart enough to know that the hatred was really a surface hatred not a deep disrespect. Otherwise if it was a deep hatred and a desire to destroy they wouldn't have been in there talking about working within the system.

> He was a smart one who understood the overriding commitment, and as a result he was able to deal with that kind of nonsense without being offended. These were the new kind of tactics. They used these same kind of tactics, incidentally, with Bob Kennedy. I had a meeting with about 300 militants with Bob Kennedy. They used the same tactics. This is just shock, to scare the hell out of the white folks. After that's all over, of course, they get around to discussing things . . . .

Asked about this tactic, Garrett said this is intended to show disrespect. "All you're doing is telling him you know, you're no big thing. Black folks have a different system of language. So they use it. They don't imply it, they use it. Like some people who can call you mister and mean dog, when they say dog, they mean dog."

Physical violence or threats of it have clearly understood uses. But as mentioned earlier, the BSU view is that Americans become concerned about this kind of violence only when it goes against their interests. They use it to perpetuate their goals, the argument runs, and therefore they have no cause to complain when someone else adopts the tactic.

A student legislator described what often happened:

> We'd have meetings and suddenly there'd be 20–25 black kids there saying how they felt about things. It began over money, then went to a general discussion of the death of white culture and innuendo but no direct threats . . . . It was mostly a massing of psychological force. They were saying, "we know what we want and we have the power to destroy something if we don't get what we want."
>
> We shouted back, and the blacks took it incredibly well, better than if we'd caved in. They came in once to a budget hearing with a demand for what was in effect the entire remainder of the Experimental College budget. They showed a few shoddy programs, we fought, and they went back and produced a better program. In the end they took the second smallest budget there.

Interestingly, some of the liberal white activists in the legislature thought they had figured out a way to deal with the black tactics.

"It was the first time that many had seen guys making demands with veiled threats," said one. "But they would really respect you if you shouted back, if you had some self interest and knew what you wanted."

In the process of moving farther and farther away from the traditional approach to a college education, the BSU issued a number of statements of purpose. One, written about late 1966 or early 1967, set down the principles that underlie many of the 15 nonnegotiable demands. It said in part:

> The Black Students Union recognizes the struggles for freedom of nonwhite peoples around the world as a positive part of our educational processes. We are a Third World organization. We adhere to the struggles in Asia, Africa, and Latin America, ideologically, spiritually, and culturally.
>
> We, the Black Students Union of San Francisco State College, seek simply to function as human beings, to control our own destinies. Initially, following the myth of the American Dream, we worked too hard to attend predominantly white colleges, but we have learned through

direct analysis that it is impossible for black people to function as human beings in a racist society in which black is synonymous with enemy, no matter what the educational attainment. So we have decided to fuse ourselves with the masses of black people to create, through struggle, a new humanity, a new humanism, a black humanism and within that context collectively control our own destinies.

THE INCIDENTS PILE UP

One of the most important influences on San Francisco State student activists was the ability to conceive and run their own programs. They developed both experience in dealing with college administrators, and a sense of knowing better than anyone else what was best for their program. That sense was heightened in BSU members by the feeling that whites, by definition, did not understand what it meant to be black well enough to know what was good for blacks.

Dean Joseph White, one of the black administrators working closely with the BSU, noted:

> The thing I think was unique about San Francisco State is that all the people in decisive roles up till about a year ago February were students. Until February there were no black administrators. Until February there were only three or four black professors . . . . The students had to run from committee to committee. They have this very innovative thing, or what they consider is an innovative proposal, and no one to carry the ball for them. There was no one on the faculty who could cut through the tape. So you have some students like Bennie Stewart who since they were sophomores have been going to committee after committee trying to articulate why black studies—only to wind up before the one they started with. It was frustrating, and gives you an idea of how the system runs you around.

This infighting first became visible in the area of student affairs, with the legislature particularly, and with campus publications that attacked the BSU.

There were complicating factors, notably infighting between the liberal and conservative whites that tied up funding for student programs. An article in the February 1968 issue of the *Daily Gater* wrapped up the events of the previous year this way:

> Held by a two to one margin by conservatives . . . the legislature refused to pass Garlington's liberal-radical programs. The president, using his only direct power, vetoed the legislative acts. Neither side could win decisive victories on the issues: the budget allocations, the Black Students Union programs, the experimental college, open process, the *Gater*.

The same issue notes in a different story what had happened as a result to one program the BSU had taken over and shaped in its own image, the much-praised tutorial program. The story read:

> The tutorial program, one of the student projects that put SF State on the educational map, is in trouble.

> Thomas Williams, program coordinator [and a member of the BSU central committee], said the program is badly in need of money and only has enough to eke out an existence through the month of March.
>
> The Shape-Up AS legislature allocated $6,000 to the program in September, a 54-percent cut from the previous year and $18,000 short of the program's initial budget request . . . .

There was evidence much earlier that the BSU had gotten tired of fighting that kind of problem. Garrity described it this way:

> We started to have complaints. The budget was up before the Associated Students . . . black people came into the room, and this was the first time that this had occurred, to our knowledge, in any college or university, and they surrounded every person in the room. One black man was standing behind each white man. He didn't say anything—they just stood there. And they were frightened out of their Goddam minds. And for the first time intimidation became a part of the rhetoric on campus. This was early fall 1966 . . . and the thing they came there for was the budget of the tutorial program. . . .
>
> But from that tutoring thing, a few days or a few weeks later it was something else. In other words, they started to gain a visibility. Just repeatedly day after day you started to hear vibrations about the fact that these cats were not going through in the ordinary demeanor of the college. They were threatening violence, they were intimidating people. It was a form of violence at that time.

Garrity then described the administration's reaction:

> We just didn't really believe that this presaged anything that would come beyond . . . and other people were saying the same thing. My point was institutionally we tried to minimize reaction to it. . . . We were guided by conventional wisdom. The conventional wisdom was that the way to truth, beauty and justice was the integrationist way—faculty member after faculty member said "What the hell's this?" It's a passing phase.
>
> I remember the black secretary that I had who was interested. I was talking about nationalism—it's evil. She was pushing the point to me that nationalism is valuable. It gives a sense of belonging, dignity. I was saying, "No, it's evil." And she was putting it to me in a very concrete way, "that's my salvation because I don't feel a part of you, whitey, I feel a part of black folks. And that's the way I've got to go." And it challenged almost every one of our liberal views about what we are up to . . . .

"What we had happen were a whole sequence of events," Garrity continued. "A name which is very big today, Jack Alexis, went into a meeting and took a great big table, and turned it over, and not only turned it over, he turned it over in a way that he threw it at the audience. That was violence. It was violent as hell. We had, we must have had, a dozen events during the fall. Jimmy Garrett and company were coming out with expressive forms of behavior which were shocking us, which people were complaining . . . about."

The tactics showed no signs of slackening off, however, and in the December 5, 1966, issue of the *Gater*, BSU member Judie Hart took half a page to note:

> The Associated Students are playing games with the Black Student Union. They have assumed that not meeting BSU's budget request is as easy as shooting a black boy in the back "accidentally." We are tired of gaming and we don't intend to get shot in the back.

The bitter barrage went on to say a BSU budget request of $9,050 had been consistently bounced back and forth between the legislature and the finance committee while much larger sums for less worthy causes were approved. It concluded: ". . . In other words, BSU, go to hell. Racism ain't even latent no more. . . ."

Another major blowup came May 11, 1967. A meeting of the legislature, called to reach some compromise over the funding of a BSU project, was adjourned after it dissolved into a shouting match and a near brawl. The issue was $2,838 asked by the BSU to finish filming plays by black writer LeRoi Jones, a visiting professor that semester, so they could be shown to on- and off-campus audiences.

Earlier, $1,584 had been voted for the project, and during the stormy meeting finance committee members complained the legislature was short of funds and the BSU should trim its request, while Garrett argued that there was no more room to trim, the proposal should be granted or cut in its entirety.

Three days later the money was granted in a meeting that illustrated both the tense mood of the times, and the BSU attitudes on the matter.

"After two hours of explanations and arguments the legislature voted 7–6 to give Jones $2,838," the *Daily Gater* reported at the time. ". . . However Pat Kimbley, speaker of the legislature . . . voted against the resolution, deadlocking the vote. . . ."

Three proxy votes were immediately opened. "Two . . . favored giving Jones all the money he asked for. . . . The third . . . favored giving Jones a reduced subsidy. Because he felt the wording of the proxy votes was unclear, Kimbley initially decided not to accept them.

> But as members of the BSU rose from their seats in anger . . . Kimbley conceded and accepted the votes. . . .
>
> Jimmy Garrett, head of the BSU, opened the meeting by saying that the legislature "can't tolerate black people doing things for themselves, because you can't control them."
>
> Jones then took over . . . "we feel that the definition of our lives is not served by Shakespeare and Moliere, we want to recreate ourselves as black people and refine our experiences through the plays and films to the communities at large."
>
> Jones then said that they wanted to use the college resources because the black communities don't have them.
>
> "If we were doing Shakespeare or Moliere, there wouldn't be any of this trouble. The fact that the material we are using comes from the lives of black people is the point of contention."

Growing anger by BSU leaders who felt they were being harassed was not eased when, 5 days later on May 19, 10 elected student officers made a formal complaint to the Board of Trustees accusing the BSU of racism and mishandling funds. Their accusations included two signed statements describing threats allegedly made after the legislative meetings, and some excerpts from Jones' writings.

After 4 days of on-campus investigation, a study team put together by the chancellor's office concluded that the "vast majority" of charges exceeded the scope of the supporting evidence, but warned that communication problems existed between students of opposing political factions.

Evidence, according to the Study Team's report, was at that time sketchy. "During the student interview," it said, "one student reported that, following one meeting of the legislature, two girls were walking across campus behind her and were talking how 'whitey' had better vote right or she'll 'get it.'" But a dispute developed over whether the two girls were students at the college. The report continued:

> Although a number of the students interviewed indicated that members of the BSU had used such tactics as packing meetings, mumbling, or finger tapping during meetings, there was no real agreement among these students as to the extent of such tactics or their effectiveness. It was also pointed out by several students who had made presentations to the panel that sharp pressure tactics had been used to some degree by members of both sides of opposing political factions. One student told the panel that remarks with racial bias overtones had been made by students representing both factions when the BSU budget proposal was being discussed in the Associated Student Legislature.

Garrett, who had turned the BSU chairmanship over to Ben Stewart by the time the report came out, complained that the summer-long battle had stalled the tutorial program, and cost the BSU a $15,000 outside grant.

With animosity growing as the school year went on, it took no great visionary to predict even more trouble ahead.

Crucial in the swirl of controversy that surrounded the BSU at the time was the beating of the editor of the *Daily Gater* in his office, November 6, 1967.

The beating came after a long series of *Gater* articles critical of and making satirical remarks about the BSU. Some poked fun at the leaders, while others stopped just short of accusing the BSU of misappropriating funds. And the charges would be picked up and repeated in the legislature during the wild battles for money.

"The word was that Garrett had control of all the community organizations, the work study program, Community Involvement Program, and was using those to further his own end," recalled a former student who was active in the BSU at that time.

"Hearings and investigations took up a lot of time and made a lot of people mad . . . the paper carried on a position counter to the facts of the matter. They became a focal point for anti-BSU feeling."

Several stories circulated at the time on what might have been the actual trigger for the visit to the *Gater* office by more than a dozen blacks. Some said it was related to the just-ended homecoming queen election in which the BSU-sponsored candidate lost by 10 votes amid charges, later proven, that 40 votes had disappeared. The election was later invalidated by the legislature.

Others blamed an article on the front page of the November 6 *Gater* alleged to contain racial slurs. The article, detailing a visit by topless dancer

Carol Doda to the campus, quotes a pair of Negro singers as announcing, among other things, "It's a Negro holiday. Today's the day the new Cadillacs come out and we're celebrating."

The *Gater* itself speculated later that an article written by Editor Jim Vaszko when he was sports editor the previous semester may have created much of the hostility. It was a satirical spoof of the then heavyweight champion Muhammad Ali.

Garrett recollected events this way:

> We were going to see three people that day. We were going to see the editor of the *Gater*, the chairman of the school of education, and the dean of students. All on the same question, Racism. . . . This was about some different kinds of racist things we thought they were pulling, so we went to talk to them . . . about Muhammad Ali and a series of things. . . .
>
> So one of the things we brought with us was a folder full of the different articles that we had documented and xeroxed, and we had given copies to the students so that everybody could see it, so that they understood why were we going to go and talk to them. One reason why there were so many people in the *Gater* office was because we were trying to build leaders, and the way you build leaders is to give them information.
>
> Question–How many did go?
>
> Answer–Fifteen. So we took them upstairs with us to go . . . and we went up there, and then the white boy [Editor Jim Vaszko] said some things, and he got hit in the mouth. He didn't get hurt, which is what he should have done. But he could have got hurt. . . .
>
> . . . We didn't expect to fight. Nobody went there to fight. The fight was spontaneous. That was the one thing that was spontaneous. The going up there was politically planned to train people on how to move on people, because we'd take people to the president's office, to the dean of students' office so they could sit and listen to white folks discuss their lives, discuss black folks' lives, and they could learn from that.
>
> Question–Were you dismayed? What was your reaction when it broke up in a fight?
>
> Answer–My reaction was that some things are inevitable, you know, and that was one of the things. . . . We had reached a point where we take a move from rhetoric to the element of action, and there was no return. We already had an atmosphere of violence. But the violence was psychological. . . .
>
> . . . The question of violence is a dual question, because violence has been committed against us ever since we had been on campus. You know. And the turnabout is that violence just expresses itself differently, because when we came back in a violent way it . . . was a response to a certain kind of violence. We just didn't arbitrarily jump on white folks, because if we had wanted to do it, we could have done that every day of the week. . . .

The next morning the *Gater* appeared with six photographs of the fight, taken by a staff photographer who had gone almost unnoticed in the general brawl. An accompanying story announced:

> *Gater* editor Jim Vaszko was beaten yesterday morning in a wild, fist-swinging melee triggered by about 15 Negro students.
>
> The attack occurred at 10:25 after the Negroes deployed themselves throughout the *Gater* office and asked to see Vaszko. A spokesman for the group was told by *Gater* reporter John Davidson that Vaszko was on the phone.
>
> The unidentified Negro entered Vaszko's office followed by four members of his group. They closed the door behind them.
>
> According to Vaszko, one of the group said to him, "I want to talk to you man."
>
> Vaszko replied, "I'm on the phone, I'll be with you in a second."
>
> "One of the Negroes ripped the phone from my hands and began beating me," Vaszko said.
>
> After receiving several blows, Vaszko fell to the floor and was kicked repeatedly.

The story said other staff members who heard the commotion and tried to come to Vaszko's aid were stopped by other blacks, and the result was a free-swinging brawl through the newsroom, a story borne out by the photographs of fights going on all around the room. One of the persons clearly visible in one of the pictures was tutorial director George Murray, later to become the focus of a suspension from his teaching job that many believe triggered the November 6 strike 1 year later.

Exactly 1 month later, on December 6, a group of black high school students brought on campus for a BSU program ran wild for a brief period, smashing some things in the bookstore. A white faculty member sympathetic to the BSU said he remembers hearing Garrett lecture the youngsters on violence, telling them, "This doesn't lead to anything, we're trying to change the institution, not break windows."

Antagonism continued to grow, particularly in the aftermath of the *Gater* beating. The BSU held a November 16 news conference, seen at the time as an attempt to repair its image, at which a statement was issued saying:

"We offer a positive program of Blackness. Our programs are work programs. Our direction is revolutionary. Our method is organization. Our goal is Black Power. Our essence is black Humanism."

"You newsmen don't really want to talk about the *Gater* office," said on-campus coordinator Jerry Varnado to persistent questioning. "You want to talk about violence. All right, let's talk about Vietnam." And he started down a list of statistics designed to show that a disproportionate number of nonwhites are killed there.

In December, the BSU issued a statement which read in part:

> Enclosed is a copy of a letter written by John Summerskill, president of San Francisco State College, to Chancellor Glenn S. Dumke regarding the fight in the *Gater* office November 6, 1967. It was sent to every member of the nearly 2,000 SFSC faculty and administration. Summerskill calls this a preliminary report based on "factual data and thorough investigation." No black students on the San Francisco State College campus including the officers of the Black Students Union have been formally contacted for interview or investigation by the president or any of his representatives. At the publication of this letter no hear-

ings had taken place regarding the *Gater* incident . . . it should be noted that on the board of appeals and review there were nine (9) whites and one (1) black.

The BSU maintains that this letter is a racist document admittedly one-sided (white sided) by the president himself.

In particular note that such references in the letter that "Negroes were intruders" as if black students have no right to be in certain classrooms on the campus. Read the letter carefully. You can see that the black students have already been convicted by Summerskill before the hearing or the trial began. . . . There is no difference in the final analysis between Huey Newton, Black Students, LeRoi Jones, Black Brothers. We're all convicted before trial in this racist school, the racist state or this racist country. Hopefully black people are learning this fact. Hopefully black people are beginning to see that their only hope is to destroy this racist nation and create one for ourselves. Our lives depend on it.

Jerry Varnado, *On-Campus Coordinator*
Jimmy Garrett, *Off-Campus Coordinator*

MOVING ON BLACK STUDIES

Documents on file with the Council of Academic Deans indicate the first suggestion for a black studies department within the regular academic framework came in December 1966 at a meeting of the academic senate's instructional policy committee. It was suggested by the Black Students Union, whose leaders had already been struggling for about a year with increasing the student commitment to blackness.

The suggestion was made at the end of the same semester that had seen the BSU's tactics of intimidation flower into common use. But those tactics weren't even hinted at in the early discussions on a black studies department, perhaps because only two or three BSU leaders were involved in those early discussions. Minutes from the various meetings, however, indicate that only a few faculty and administration members appeared to have caught the sense of urgency that marked battles in the AS legislature. And perhaps because of this, it took a year for any substantive progress toward the department the BSU wanted. During that year, the polite demeanor of the BSU on this issue slipped away.

"The first confrontation in today's terms was a nice, quiet little session," said Garrity, who hosted it at his home. "LeRoi Jones was visiting professor, and he sat in there and never opened his mouth. Nice and quiet, and he said you know, we've got to do something. Certainly, we're all for it. And we were all happy and working together, and we had committees, and we were theoretically solving the problem."

Administrators were even ahead of the BSU in some ways. They insisted from the beginning it would have to be a program including Orientals, Mexican-Americans, and other minorities, not just blacks.

President John Summerskill had called a series of open meetings in 1966 to explore the general problems of black students, including the drop in the percentage of black students over the past several years, and the problems of courses felt to be irrelevant. Up to that time, most of the formal work done

355-234 O - 69 - 9

by the BSU on courses designed especially for blacks had been in the experimental college's Black Arts and Culture series, and in their high school tutoring program.

"When the results of the experimental college began to show itself, it became clear that more people ought to be involved in them," said a former student who was a BSU leader at that time. "We had dialogue on the changes that would give black students a more positive relationship to education. . . .

"We began to negotiate with the school in terms of getting credit for them—the reception was always poor. So what it involves is a re-education of the administration, and that is a long, slow process. It conjures up all sorts of fears of loss of power, and that sort of thing. The argument is always 'how badly do you want it? We will give you just as much as we feel we have to and no more.' This went on from then to now."

In March 1967, 3 months after the formal suggestion was first made, the IPC unanimously voted to start a program of black studies, and in April Garrity hosted his "nice, quiet little session" for an informal discussion with a select group of students, faculty, and leaders of the black community. Included from the BSU were Garrett and Stewart.

Six weeks later, at the May 31 meeting of the Council of Academic Deans (CAD), Garrity reported on the evening of informal discussion. He said no conclusions had been reached, and no determination had been made of what to do next, but there had been a full discussion. Garrett, he said, had asked for—

> All academic program at San Francisco State College wherein the Negro student could get something to help him find his place in American society, his self-identity. He asked that a department be established with a major and a budget for staff and that the control of that program be given to the Negro students.

The wording "to help him find his place in American society" points up just how fast the BSU position was changing. A year later they would issue the letter complaining about Summerskill's handling of the *Gater* incident investigation, and urging blacks to "destroy this racist Nation and create one for ourselves."

According to CAD minutes, some homework had been done between the gathering at Garrity's home and the May 31 "CAD meeting."

Some of the ideas had been refined, and the academic senate's executive committee had been notified of what had taken place. The deans discussed the matter at length that day, in ways which appeared reasonable at the time, but which were later pointed out by black students and faculty as examples of deliberate stalling where black needs are concerned. The points they raised included:

Whether the name "black studies" was proper in an unsegregated school, whether a "Negro American Studies Department" might not be a better choice, concerns the School of Education has had about impressions of anti-Semitism and pro-Nazism in meetings run by the BSU, Garrett's failure to show up at a School of Education meeting because of prior commitments, the academic community's duty to live up to rationality and humanism, the duty of a college to embrace educational problems and not problems of a minority unit alone, the failure of the college to set up institutes on Negro history although there were institutes on other groups, the possibility the Negro faculty might form a communications link with the Negro community, asking 10 or so distinguished scholars "maybe mostly Negroes" to meet with the deans to discuss a first-rate program, the "tremendous dynamism now operating within the Negro student community which needs a base for operations," a survey to see what the college is already doing, the need to show that "American education and American culture does a good job for all Americans," a black identity crisis that might be more important, whether the vocabulary used at Garrity's home had been less sharp and abusive than that used in student meetings, whether there was a consensus for a program of Negro-American studies, whether the problem is explosive and needs to be dealt with immediately, the need to keep from condoning separatist movements on campus, and the challenge to higher education to accommodate to change.

At the end of this discussion, much of which indicated unfamiliarity with what had been going on in the BSU over the past year, the CAD continued the discussion to its next meeting, a week away.

At its June 6 meeting, the CAD approved a resolution that read:

> San Francisco State College shall accept the judgment of a significant number of its students and faculty that the present curriculum does not adequately meet the needs of black students and other minority group students nor adequately confront and comprehend the history and present realities of the cultures and communities of Negro-Americans and other minority groups in the United States and the world.
>
> This college shall therefore seek the means necessary to meet those needs and to comprehend these realities. This college shall support fully whatever means are essential for the fulfillment of the intentions of this resolution.

Garrity translated that to mean that the CAD "is suggesting that a faculty person be hired and assigned to take a major role in the planning and working on this problem. Also each school will try to fund a person to participate in this effort . . . possibly in a seminar meeting regularly."

During the summer months, CAD minutes indicated some action exploring the difficulties of hiring a black studies planner and getting a funding grant from private sources, but no real progress for a variety of reasons.

There was little, by that time, disagreement on the need for some sort of emphasis on the history of minority groups. A Council of Academic Deans report adopted September 19, 1967, noted in part:

> . . . There can be little doubt that in the period of increasing unrest among black and other minority groups an attack on the problem of the relevance and meaning of a college education for these groups demands a high priority indeed. . . .
>
> In the eyes of many, the educational problem of black and other minority students from kindergarten through college is the problem of relevance, estrangement, and identity. It is hypothesized that the high drop-out rate, the low grades, and the general lack of motivation among large numbers of minority students are due not only to a general feeling of separateness, but also to a more specific folk recognition that education under the authority of the white community fails to focus upon subject matter that is germane to the life experiences of the people in the minority community.

The same report, however, also detailed the kinds of things the BSU was finding increasingly frustrating.

Early attempts to come to grips with the problem, it said, "were discouraging in that they dramatized the inadequacy of a support, the lack of a coordinated strategies, and the uncertainty of a sound intellectual foundation."

Recognition of that led to setting up a task force of faculty, administration, and representatives of the BSU "to launch an immediate, urgent, and thoroughgoing exploration of the problem with an eye toward discovering some beginning answers in the near future."

But the BSU, however cooperative it may have been on one level, was at another level growing more and more tired of what appeared to it to be unreasonable delays.

Then came the fall 1967 semester with its confrontation tactics, its threats of violence, criticism of the BSU, and the *Gater* incident.

Administrators said they felt as if they were running from one crisis to the next with no time for any long-range planning. Minutes from the CAD's January 16, 1968, meeting include the following:

> Dean Pentony said that . . . because of the events of the fall, the Task Force [authorized June 6] had not been able to move far from its organizational meeting. . . . He commented also that he felt that the college's credibility, particularly with the task force idea, was reaching nearly zero with the blacks and also vice versa. He said he felt that if the IPC resolution goes through our group and the [Academic] Senate, and if the black students don't get a chance to participate, they'll boycott the program. . . . Dr. Garrity said he felt the IPC was committing the college to black studies as a program and as a program educationally sound, while the CAD had come to a point of feeling uncertain about the educational soundness.

The CAD at that meeting did endorse the intent of the resolution to start a black studies program which the IPC had adopted the previous March. Pentony, however, was right in his assessment of the credibility gap. Blacks by that time felt the college was deliberately stalling.

"They appointed a task force," said Vice President Glenn Smith later, "and the task force dropped the ball. They didn't meet."

Faculty and student interviews indicated a number of things happened in the fall of 1967 to create that credibility gap, including the student infighting, and the handling of one discipline problem in particular by President John Summerskill.

Summerskill suspended several white staff members of the campus newspaper, *Open Process*, after it printed a poem the administration termed obscene. He lifted the suspensions the next day, partly, Smith said, on the advice of the American Civil Liberties Union. But he had earlier suspended six black students involved in the *Gater* beating, and when they remained suspended until the spring semester, several BSU leaders termed the difference in the handling of the two cases another example of racism.

The impressions of unwarranted delay, though, extend beyond the black students.

"Summerskill and [Robert] Smith [his successor] were committed," said a black faculty member who had been involved from the beginning. "People in the IPC and the committee ran them around in circles."

The Reverend A. Cecil Williams was one of the handful of black community leaders who met with college officials and black students almost from the beginning. The administration position, he said, did not seem reasonable.

> I had a feeling that they were caught up in the bureaucracy maze for one thing. That the real issue at hand here was those administrators didn't have any power to act. That the problem that they faced was with the Board of Trustees who undoubtedly had been very reactionary to any significant movement in the demands of the students, were in fact unable to be moved to the degree that something significant could come out of it. And what they were doing was trying to buy off the students to a great degree. They offered them small measures of things that certainly were unreasonable to the students. We understood that also, we talked about it with the students.
>
> First of all, they couldn't understand the philosophy projected by black people . . . basically a self-determination philosophy. The real problem with most of the men who gathered . . . was that they were probably liberal, or liberals, but they wanted to act like liberals usually act, and that, you know, they just didn't understand . . . .
>
> Question–You mean, "Here, boy, lemme give you a hand?"
>
> Answer–Yes. They just didn't understand at this particular point that there's a new mood and a new tempo in regards to complete direction, a new direction in the black community. And basically, they didn't even know how to react to it . . . .

The philosophy the college projected in those discussions, in Williams' view, was–

> Let's talk about it, let's make sure that we understand you and you understand us, and reason is more important than. . . . You know, John Summerskill is a liberal man and we need this kind of man in the educational system, and . . . we'll get more from him than we will from, say, a person who's conservative. Just give us time to do it. They talked in time spans of like two to five years, these kinds of things. They wanted to talk about the critical problems they were facing, in regards to other schools within the academic community, what they were trying to do with them. And also, they went on to say, we cannot in fact let this studies department . . . overshadow any other department, we've got to work it together, it's got to be integrated into the total kind of process that we have, and we've got to do it the same old way that it has been done. And what they were talking about was working through the bureaucracy maze. . . .

Others talked about feeling that the students were being placed on the same old "treadmill of conversation" that they had tried for so long, and grown so tired of.

The American system of getting things done by compromising, watering down, "is archaic," said a black elected official. "It's a game that us adults play. It's a game that gets a lot of people hurt. It is a very serious game. It doesn't address itself to the real issues. You get caught up in emotion, the sound and the fury, words, outward appearances, but you don't deal with the basic issues. That's the dilemma, really."

Translated, that means that by November 6, 1968, the day of the strike, SFSC still had no black studies department, although there were 18 black studies courses and plans had been approved to grant a degree in black studies beginning in September 1969. Blacks who were freshmen when Garrett first suggested the idea were now Juniors.

"I think it got to the point of strike because they [the students] had literally gone through 18 months of negotiations," said the official. "I know that this is true because I was involved in certain parts of it. . . . And they really attempted to use democratic, legitimate avenues of redress and grievance and committee meetings and more meetings, and the strike came about because I think they . . . legitimately damned tired of promises that were broken, of extended negotiations that weren't going anywhere, that didn't seem to be productive. They got Nathan Hare on campus which was one success, but then Nathan Hare was left for months without even a secretary. . . ."

The administration during this time was convinced it was acting with unusual sympathy and dispatch.

". . . Part of the absolute nonsense of the current situation is [the idea] that the radical and black, etc., have not had access to the holy sees of power," said Garrity. "As a matter of fact the guys who did not have access were the conservatives, the reactionaries . . . . Jimmy Garrett spent more time in Summerskill's office than [presidential aide] Glenn Smith and I put together . . . any radical faculty member could get in and spend an hour, and [Dean DeVere] Pentony could spend ten minutes, and a conservative . . . couldn't get inside the door."

But the BSU was beginning to operate on a different theory–that the president's office at SFSC was in fact powerless, that real control lay with the chancellor's office and the Board of Trustees. The realization dawned slowly, several people said, as Summerskill kept agreeing with BSU ideas, but seemed unable to deliver what they thought he was promising.

"Summerskill . . . was a good man but he is in the wrong century," said Garrett. ". . . We talked to him every day, but he was wishy-washy. He couldn't decide whether or not he wanted to be a white college president or a human being. . . . He could have reformed us right out of existence. He could have organized in such a way to make that black studies program live and the Black Student Unions around this country may never have gotten developed. But it wasn't him. He did not have the confidence of the faculty, or those administrators. So we got hung up in committees, stuff like that. He was allright, but he was just in the wrong century."

The black elected official, involved in some of the conferences with Summerskill, tended to agree. There was no progress in Summerskill's case, he said, "because he made a couple of moves that were rather progressive moves for a college at that time . . . where he lost political support in an otherwise Republican conservative State. And I think he was frowned upon because of his involvement with the black students, and I think it just made his life much more complicated, and the support that would have ordinarily accompanied him had he played the Hayakawa role just dropped away."

The official said Summerskill confided to him before he resigned under pressure that he–

> resigned on principle, and that principle was that he knew clearly that he was not making the decisions to make San Francisco State grow, as a

> college or university, and that the dilemma he found himself in was insurmountable. He had to grapple with the State legislature, to grapple with the Board of Trustees, and he had also to grapple with the administrative hierarchy in the system . . . so that he could not function as a president making independent decisions. It was all interrelated, complex, very difficult to move, having to satisfy too many parties in order to get something done. . . .

This comment reflects the attitudes of many students and black community leaders who discussed their feelings, and again indicates the difference in outlook between the black and white community spokesmen. Time and time again in civil-rights discussions, in other parts of the Nation, black adults who try to keep abreast of the problem say the black community cannot afford to let another generation of its young people be crushed by the Nation's failure to meet their by now special needs. The problem is seen as of the utmost urgency to them. But over and over again they complain, at SFSC and elsewhere, that they see whites in power who treat the problem like any other, processing it through the normal channels as if the question were one of getting funds to put up a building, and not deciding the future education and income of black children. This difference in outlook produced a communications gap at SFSC almost impossible to overcome.

"You've got to take it one day at a time," said a black administrator. "It can't come overnight. But night doesn't have to last 400 years."

By spring 1968, a sense of the importance black students attached to this proposal was beginning to filter into faculty and administration, and work speeded up considerably. Dr. Nathan Hare, a black psychologist and prizefighter who had been let go from Howard University in Washington, D.C., the previous year for his statements against the Howard administration, was hired by Summerskill at the advice of Garrett and over the objections of administration, staff, and some community people to coordinate the program.

After the strike started, Garrity issued a list of steps taken over the past 2 years to get a black studies department going, and a covering letter that noted:

> At times it even appeared that there are some elements of the community who believe that students and faculty are in favor of a black studies program while the administration is opposed. That belief is not based on truth. . . . While it remains necessary to seek additional major support for this and other programs of ethnic education, it is clear that considerable progress is now possible through effective use of the resources recently made available.

By that time, however, neither the BSU nor the black community was listening. They were not laying all blame on the administration. Both academic senate faculty committees and the Board of Trustees, dominated by appointees loyal to Governor Reagan, were given a larger share in many cases. Their argument, however, was that 2 years of approaches to a problem which they knew to be so crucial was either inexcusable inefficiency or racism, depending on how radical you were.

For their part, administrators laid much of the blame on problems raised by the black students and others that they had to use their time to deal with the college's presidential problems and the failure of the man they had chosen to coordinate the program, black professor Dr. Nathan Hare to deliver.

Garrity said the steps the school took shows "that the college administration has moved with unusual speed in the implementation of the Black Studies Program. In fact the accomplishments to date have gone considerably beyond both the timetable and the faculty positions requested by Dr. Nathan Hare and Dean Joseph White. His list read:

> February 9, 1968: Appointed Dr. Nathan Hare to be Special Curriculum Supervisor at the rank of lecturer with pay based on academic rank of associate professor and with the assignment to "help design a curriculum of black studies." Dr. Hare became a member of the staff of the vice president for academic affairs.
>
> Spring semester, 1968: At least 14 black studies courses offered under joint auspices of various currently established departments and of the curriculum coordinator for black studies.
>
> March 11, 1968: Reported in faculty footnotes: "Actually this is probably the first move at any college to try to solve the black people's problems through education."
>
> April 16, 1968: Proposed a department of black studies to be created in two phases. Phase 1 would "pull together some of the currently experimental courses into a new department by September 1968" [p. 7, Dr. Hare's proposal]. Phase 2 would establish a black studies major by September 1969. The curriculum "has been constructed but certain rough edges are still being ironed out."
>
> "Professors and staff must be added at appropriate rates, beginning with three professors by September 1969, and accelerating to a full departmental staff with each succeeding year" [p. 8, Dr. Hare's report].
>
> April 12, 1968: Reappointed Dr. Hare for 1968–69, invited him to teach in addition to administrative assignment if he so desired, and agreed to adjust his administrative duties to permit this arrangement.
>
> August 2, 1968: Proposed that a B.A. degree in black studies starting in 1969–70 be approved by the trustees [see record of approval below on October 24]. Dr. Garrity's letter to the chancellor's office [Dr. Gerhard Friedrich] stated on p. 7, "It is anticipated that during the coming year a complete major program in black studies will be developed and presented for consideration by our college curriculum committee."
>
> September 1968: Appointed Dr. Joseph White as dean of undergraduate studies.
>
> September 17, 1968: Created a department of black studies and named Dr. Nathan Hare to be acting chairman.
>
> Fall semester, 1968: More than 20 black studies courses offered under joint auspices of black studies and established departments.
>
> September 30, 1968: Confirmed September 24, 1968, oral agreement committing 1.2 positions for immediate use.
>
> October 21, 1968: Memo to President Smith states that the black studies courses now in session will be transferred to the black studies department in spring or fall 1969. The black studies department is assigned for administrative assistance and supervision to the dean of undergraduate studies.

October 24, 1968: Approved black studies degree. First such program in California State colleges. *To be implemented, September 1969* [date suggested by Dr. Hare in his April 1968 proposal].

October 24, 1968: In a joint meeting approved the black studies B.A. degree proposal and recommendation for 11.3 positions.

November 4, 1968: Revised proposal for black studies B.A. degree presented to Vice President Garrity. Three faculty positions are "needed to initiate the proposed degree program" [p. 8] [later increased to 11.3 positions].

December 5, 1968: 11.3 positions to be taken from regularly approved programs and given to the black studies department in order to permit it to expand in spring 1969, without waiting for a budget allocation [which could not start until fall 1969 at the earliest]. CAD approved "the implementation of the black studies department with full faculty power commensurate with that accorded all other departments at the college. This power includes the selection of faculty and shaping of the program" (quoted from letter to President S. I. Hayakawa from CAD).

December 17, 1968: Requested Dean Joseph White as "chief academic officer responsible for the black studies program" to develop and forward to the vice president's office by January 10: the courses in black studies to be offered in spring 1969; the selection and assignment of faculty and the need for office space.

January 2, 1969: In a letter to Dr. Gerhard Friedrich at the chancellor's office stated the college's intention "to begin the formal offering of the [black studies] program in the spring semester 1969, which advances the timetable of our original submission."

[*Note:* A study of the above chronology and of the full records reveals that the college administration has moved with unusual speed in the implementation of the black studies program. In fact, the accomplishments to date have gone considerably beyond both the timetable and the faculty positions requested by Dr. Nathan Hare and Dean Joseph White.]

There was a great deal of confusion on campus at the time about what had actually happened to the program. Blacks were saying the college had sabotaged it, and Garrity's chronology might have managed to convince many the program was at least still alive had it been issued earlier, and had blacks by that time not been occupied with other problems.

One was simply the loss of a safety valve. Summerskill resigned in May 1968, putting an end to the close relationship that had developed between the president of the college and top activists in the BSU.

His successor, Robert Smith, came with tremendous backing from the faculty but was not well known to the blacks. One community spokesman described him as a good, liberal man, without the empathy Summerskill had for the problems of black students. At least, the empathy did not come across.

The result was a major change in BSU approach, illustrated by a story one professor likes to tell. Immediately after the beating of the *Gater* editor, he said, he saw George Murray fleeing from the building across a short stretch of lawn to the Administration Building. The administrator hurried toward the rapidly growing commotion Murray had just left, saw what had happened, called police first, then telephoned Summerskill to inform him.

"There's one thing to be thankful for," Summerskill is said to have replied. "George Murray wasn't involved."

"What do you mean, wasn't involved?" the administrator exploded.

"He couldn't have been," Summerskill is quoted as saying. "He's right here in my office."

Instead of using the new president's office as a refuge, Smith was treated to the already-described name-calling tactics.

Part of the BSU attitude toward Smith was due to a change in its own leadership. Garrett had left school in June, turning the reins of the BSU over to a central committee which had been formed partly because the workload had grown too large for one person to handle, and partly as a reaction to Garrett's own intensely personal brand of leadership.

He had tried the previous year to develop new leaders within the BSU. Taking people with him to discussions with administrators was one technique discussed earlier. Another was to appear at student legislature meetings with two lieutenants, usually Stewart, who succeeded him as chairman, and Jerry Varnado. Garrett would make the opening statement, then sit back and give Stewart and Varnado experience at handling the argument. He stepped back in if needed, but as time wore on toward the end of the spring 1967 semester, he gave them more and more of the responsibility.

With Garrett out of the picture, however, whites discovered that neither Stewart nor Varnado was as accessible, as easy to talk to, or as willing to bargain as Garrett had been. They set their own style and their own directions, and from the point of view of the whites involved, the BSU had closed one more door to communications.

Summer 1968 was a rough time for black activists around the country. Assassinations, election campaigns many thought were racist, and repeated small rebellions in the ghettos put tempers on edge. The Huey Newton trial and all the other local issues already described strained the already tenuous communications between the BSU and moderate whites, so that by the time the fall semester began, and the University of California regents began to crack down on Eldridge Cleaver, many of the college faculty and administration were convinced they were sitting on a tinderbox, waiting for a spark.

A DIFFERENT POINT OF VIEW

Some significant points about what has been said up to now need to be brought out here. While the Study Team made no attempt to exhaustively survey the opinions of all black professors at SFSC, they did talk to every black administrator and most of the actively involved black faculty and administration, as well as the most involved black community spokesmen.

Not a single one of these black adults was willing to say that the black students had been dealt with fairly by the college. A few were privately angry at the tactics used by the BSU, while others either supported the tactics or else considered them inevitable given the present situation. But they agreed that the overriding issues were an education relevant to the needs of black students, and an approach to black problems that still contains a great deal of racism.

Racism is one of those emotional words which has been thrown around so much in the last year or so that it has lost most of its meaning. But the black administration and faculty at SFSC see many concrete examples. While white administrators may congratulate themselves with the recent sharp increase in the number of black administrators, for instance, the black administrators all spoke in rather bitter terms about the fact that the college had not seen the need to put blacks in these positions until recently.

"They're scared of blacks," said one black professor. "Tom Williams [a BSU member] had set up some kind of community education program and he wanted to use a couple of rooms. . . . They called a series of meetings. I sat in on a few meetings. They said what if our typewriters get broken? Williams said he'd take out extra insurance. Other groups have used the facilities, and they don't get questions like that. The objections were clearly racist in origin. The students are becoming increasingly militant, increasingly bitter."

These involved black adults saw the State-college system piling mistake upon mistake in dealing with minority student problems, without any individual of substantive power being knowledgeable enough about black attitudes to catch what was going on. Some felt this compounding of error upon error was really a series of innocent mistakes based on lack of understanding of the problem, while others felt it pointed out a basic racism in whites—the stubborn refusal to understand. Either way, however, blacks came out on the short end—again, many said. And that is the significance of the support given to the black students by San Francisco's generation of black leaders over 30.

Several of the black community spokesmen who said privately they thought the BSU was mistaken in its tactics—violence and nonnegotiable demands—refused categorically to say so publicly because, they explained, the students did have legitimate grievances. And white society has proved by its actions time and time again that if a black spokesman utters words that appear to criticize the actions of other blacks, those words will be picked up by whites in power and used as an excuse for not doing anything about the basic problem.

They see Governor Reagan's position of not dealing with the issues until the campus quiets down as an ideal example of this. If you don't want violence, they argue, then get rid of the frustrations. An attitude like Reagan's will probably, they feel, be used to stall remedies indefinitely, because nothing is done when campuses are quiet, and when they are not, that fact is used as an excuse for doing nothing.

For reasons like this, some of the black community spokesmen who had the strongest reservations about the student strike when it first began have become vocal supporters of the students.

This divergence of viewpoints is another item that seems unlikely to be smoothed over in the near future, particularly in a State like California where black leaders generally feel the State leaders have little sympathy and almost no understanding of black problems.

ON THE BRINK

Both the violent incidents and the faculty debate on the particulars of black studies continued into the fall semester of 1968 with the tactics of each side making the other more recalcitrant.

Administrators accused Nathan Hare and the BSU of failing to do the work they had promised on the black studies department. Hare and the BSU shot back that the work had not been done because it was obvious that the college did not really want the kind of program the BSU wanted, and was stalling on money and manpower. Incidents of violence upset the faculty and staff.

Academic Senator Ralph Anspach resigned from the IPC with a blast at delays and decision changes on black studies which he said contributed significantly to the "frustration of the blacks on this campus and hence were instrumental in precipitating the deplorable and unacceptable turmoil in which we now find ourselves." Twice during the series of meetings in Anspach's following description, Hare walked out in anger:

> [The IPC] on October 24 adopted by a 5–0 vote . . . the program of the black studies degree major and decided that the department be staffed with 11.3 faculty positions. . . . Five days later . . . an administration representative and the senate's executive committee prodded the academic senate to pass a mysterious and apparently useless resolution once again reaffirming the senate's approval in principle of the black studies program. . . . On Monday, November 4, the IPC called a special meeting and . . . was informed ex cathedra that the administration and not the faculty had the power to make staffing decisions. The IPC acquiesced in this and rescinded its previous recommendation . . . it gave the administration the right to staff the black studies department with as few as three positions for 1968–69.

Garrity told the Commission that the IPC had in fact entered a policy area that was none of its business. Neither Hare nor the BSU paid much attention to such cleanly drawn lines, however.

"There was no compromise because the BSU was testing their wings," said a black administrator. "The students really felt strongly [against] that all this questioning had to occur. They felt the concurrence of Nathan Hare and myself should have been the decisive factor. The school's response when it got to that point [a strike] was 'OK, let's talk,' which is precisely what they were sick of. Especially then, because they were now veterans, not seniors who suddenly thought they wanted a black studies program."

Why didn't the college listen?

> Their habituation level had gone up to the level where it didn't penetrate. At a meeting of the Council of Academic Deans, Jerry Varnado began pointing at people around the table. "Let's see, that's an enemy there, here's a pig, there's an enemy there." . . . it didn't bother them, they just sat there.
>
> At another meeting . . . they got an empty wastebasket, tore up paper, dropped it in, lit a match, dropped it in, shoved the wastebasket across the rug and said "it could be as easy as that." They had gotten used to it. If black people wanted the speaker's platform, they just go down and take it. If no whites were allowed in to hear LeRoi Jones, well, everybody just figures out a reason why.

Many on the SFSC campus believe that the trustees' order to President Smith to reassign George Murray to a nonteaching job played a large role in turning the already planned student strike from a one-day affair protesting the lack of a black studies program to an ongoing walkout with a list of 15 nonnegotiable demands. Many believe relations had deteriorated to the point where had Murray not been handy, there would have been some other incident seen as so repressive that it triggered the same thing. But Murray, in this case, was it.

The trustees acted when Murray, after being involved in the *Gater* beating the previous year and traveling to Cuba during the summer, stood on a cafeteria table in late October to announce a student strike November 6 to protest the slow progress on black studies. He was reported to have urged students to bring guns to campus on that day—that is the quote that was bannered in the newspapers. Administration officials say they have been unable to prove that Murray said that, and the afternoon *Examiner* newspaper several days later mentioned in the middle of one story that Murray's suggestion to bring guns did not appear to be linked with his call for the strike. By that time, however, the damage had been done. His suspension without a hearing was looked on as a racist act by the BSU, and was opposed by many faculty. It was clear Smith had wanted to resist but could not. He immediately became the focus of the strike, and to the BSU a perfect example of why they could not trust whites to give them what they needed, and would have to from now on push for a completely autonomous department.

Newspaper stories usually identify Murray as the minister of education for the Panthers, or the student who advocated shooting conservative Superintendent of Public Instruction Max Rafferty, or the SFSC instructor who compared the American flag to a piece of toilet paper in a speech at Fresno State College. Murray did all these things, but he is a much more complex figure than they would indicate.

"Three or four years ago George Murray was well groomed, had his hair cut, knew how to make it in middle-class society," said a teacher who knew him then. "George was the sincere one who did the work. He worked very hard. I saw that guy change in 2 to 3 years from a very respectable, approachable guy to one who talked fuck this and fuck that. Certainly he wasn't this way two or three years ago. Now there's a certain rhetoric, a certain way you present yourself. George is brilliant."

Judging from the comments of the man responsible for recommending Murray as an instructor in remedial English, Murray kept that approachability and tendency to work hard in the classroom, whatever else he may have done outside.

"He ran a fairly tight class," said Patrick Gleeson. "Lots of questions. He'd listen very carefully to students, then bear down on what they were really saying. . . . Murray did not teach separatism. He was generous in talking about the dilemma for the Jewish guy in one of Richard Wright's stories. . . . Murray was . . . teaching what black consciousness was. It was not patronizing with him, he tried to relate it to their [whites] experiences so they could understand. . . . he worked hard to let them reveal to themselves the implications of what they said when they made comments that were racist, so they wouldn't be embarrassed or put down by him."

By special arrangement, the BSU sent a lot of blacks to Murray's English section, because in teaching what black consciousness was he was giving students what the BSU thought they needed to know. His firing convinced them they might never get their program through a white college administration.

"They would give us a black studies department tomorrow if we didn't want to hire Stokely and George Murray, people who relate to us," said a black administrator. And that, too, is what the BSU means when it talks about "self-determination."

STRIKE TACTICS AND GOALS

November 6, 1968, marked a deliberate shift in the public pronouncements of the BSU and TWLF. On that date their strike began, and on that date they added power to the cries of racism and injustice they had raised over the past 2 years. Power in the form of an autonomous department of black studies, a student-controlled department of ethnic studies and a nonnegotiable policy on their 15 demands.

"I'd just like to lay down these three principles on which our struggle is based," Ben Stewart told the campus newspaper *Open Process*. "The first is our fight against racism. The second is our right to seize power in order to control our own destinies. This means not only talking about this principle but inflicting political consequences when that principle is disregarded. And the other thing is very revolutionary and probably anti-American, because American means no power to the people, only power to the few. That is, that the 15 demands are nonnegotiable, which means that we want them all . . . no piecemeal programs, no compromises–we want all of them. . . . We say the spirit of the people is greater than the man's technology, and once the people have a sense of this and they break that old slave-master relationship by not merely asking what the slave-master is willing to give us, then the day of the slave-master is over."

To successfully demand power your political consequences have to be quite severe, and the most radical students decided they had a promising plan, a rather sophisticated variant of guerrilla warfare which the administration admitted was proving exceedingly difficult to combat. Stewart outlined it just before the strike to a nonwhites-only meeting of TWLF:

> It just so happens that the members of the BSU Central Committee have been analyzing how student movements have been functioning. Taking over buildings, holding it for two or three days, and then the thing is dead. Most of your leaders are ripped off and thrown in jail, or the masses are thrown in jail, and there's no one to lead them. From our analysis of this, we think we have developed a technique to deal with this for a prolonged struggle. We call it the war of the flea . . . what does the flea do? He bites, sucks blood from the dog, the dog bites. What happens when there are enough fleas on a dog? What will he do? He moves. He moves away. He moves on. And what the man has been running down on us, he's psyched us out, in terms of our manhood. He'll say, what you gone do, nigger? You tryin' to be a man, here he is with shotguns, billy clubs, .357 magnums, and all you got is heart. Defenseless. That's not the way it's going to go any more. We are the people. We are the majority and the pigs cannot be everywhere, everyplace all the time. And where they are not, we are. And something happens. The philosophy of the flea. You just begin to wear them down. Something is always costin' them. You can dig it . . . something happens all the time. Toilets are stopped up. Pipes is out.

> Water in the bathroom is just runnin' all over the place. Smoke is coming out the bathroom. "I don't know nothin' about it. I'm on my way to take an exam. Don't look at me. . . ." When the pig comes down full force, ain't nothin' happening. He retreats. When they split, it goes on and on and on . . . .
>
> We should fight the racist administration on our grounds from now on where we can win. When he disrespects our humanity, then he pays. . . . Pig stepped on my shoes. I told you about that. WHOP! [laughter] . . . A young brother . . . looked at me and smiled. He said, "Man, you ought to know better . . . you're out here on this white man's college campus, you can't be doin' none of that. You're in the minority. . . ."
>
> So I said look here, brother . . . say we're 10 percent. Do they ask the black community . . . well, they're just 10 percent Negroes up there at San Francisco State college, so we're only gonna ask the black community for 10 percent of their taxes. Hell no! It don't go like that. They get us all. And some of your mommas and daddies never have and never will be able to go to State, and some of your young sisters and brothers will never be able to. . . .

"The administration doesn't understand the new student language," said white Prof. Ralph Anspach. "When they talk about a strike, they mean a strike in the old labor union sense of the word—close the institution down."

For several days in the next couple of months they succeeded in doing just that, with the help of striking American Federation of Teachers professors and a variety of classroom disruptions, wastebasket and washroom fires, ransacked offices, smashed windows, small bombs, police-student melees on campus, and threats.

The tactics had a double purpose. First to close down the campus both by causing such disruption that work was impossible, and by making students, staff, and teachers afraid to set foot on it for fear of harm.

Second, to gain power either by forcing the administration to grant the demands, or by forcing it into such repressive counteractions that support for the strikers would grow. Tony Miranda, 20-year-old TWLF activist, described the philosophy behind the strike:

> We decided first of all that student movements up to this point had been absolutely worthless in terms of effects. In terms of physical gains . . . the one-day strike was a test of strength, to find out who was supporting us and in terms of what we could get. It was planned that way.
>
> FSM [Free Speech Movement] at Berkeley did not gain free speech. Student movements traditionally have not meant a thing. The thing that went down at Columbia did not gain a thing for the people in Harlem. They're still building that gymnasium and people are still being arrested and persecuted.
>
> What it boils down to is that we're tired of fighting symbols. . . . In other words we want to talk about fighting the military-industrial complex. Kicking ROTC off campus just don't make it in terms of symbols.
>
> We decided our demands were going to relate to right now and to what we need. Educational demands. And educational issues. Each of

the demands are interlocking or relate to what has been going on at State for the last six years.

When we called the strike first of all we needed to test our backing. Our constituency. What happened was that we had more support than we thought we did. We decided that we were not going to make a symbolic fight . . . but that we are going to get it. We are going to fight for it. We can no longer afford to wait. That's what it boils down to.

The decision to continue to strike has been made all the way along. We decided to have a one-day strike, following that we sat down and decided to have a continuous thing. It was a predetermined decision, but we had to make our decision on the basis of what was going on. . . . The BSU called the strike. Then Third World joined the strike two days later. . . .

The strikers always maintained, up to this point [Feb. 9] still have, a gradual steady increase, which is slow and a day-to-day process, with occasional setbacks which are very small. Your mainstream of support continues to grow.

With the advent of police on campus you got a large increase, because people just happen to hate the pigs. At the point of the [Nov.] 13th, I would say it was people who were interested mainly in hating the pigs.

The convocations heightened it. We would have meetings right after the convocations, and mobs of people were coming in whom we didn't have before. And basically out of the convocation we got a lot of support. The contradictions that were shown in evidence by the position of the administration [during convocation] and it showed the stupidity of how the administration was thinking.

For instance, a woman gave . . . $75,000 . . . to black students generally, and the administration blocked it and sent back the money, and when this question came up at convocation they didn't have an answer. Then they came back and gave their answer—no discrimination is allowed. And they didn't have the right to do it, because it wasn't willed to them. And things like that. Helen Bedensem [financial aids officer] had sent back $119,000 to the Federal Government because she said there weren't enough needy students.[2] These are the types of things that people are just beginning to really realize have been going on. How the contradictions were heightening. So we had that and that was something that white students could relate to.

So when the convocations were over, the pigs started coming down on people's heads and that also made them realize what is going on. Not only are they lousing things up by their attitude, but they are using pigs to stop us to get what we want . . . and it got many people very upset. People became involved and became educated to the real issues, and they became educated to the actual reality of pigs on the campus. It was a twofold educational process.

"People are learning more in a day on strike than they learned in two years," said BSU member Terry Collins. "I've had white girls tell me that. With the strike, they can't fool around talking like they do in class, they've got to learn. It's a political learning process."

Disruption of classes appeared to grow naturally from tactics the BSU had been developing right along. Teams of strikers, some all black and some all white, would rush into classrooms, announce that class is dismissed, and either leave, or leave with a vague warning that there might be consequences if the class continued. Sometimes the intruders were reported wearing stocking masks. They moved so fast that plainclothes police could do little to catch them.

This compares with 1967 as described by James Garrett:

> There were a number of little skirmishes going on. Black students began to pull together on different kinds of things. We would have our cultural program three times a week . . . little battles and little fights and little arguments. . . . and we tried petitioning the school several times saying that certain things were coming from a racist's position. The school wouldn't listen.
>
> Question–Whom did you talk to?
>
> Answer–Faculty, we had meetings with the executive committee of the faculty, we would have meetings with chairmen of departments . . . the leadership of the college would combat us constantly . . . but if we called any of them a racist for what he was doing, what we thought was racist coming from some real negative stuff we would go to the chairman of the department, and they would just tell us to go to hell, so we would go back to the teacher's classroom and disrupt his classes what we were doing was pointing out to him how he was being a racist. You see, you destroy the whole discipline thing, because we would study all night and come back the next day and eat him up, you see, so he couldn't deal with us. So we did that for a while. People got riled up about it, and they got scared of us, and stuff like that. And then the *Gator* thing finally got violent.

"Violence is something which can only be used when people are politicized," said Miranda. "In other words, before you can engage in violence, you have to have people politically sophisticated enough to be aware that (1) this is not a nonviolent country, and (2) that violence is going to be necessary. That we are beyond the age of pacifistic sit-ins. Pacifistic sit-ins gain you a cracked head, a set of co-opted demands. As I said before, no decision has come down from the Central Committee related to any of these things. . . . Our goal is not to destroy the institution. Our goal is to make the institution address itself to our needs and have an education which is relevant . . . ."

Leading members of BSU and TWLF were careful not to be caught damaging property themselves. An SFSC student caught in a police sweep described what she saw:

> The squads [of police] were coming, you could see the police. He [an unidentified black student] said . . . make your presence known as you leave. Well, the point is we were moving sort of fast because we were trying to get off campus, but there was no intention on the part of most people to do any rock throwing, but suddenly there was this tremendous volume of rock throwing.
>
> It was particularly nasty because the way they were throwing they were coming down on the heads of the marchers to begin with and also hitting the glass windows. I saw a shower of glass coming down on a

355-234 O - 69 - 10

> girl. A number of people in the group began shouting "Stop, you're going to hurt people inside." The number of people throwing was quite small, I didn't see any blacks throwing.

Tactics were often unspecific. One melee witnessed by several Commission researchers began when TWLF announced a rally would be held on the Commons in defiance of a ban on them there by Acting President S. I. Hayakawa. As the scheduled hour approached, a few dozen students began to gather on the Commons at the lower end, while helmeted police took up very visible positions at either end of the grassy lawn. A crowd of about 250 persons quickly formed, most hanging back along the asphalt paths that cross the grass as if they wanted to see the action, but did not want to get involved. A half-dozen students, one Oriental, one black, the rest white, crisscrossed the grass shouting loudly "on strike, shut it down," the strike rallying cry. As the crowd grew larger, police made their move. The group at the lower end of the Commons marched south in a line, and without any bodily contact, the crowd began to move toward the main path which ran in front of the library close to the second line of police. Shouts of "pigs," along with assorted obscenities, filled the air. As the crowd neared the library, a few stones were thrown to the police who stood in front of that glass-doored building. When the police moved forward in response, several students inside the library gave the doors booming kicks. A knot of policemen rushed back to the library, and as they broke away on the run a barrage of stones swirled down upon the line of officers. They came from the rear fringes of the mostly white crowd, and as there were no rocks nearby, they would have to have been carried with the people who threw them. At the same time, most of the BSU and TWLF leaders remained at the north end of the Commons, where other officers were busy making wholesale arrests from inside a double ring of officers that had surrounded the crowd on the speakers' platform. The stone-throwing crowd was driven off; campus order was restored without further incident.

In general, bringing police on campus appeared to bring in many students who otherwise would not have gotten involved. Their response was similar to but less intense than that of students at the Democratic Convention in Chicago last August. Rocks and sticks were thrown, shouts of "pigs off campus" and "oink, oink" were heard, along with a variety of obscenities. Few appeared to pay much attention to Hayakawa's statement that "there are no innocent bystanders."

The variety of acts committed in the name of the strike included class disruption, bombings, arson, vandalism, epithets, and implied threats. The Study Team tried without success to track down newspaper reports of direct threats, particularly to members of the football and basketball teams. Those coaches were generally uncooperative, and team members contacted all said they either did not wish to discuss the matter with the Study Team or had not been directly threatened.

Complaints most frequently lodged against police included clubbings, beatings, and the failure to distinguish the innocent onlooker from the active stone thrower. Both BSU and TWLF tried to exploit these complaints to the limit, with considerable success. A number of students interviewed said that after watching police in action, they were more afraid of being attacked at random in a police sweep than they were of being attacked by strikers. Most of the 731 arrested were white.

The implied threats generally took the same form as BSU tactics in the student legislature battles a year before. Students were jeered and warned if they crossed picket lines, and a strike-support booklet put out largely by SDS included the following item:

> ATTENTION SCABS WHAT ARE YOU DOING
>
> By crossing the picket line you have consciously or not put yourself in a position against the strike of the BSU-TWLF. This is a strike against racism . . . that recognizes the right of the oppressed Third World people to self-determination by any means necessary . . . by crossing the line you have made your choice–there is no middle ground.
>
> You are being used by Hayakawa and the trustees to break the strike . . . [the administration] has appealed to your narrow self interest by constantly pushing the attitude on you that "*I* have a right to go to school, *I* want to get *my* education."
>
> Too many scabs have given lip service to the support of the 15 demands but still go to class. . . . What you are really saying is that you support the right of Third World people to better their conditions, but you don't support their efforts to achieve that better condition. . . . Friend, that is a pretty racist attitude . . . the selfish individualist attitude of you scabs . . . can no longer be tolerated. . . .
>
> Historically, workers on strike have not dealt so kindly with scabs as we have with you. In the current steel strike in Denison, Texas, the workers are armed and there have been several shoot-outs with scabs. Scabs have been beaten in numerous strikes. Not even police have been able to protect scabs when working people have been fighting for their lives against the bosses . . . though we know you aren't the enemy . . . you are objectively acting as agents of Hayakawa and the trustees and as such must be dealt with accordingly.

Several members of TWLF said classroom disruption was planned in advance as an important educational tool. A variant was classroom "education," where strikers would enter a room with the permission of the professor to discuss the strike issues.

Both BSU and TWLF members pointed out when questioned about the bombings that anyone, including rightwing strike opponents or the police, was capable of sneaking a bomb onto campus. Some said it would make no sense to risk injuring people because that would lose the strikers' support. They avoided answering or indicated they did not know personally of any when asked if bombs had been a tactic of the central committee. One black college employee did say it seemed to him that some BSU members did know enough to give indirect warnings to stay away from a particular area. His observations, however, were not confirmed by others.

Many activists drew a sharp distinction between the kind of violence being committed in the name of the strike, and the kind being dealt out by police.

"In this society people are taught to relate the destruction of property to individuals," said Miranda. "They are taught to accept the beating of someone by a police officer or the just plain beating of someone. They are not at all acceptable to the notion of a $200 typewriter going through a $15 window."

"We break property," said Carlton Goodlett, "but they don't hesitate to take lives."

Although large numbers of individuals condemned the violence on both sides, there were substantial numbers who felt that given the history of both the Third World fight at SFSC and the struggle by blacks through the country's history, the issue was not so simple that they could just come out against violence. Some representative comments:

> In 1936 the University of California . . . rejected the petition of the Negro students that outstanding Negro students of social sciences and sociology . . . be brought to the University as summer school professors . . . .
>
> And 15 years ago a prospectus was sent to the University of California asking that they establish an institute for the study of California's racial minority . . . which the University rejected summarily . . . 18 months ago the California Negro Leadership Conference penned letters to both the University of California and the board of trustees of State colleges predicting that if it didn't respond favorably to the demands made by members of my generation they could expect to have mass confrontation and violence.
>
> –Dr. Carlton B. Goodlett, *President, California Negro Leadership Conference.*

* * *

> People accuse you of being violent when you shove a man off your foot after you've asked him to please stop standing on your toe. And the myth that this is violence is a myth and has no basis in fact. A cornered mouse will eventually do something in his own defense, and that is the frustrating position that poor people are always put into, which inevitably leads to some kind of aggression in self-defense.
>
> –Hannibal Williams.

* * *

> Violence is teaching black students that they are citizens. Violence is teaching people that they can get a measure of justice in this country comparable to the kind of justice that John F. Kennedy would have gotten, had he lived, or that Ted Kennedy will get. Violence is teaching black people that all cultures are the same, which means that all cultures are white. . . .
>
> –Garrett.

* * *

> Society is geared to economics. If you are denied money, that's like shooting somebody. My definition of violence is quite different than what the newspapers say when they talk about violence. Look at violence where Chinese people earn 55 cents an hour and are denied admission to unions. Where a farm laborer's average income is $1,300 . . . .

Look at the kind of violence we see in the school system where Third World people are systematically placed in second, third, or fourth tracks; the sociological violence of an institution like the Welfare Department where people are subjugated to degrading questionnaires. . . .

–Miranda.

* * *

THE CASE FOR BLACK STUDIES

Black people's lives are built on a different set of experiences from white folks. You see this historically in the persecution black people have undergone in this country. You can also see it culturally, in our music, art, dancing, writing, and so on. . . .

–Ben Stewart.

The struggle at San Francisco State and the BSU's throughout the State is a struggle for the seizure of power and the implementation of one primary point, which is the determination of our destiny educationally, politically, socially and economically. In other words we are struggling for freedom and the goal is the seizure of power to bring about that freedom.

–George Murray.

Like the student strike, an autonomous department of black or other ethnic studies is looked on by TWLF as a necessary political tool, as well as a way of informing minorities about their history.

To the most radical, the problem is not just that black, brown, and yellow people have not been informed of the cultures they come from. They also have not been allowed to learn the truth about the deliberate, planned way in which the whites who ruled this country lied, stole, cheated, murdered, brutalized, and in the case of Indians committed genocide to make sure they stayed safely in power.

"The educational system robs us of learning the correct political line for our contemporary roles in bringing about change and liberation for our people," said Stewart in a campus newspaper interview. "Because what they want to teach us in political science classes is the beauty and the good side of capitalism, that our poor, poverty stricken communities just represent accidents or miscalculations. But we're not going for that, because we're dealing strictly with reality."

". . . The educational system is no accident," added Miranda. "It's not simply a matter of not including what our culture is about, what our history is about, what our economics are about, what our politics are about. It's a process of miseducation. It has a purpose. One is to teach us not how to change our community, or even how to live in it, but how to escape it by denying that we are a part of it."

There's lots of talk in BSU circles about white techniques to accomplish this. How does the white man teach minorities to escape their communities, for instance? Two simple ways. First, by not teaching them about their own cultures he forces them to look to his as a model. Second, he rewards the minority spokesmen who agree with him, giving them lavish praise, money, and good positions. One man frequently mentioned as being in this position is Acting President S. I. Hayakawa, a Japanese-American, who has been accused of being installed by the trustees to deny to the general American public that legitimate TWLF needs exist.

The result of this education, as these activists see it, is that minority group individuals keep trying to grow up to be "good white people," as one put it, only to learn when it is too late that they can never be white because their skin color, or language, or name, sets them apart as targets. By that time, however, they say, most are hopelessly committed to keep trying, lured on by the "myth" that the country really is working toward, say, school desegregation, like she says she is.

An example might go something like this: A black student who wants to become a top anything these days is quite likely to apply to an almost all-white school, because they have the best education. Once there, one of two things will happen. Either he will vanish completely from the black community, which will never get the benefit of his education because he is happily living, laughing, and loving with whites. Or if he sees his responsibility to help the people he comes from and begins to act in a way the white community thinks is out of line—say he calls the country racist—they will simply rein him in by threatening to cut off his education.

In this context, Eldridge Cleaver and George Murray are viewed as political casualties, attacked not because what they said was wrong, but because whites did not like it.

"The average white doesn't want to drastically change the structure because the present structure meets his needs," said a community organizer active in the San Francisco area.

With that set of assumptions, it is easy to see why the BSU Central Committee concluded that they would never be given an autonomous department of black studies, and would have to fight for it.

"You must understand the importance of your fight, the white power structure does," Stokely Carmichael told the same TWLF meeting before which Stewart outlined the tactics of the flea. "You should not underestimate what you're fighting for. It is vitally important. Because you're now beginning to challenge real attitudes."

In trying to organize the BSU, said Garrett, it was necessary to teach the students that they were oppressed. "They are educated to believe that they are not over oppressed, and if they get an education they can be not oppressed at all."

Most of the talk about black studies departments does not reach this level of analysis. People talk about the genuinely different culture blacks grow up in in this country, genuinely different attitudes on many aspects of life, and the need to tell the truth about what whites have done without attaching the extreme political significance of the set of assumptions just outlined.

But there is still a difference between what they talk about, and just teaching more facts about black history.

"Let me see if I can rephrase it this way," said Edward O. Lee, the only black State college trustee. "You can't take people who have taught a history course for years and have consciously or unconsciously omitted the participation of black people and then expect them all of a sudden to say in my U.S.

history course I am going to include the participation of black people. Human nature doesn't work that way. So, in order to make sure that black participation is given its fair hearing . . . it's nice to say, for instance . . . that before the Civil War the blacks were slaves. But I would prefer . . . to make up for the years of omission in U.S. history from a black institution standpoint. How did blacks really view the existing society?"

> Question–What you are really doing then is changing the overview–not just inject courses that say what role blacks played but also give their viewpoint.
>
> Answer–"That's right. . . . The board is very concerned . . . that the black studies department might be staffed by all blacks. . . . I become quite irritated when board members begin to express this simply because I did not see the same criticism about departments that were all white. Nor do I see them talking in terms of integrating all white departments right now."

Nathan Hare, in his conceptual proposal for a black studies department attached as appendix 5, uses two key concepts new to American education to help get across what most blacks seem to talk about.

"The whole problem is that they want to hire a whitewashed-type Negro," said Hare. "Somebody who thinks white just like them. They want to experiment, do research, and get grants. They don't want the blacks to move up in droves, either."

His community-based approach assumes that blacks–and by inference other minorities–can reap enormous benefits by banding closer together, a position the BSU has taken ever since it appeared on campus, and a position quite in line with the feeling of the black community spokesmen interviewed by Commission investigators. Most said they felt there was more to the problem than just teaching more facts about the history of blacks in this country, and that feeling appears to be on the rise in the black community, whether whites realize it or not.

The quotes used in this report do not convey the table pounding with which some of those interviewed, particularly black community spokesmen over 30, emphasized their sympathy with the students' cause, or their joy at what Assemblyman Willie Brown called "an incredible display of unity."

This unity was not automatically achieved among the black people that whites are accustomed to seeking out when they wish to find someone to tell them how the masses of blacks feel on some issue or other. It took at least two community meetings and numerous telephone calls before the group decided to come out united in support of the student grievances.

But neither was it in any sense forced. BSU Central Committee members had worked with some of these community spokesmen for periods of months or years. They came when asked to explain positions some black adults had questions about.

Perhaps most important, the initial link that drew them together was a common feeling that in this situation as before, whites in power would probably use any excuse they could get their hands on to avoid dealing with the basic issues.

"I would say that in a general way what most of the people who have come out here have said is these are our black students, these are our finest, these are our future, these are our hope," said Berkeley City Councilman Ron Dellums. "They are saying that this institution is not relevant to them, that they are not receiving an education, they are receiving an indoctrination. Then if that is true . . . I am with them in attempts they make to change it.

"Some people got hung up on the tactics, and I say that is a bad bag for us as community people to get into. . . . I am not sure that the black students are throwing the rocks through the windows . . . but even if they were, even if I could become the tribal chief of all black students across the country and raise my hand and stop all the window breaking, you know damned well you would not respond to this. So let's quit . . . that issue and start dealing with the basic issues. . . ."

To several, the issue was the right of all black students to get the best education they can, and not be shunted off into some second-rate junior college because of low grades produced by an inferior high school education in the first place.

Perhaps the best view of black thinking, however, comes from a sample of opinions about one of the community meetings where the black community decided what position it would take.

An estimated 200 persons attended, representing 150 community groups around the Bay Area, and the meeting was memorable because Hayakawa, invited to discuss the issues with the community, almost came to blows with them instead.

He began by telling them how he, as a Japanese-American, had suffered too, and therefore understood black problems, and right there ran into trouble with Mrs. Elouise Westbrooks, a community-relations worker.

She said:

> I think that we have heard that so oftentimes from the white community . . . how hard they worked and what they had been through. To me I felt like it was a waste of time and energy to sit there and listen to it, so I said to him that as much as we would like to hear the hardship that he had gone through, that I would appreciate it very much if he would get down to the issue, because we all had to go back to our individual jobs.
>
> So I think that kind of stunned him, because he wanted to tell how liberal he was and all the things he had done to help black people . . . so people kept on asking him to get down to the issue and after a while he got kind of huffy and angry. . . . He did threaten to go out because they would ask him direct questions about the 15 demands.
>
> I kind of felt like it was a slap in the face and I think I told him so, that it was like a slap in the face for him to treat us the way that he did because we came over there with good faith to talk with him as one race to another race, and we didn't have anything against him as a man but what we were trying to talk about was the issues. . . .

Mrs. Westbrooks said he never did get to talking about the demands. "I think he understands them very well, but I think . . . he has been oriented by the white world . . . so to me, I just feel like he was just doing more acting than really being real Hayakawa. . . ."

From Dr. Washington Garner, a police commissioner: "I think he's catering too much to the establishment and I think this is the reason that we're having the problems that we're having now . . . they are not paying any attention to the cries of the young people or trying to satisfy their demands."

Asked whether he felt Hayakawa understood the problems at San Francisco State, Garner replied, "Yes, I think he has, but I don't think that he is trying to do anything about it. I don't think he is trying to implement the understanding that he has . . . but I just think that he is listening to others rather than to what his conscience dictates. . . ."

Others run along similar lines. "We were confronted with a man that had completely no understanding of social change. . . ." "I don't think he understands . . . what the people in the black community were saying." "I don't think he knows anything at all about the black community."

Hayakawa eventually walked out of the meeting while it was still in session.

Chapter VII

THE OUTLOOK FOR THE FUTURE

The story of San Francisco State is an unfinished story. The teacher strike and the student strike have ended, the violence has subsided, and an uneasy peace prevails. But the deeply rooted problems which underlie San Francisco State's crisis–and which plague many of the country's higher education institutions–remain to be solved. Among these problems are long standing social and economic injustices and inequities and the reluctance of the so-called establishment to respond rapidly to the need for change.

The patience of those adversely affected has been over-estimated. The student leaders in controversy with the administration were prepared to go to direct confrontation in order to change the systems and beyond that to violence.

Sizeable numbers of students and faculty, augmented by elements in the community as the action built up, were willing to follow this leadership. When people do not feel for their safety and such direct-action strategy is used, violence is a virtual certainty.

The violence mirrors the turmoil, the sharply divergent outlook, and the economic and social imbalances which bitterly divide the American people today. It is misleading to attribute the causes of violence to outside agitators. The causes lie much deeper. The ugly consequences of violence have obscured the major reasons for the disorders and have obstructed the way to peace.

San Francisco, justly proud of its tolerance, will not permit property destruction or personal assault as a justification for "getting attention." San Francisco State cannot and should not become "surrogate" for the whole of San Francisco's social and economic ills. As has been said so often, an educational institution is of necessity fragile and is not built to withstand direct and violent attacks aimed at its heart.

Today at San Francisco State the groups involved in the conflict for the most part are polarized. The students are committed to their struggle as no generation of students has ever been. The faculty is fragmented, often unhappy, and increasingly militant over its rights and responsibilities. The administration is charged with the duty to manage, but is essentially powerless to act, caught between the conflicting pressures of the other groups. Trustees of the State colleges are determined to take a stand at San Francisco State; it has become for them a watershed of decision, the crucial point as they see it in a struggle for the preservation of the institutions of higher education.

The political leaders and the public at large are bewildered and angry over the turmoil and violence on the campus, at San Francisco State and elsewhere. But the issue will not be disposed of simply by saying that many people do not like it. The fact is that the "New Left" openly espouses violence as a key tool in the drive to lock the academic community securely into the general struggle against the community at large. It indicts all higher learning as the uncritical servant of business and the military, rather than helping the poor and the uneducated to advance. It seeks, in extreme form, the destruction of higher education and its visible institutions as they are presently constituted.

Californians are disturbed all the more because they have taken great pride in their publicly supported colleges and universities and have generously supported their more than 100 junior colleges, State colleges, and universities. Ultimately the progress–indeed the survival–of California's public institutions of higher learning depend upon broad-based public support. Operating funds require legislative appropriations, and capital expansion is financed through the issuance of bonds which require approval by the voters of the State. These are political and economic facts of educational life in California.

In the final analysis, the State colleges must therefore respond to the voting public. But the degree of response they should make, and the degree of insulation which the method of governance should afford them, are vitally important questions raised by the crisis at San Francisco State.

The present reevaluation of aims and purposes of education at San Francisco State must be pursued vigorously. On the part of the administration, patience, firmness, and recognition of curriculum deficiencies will be needed. On the part of the student leadership and their faculty supporters, there must be lasting recognition that the language of the gutter, the shock rhetoric, a willingness to "mount the barricades," vandalism, and personal assault do not constitute a valid or effective means of getting better education for themselves and their followers.

The Study Team talked with State legislators in an attempt to assess political reaction–and thus to some degree public reaction–to the turmoil at San Francisco State. Because disorders were occurring on other campuses, particularly at the neighboring Berkeley campus of the University of California, the reaction goes beyond San Francisco State.

The legislators interviewed are Democrats and Republicans, liberals and conservatives. For all of them, campus unrest is an immediate and important issue. Uniformly, they feel that the legislature must make some response to demonstrate its political credibility to the voters. Their views of the public attitude differ sharply. The more liberal of the legislators see the public response as a rejection of the new doctrine that colleges and universities should be powerful "relevant" agencies for social change, rather than instruments for indoctrination in the traditional wisdom. The most conservative see the public reaction as a justifiable response to a coercive effort by radicals to impose their views on the majority. Where one legislator sees the unrest as a struggle for Negro manhood, another sees only "creeps" and "bums" agitated by a hard-core preaching revolution imported from Cuba.

A special committee has been created by the State assembly, consisting of members of the Criminal Procedure Committee and the Education Committee; the combined membership will hear bills relating to campus conduct–more than 50 of which have already been introduced.[1]

Liberals and conservatives alike agree that some form of legislation regulating campus conduct through criminal sanction will pass in this session. They feel it is a political imperative, notwithstanding the recognition among most of those interviewed that, realistically, there is nothing the legislature can produce which will give college administrators and law enforcement authorities any greater legal foundation than they already have for dealing with conduct on the campus. Nor do most of those interviewed believe that the new criminal legislation will aid in solving the causes of the violence.

It is unlikely that there will be any reduction in appropriations for higher education in general. The education committee in the assembly has already begun work on a $2 million supplemental appropriation necessary to prevent enrollment cutbacks at the State colleges. While there were some urgings in the last session that the legislature punish the dissidents by cutting back college and university funding, most of the legislators believe that they should continue to reflect a general attitude among California's voters that education is "good," and that it would be inappropriate to deal with the disorders by reducing appropriations.

It seems equally unlikely that there will be any substantial increase in support for higher education. The legislators keep a sharp eye on the political weather vane. The voters rejected a $250 million bond issue for higher education construction in the November 1968 election. The bond issue lost, and it lost badly; only a few counties supported the measure. The Governor did not support it. One University of California official, knowledgeable about the bond issue's defeat, attributed the loss to two things: campus unrest and a general taxpayers' revolt. (In a number of local elections, voters have rejected proposals for tax-rate increases and bond issues to finance public schools.)

Special programs, such as the Educational Opportunity Program (EOP), may suffer. The Governor vetoed appropriations for the EOP from the State colleges' 1968–69 budget, and a trustees' request for more than $2.4 million in EOP money was not included in his budget for 1969–70.

Faculty salaries are the area most vulnerable to attack. Several legislators expressed the opinion that there might be no salary increase. There is a feeling that the few teachers who went out on strike acted irresponsibly, and their actions may be the cause of the legislature's refusal to provide more money for salaries. In view of the fact that economic parity for faculty salaries has been a prime issue with the teachers, it would be ironic if the strike were ultimately to retard the upward progress of faculty salaries.

There has been no dearth of comment from political officeholders or from political aspirants on the subject of campus disorders. Higher education in California is woven inextricably into the politics of the State. This is not a new development, nor a surprising one in view of the massive public financial support given to the higher education enterprise.

While all public officials are generally concerned about the state of higher education in California, there are two whose viewpoints are particularly relevant to this inquiry—the Governor, and the mayor of San Francisco. Many people view Governor Reagan and Mayor Alioto as potential opponents in the 1970 gubernatorial race, but that is not the reason they were chosen to summarize and highlight the comments they made in the course of interviews with the Study Team. Other public officials could choose whether they would become involved in the San Francisco State controversies. For both the Governor and the mayor, deep and direct involvement was an inevitable consequence of office. The Governor is the chief executive officer of the State, with overall legal responsibility for peacekeeping and public safety; his administration, through the Department of Finance, constructs the budget of the State-college system, as finally submitted to the legislature; and he is an ex officio member of the governing Board of Trustees.

The mayor has the primary responsibility for peacekeeping and public safety in San Francisco; it is the San Francisco police force which has been called upon to quell campus disorders; and it is San Francisco taxpayers who bear the cost of providing the extra police services to maintain order on the campus—an estimated $700,000 so far. It is not the purpose here to detail the involvement of these two public officials in the recent events at San Francisco State College; to the extent that their actions were deemed relevant, these particulars have been dealt with in other portions of the report. The purpose here is to summarize comments made to the Study Team so the reader may make his own analysis.

GOVERNOR RONALD REAGAN[2]

The Governor does not believe that the violence is spontaneous—although some of the participants in a crowd disturbance may act spontaneously in the highly charged emotional atmosphere of the moment, once a disturbance has started. He believes there is an element that wants a confrontation with the established structure, and that some of them must be described as anarchists. He sees radicals provoking confrontation as a tactic to secure a "cushion of support" among moderate students; this gives the radicals their power.[3]

Governor Reagan says the stationing of police on campuses in force can be preventive; he argues that a premature reduction in force can result in the immediate escalation of violence—a development, as he sees it, at San Francisco State. At the same time, he states it should be recognized that there is a limit to what can be expected from law enforcement, a limit to what can be accomplished in this way, and a limit to what any government can afford to do. Basically, this must be a society where individuals are bound by their own inner restraint.

The Governor senses a reluctance on the part of the academic community to play their part in this battle. While he believes that the real answer lies with the college administration, the academic community has no tradition of dealing with violence, and is not prepared to deal with it. Unfortunately, he says, many people in the academic community are confused by their own sympathy with some of the demands that are being made. "What they have failed to appreciate is the necessity of dealing with violent tactics."

"The point is that the violence itself becomes the issue. You cannot give in to violent tactics. The question that must be asked, if you do, is: who will use force tomorrow?" Much of what has taken place at San Francisco State results from the earlier appeasement. At this point, the Governor contends, society must simply say, "No"—that nothing will be done on the basis of threats and violence.

The Governor wants college administrators to take definite, tough measures to deal with troublemakers, such as Father Hesburgh has established at Notre Dame. Expulsion is an effective remedy, because it is permanent. The hard-core troublemakers should be identified, isolated, and separated from the rest of the students. People who have no legitimate interest in the institution, such as nonstudents or those who have long since been graduated, should not be allowed to agitate on the campuses.

The Governor considers the legislative proposals he has made to be emergency measures which are based on the suggestions of California's college administrators; that this is what they have told him they need to deal with the situation.

He believes it would be a mistake to focus on who the dissidents are, rather than on what they are trying to do; "attention should be focused on the damage they are doing, and the potential injury, not only to people, but to the educational institutions themselves."

It is Governor Reagan's position that public employees do not have the right to strike; that they simply can't strike against the people. "The government, unlike a private business, can't close its doors–it must continue to provide service." On the other hand, machinery can be set up which will assure access for public employees to the highest officials of government. But once a decision is made by those officials, it must be a final decision. There is a study now underway in the Governor's office with regard to grievance procedures for State employees. With respect to the State-college teachers, the problem as the Governor sees it is that under State law, public officials cannot meet with any one small group especially when it does not represent the faculty. Several faculty organizations have told him that they do not consider the American Federation of Teachers representative of the faculty.

Nor does the Governor see San Francisco State as a racial confrontation between blacks and whites. How can it be, he argues, when there are a far larger number of black students going to school–often in an atmosphere of threats, fear, and intimidation–than are out on strike? Most of the students, he believes, "are just confused."

Governor Reagan supports the concept of the Educational Opportunity Program as a worthwhile effort to help students who have exceptional potential but who, either through family failures or failures of the schools, are not qualified under the regular admission standards. But in California, he believes these programs are dealing with a problem that should be dealt with by the public community colleges. There are more than 80 such colleges in the State, and those are the institutions to which these students should be admitted in the first instance. The Governor perceives a high likelihood of failure as a danger in admitting them to the State colleges. If the EOP students are not able to compete, he says, then, with the most noble of intentions, the result may be "a very real psychological crippling."

While Governor Reagan has supported black studies programs as a trustee, he feels one really must ask whether the demands for a completely autonomous department is not in reality a request for "sanctuary" from the rigors of the institution, a shelter from the normal standards. If it is, he asks, then what will students in these programs have learned when they leave the institution, and will they be able to compete in the outside world? On the other hand, the Governor thinks a black studies program might be justified for its symbolic value alone. He is opposed to a black studies department restricted to blacks. He feels it might be more useful to get whites into the black studies department to learn something about black people.

MAYOR JOSEPH ALIOTO

The mayor does not see the campus disorders as part of any Communist conspiracy. But he does see a need to recognize that a certain hard core (like the Maoists, who think that the Russians are part of the "Establishment") has to be isolated if the violence is to be dealt with effectively. At the same time, the mayor says one must recognize that the great majority of students and the teachers are concerned with the real educational issues that are being raised.

Mayor Alioto argues that the use of militia and talk about education being a privilege only serve to radicalize those students and teachers who are legitimately concerned.

"You can't just talk tough" says the mayor. Public officials can only afford to be tough if they are willing at the same time to work with the militants for the constructive solution of legitimate demands. There are, he argues, some very militant people who are still willing to work within the system. For example, he was able to get some young blacks he regards as quite militant to work with him by going out to the San Francisco State campus to try to cool off the situation.

Mayor Alioto sees the violence as an indication that society needs to define some new areas of rights for teachers and for students. "We ought to examine the lag between law and life." Injunctions have been issued and ignored in public employee strikes across the country: society says there is no right of public employees to strike, yet they go out on strike anyway. The fact that we either despair of enforcing these injunctions or that we are afraid to enforce them, the mayor argues, indicates that society needs to establish new grievance machinery, and to redefine some rights. Too many people, notes Alioto, have forgotten about the violence which attended the women's suffrage movement, and the violence that occurred in the organization of labor unions until the Wagner Act was passed.

"We don't need new legislation to deal with campus disorders," he says. "We don't need new laws, there are already enough on the books–we just don't enforce them." What is needed, he believes, is a clear definition of the rights of teachers and students, and the creation of procedures which will give students a clear definition of the results that follow misconduct.

Mayor Alioto thinks the San Francisco Police Department has done a very good job; he is reluctant to bring in outside police forces or to use the National Guard, because this tends to inflame the situation. Alioto says he made it clear from the beginning that once the college administration called the police, the San Francisco Police Department would make the decisions in dealing with any situation: Procedures were established which allowed police to absorb two or three rocks or bottles, so that one person could not cause a confrontation. It was also decided that occupation of any building by force would not be permitted, nor could any doorway be closed or blocked. Ultimately, it was necessary to ban meetings in the area where violence had occurred before, with an area perhaps 100 yards away designated as the area to remain open for speeches and rallys. This, the mayor believes, fully protected the exercise of free speech. He notes that, as a result of these rules the on-campus violence now seems to have come under control. "It is limited now to surreptitious nighttime bombings." The police have improved their tactics, he believes, recalling that in one recent incident some 400 arrests were made without any violence.

The mayor blames the trustees for some of the violence last fall. He believes there would have been less violence from the outset if he and college

President Robert Smith had been given an opportunity to prepare for the trustees' actions in the Murray case. "Bob Smith and I asked the trustees for just a few days' delay to nail down solid evidence, so that Smith could proceed with a disciplinary hearing." And, the mayor states, there would not have been the kind of major violence that occurred on November 13 if city officials had been given a brief delay, and had an opportunity to set up police procedures in advance of Murray's suspension.

The mayor sees an important comparison between San Francisco State College, where local public officials have little influence, and City College, where they do. Black studies programs have moved at City College, he says. "Legitimate issues have not been permitted to fester," where, on the other hand, he argues, they were permitted to fester at San Francisco State and "the hard liners, who like to exploit these situations, were able to take advantage of it." It is for this reason that the mayor favors local control over curriculum and personnel. He believes there should be a local board, appointed by the Governor, consisting of residents of the region from which the students are drawn, and members from that local board should be appointed to a statewide board which would handle financing of the entire system.

From the outset, the mayor saw a need for some form of mediation. The students had nonnegotiable demands, and the trustees did not want to talk to the students. That was the reason for the creation of the Citizens' Committee. "It was the only thing which kept the parties talking."

While there are legitimate issues, the mayor finds some of the student demands unacceptable. He is opposed to creation of black studies departments free of the controls normally exercised on other departments in a college. Nor can it be open only to blacks—"you can't have black racism any more than you can have white racism." As for amnesty, the mayor says he has made his belief clear from the beginning that there should be no amnesty for serious offenses (where violence was involved).

"Those who use violence ought to be willing to take the consequences"; they should not complain, he says, when they are apprehended. On the other hand, he sees no problem in giving amnesty for offenses such as failure to disperse; it is a traditional method of settling disputes.

ACTING PRESIDENT HAYAKAWA

Finally, one cannot discuss the outlook for the immediate future of San Francisco State without considering the perspective of Acting President S. I. Hayakawa.

Acting President Hayakawa draws a distinction between the white radical students and the black radicals who have been involved in the protests and confrontations at San Francisco State.

> The black radicals want a better America. And they may use revolutionary methods at moments, but they are willing to give them up as soon as it's clear that the administration is willing to do something to improve the quality of their education and their opportunities within the system. White radicals, like the SDS, don't want to improve America. They just want to destroy it and louse it up in every way possible. So I have nothing to offer them.
>
> There are many reasonable demands the blacks are making, which I'm fully prepared to work upon, very hard. This is a community with many, many nonwhite minority groups here. You have to pay serious attention to what their needs are.

* * *

San Francisco State is certainly unique, but then so is every institution of higher learning. In a very real sense, the problems which plague San Francisco State are akin to the problems which beset most public universities and colleges and many private ones, particularly in metropolitan areas. The problems of black students and other minorities are not peculiar to San Francisco State. Institutional inflexibility and communication breakdowns are characteristic of many colleges and universities. Trustees, administrators, faculty, and students throughout the system of American higher education are reassessing

APPENDIX 1

TEN DEMANDS OF THE BLACK STUDENTS UNION

1. That all black studies courses being taught through various other departments be immediately part of the black studies department and that all instructors in this department receive full time pay.
2. That Dr. Hare, chairman of the black studies department, receive a full professorship and a comparable salary according to his qualifications.
3. That there be a department of black studies which will grant a bachelor's degree in black studies; that the black studies department chairman, faculty, and staff have the sole power to hire and fire without the interference of the racist administration and the chancellor.
4. That all unused slots for black students from fall 1968 under the special admissions program be filled in spring 1969.
5. That all black students who wish to, be admitted in fall 1969.
6. That 20 full-time teaching positions be allocated to the department of black studies.
7. That Dr. Helen Bedesem be replaced in the position of financial aid officer and that a black person be hired to direct it and that Third World people have the power to determine how it will be administered.
8. That no disciplinary action will be administered in any way to any students, workers, teachers, or administrators during and after the strike as a consequence of their participation in the strike.
9. That the California State College Trustees not be allowed to dissolve any black programs on or off the San Francisco State College campus.
10. That George Murray maintain his teaching position on the campus for the 1968-69 academic year.

FIVE DEMANDS OF THE THIRD WORLD LIBERATION FRONT

1. That schools of ethnic studies for the ethnic groups involved in the Third World be set up, with students for each particular organization having the authority and the control of the hiring and retention of any faculty member, director, and administrator, as well as the curricula.
2. That 50 faculty positions be appropriated to the schools of ethnic studies, 20 of which would be for the black studies program.
3. That in the spring semester the college fulfill its commitments to the nonwhite students in admitting those that apply.
4. That in the fall of 1969, all applications of nonwhite students be accepted.
5. That George Murray and any other faculty members chosen by nonwhite people as their teachers be retained in their positions.

APPENDIX 2

COMMENT ON THE POLICE

The San Francisco Police Department—as a result of its 1968-69 duties at San Francisco State College—probably has more knowledge of effective tactics for coping with large-group student demonstrations than any police department in the Nation.

Most observers agreed that the police efficiency in controlling or dispersing crowds increased steadily as the student strike lengthened. The police seemed more assured and effective in their tactics in late January than in mid-November.

The performance of the police drew high praise from the mayor and college administrators. "They gave us the only help we got," said one beleaguered college official.

Student strikers (and many nonstrikers) would disagree.

The confrontations at San Francisco State brought charges of police brutality—as has almost every other major confrontation between students and police, whether in the streets or on the campuses.

When he reopened the campus in early December, San Francisco State College President S. I. Hayakawa repeatedly warned students over his powerful loudspeakers: "Do not form crowds. Do not join crowds that already exist."

"There are NO innocent bystanders in this situation, because a bystander, even if innocent in intent, serves to shield with his body the activities of troublemakers."

Such orders were often greeted with choruses of boos, obscenities, and shouts of, "ON STRIKE! SHUT IT DOWN!" Police were many times pelted with rocks and other objects thrown by members of the crowd, and they were continually subjected to shouted epithets from the students. "Pigs off campus!" was one of the most frequently used chants.

There was hostility. There was bloodshed. There was confusion. Inevitably there were instances of police overreaction.

Other investigators in other reports have dealt extensively with analyses of police in a rapidly changing urban society. The problem is agonizingly complex and delicate.

The Study Team conducted an investigation into police performance. However, it would not aid in understanding the *causes and prevention* of conflicts like San Francisco State to detail here all of the comments by advocates, both for and against the police.

Indeed, much of the material which would be essential to a full and fair exposition of this subject cannot be obtained pending the outcome of criminal actions, disciplinary proceedings, and civil suits for personal injuries.

It would be unrealistic to believe that confrontations such as those which took place on the campus of San Francisco State College—sometimes involving thousands of students and hundreds of police in roving combat across the campus—could occur without some injuries to both sides.

It would be as unthinkable to condone police abuse—such as the unwarranted clubbing of demonstrators or mistreatment of prisoners once inside police vans as to condone the violence of student agitators— such as planting bombs, starting fires, and throwing rocks. But these allegations are not the things upon which to focus if one is to understand the role of the police in campus confrontations.

American college campuses are not enclaves from which police are barred—like some South American universities.

Indeed, it is clear as a matter of California law that a policeman's duty to keep the peace does not stop at the campus gates. On the State-college campuses general agreements have been worked out between local administrators and police; the police generally do not enter the campus in force without invitation, but this is a matter of practice, not a legal requirement.

The police have been called onto the San Francisco State campus by each of its last three presidents.

Former President Robert Smith told the Study Team:

> This puts me at odds with some of the faculty, [but] . . . police are part of any society.
>
> I have no big thing about not calling the police for protecting people's safety.

The first essential fact is that the institutions of higher education are without any means of protection against overt violence save regularly organized police forces. The second essential is to understand that in urban America, 1969, a great many students—probably a majority—bring with them to the campus a tremendous hostility to the police. The hostility is not restricted to those who are black and poor.

What is important to an understanding of the campus confrontations is that the reservoir of hostility among students provides a ready tool for those who would use it. If a police overreaction can be provoked (or if through error or lack of proper control or their own hostility the police should overreact), radical activists win immediate converts among the so-called "silent majority." Previously uncommitted students are "radicalized." The police are the common enemy, and "getting the pigs off campus" becomes the common goal. The appearance of the police on campus may then be enough in itself to turn a calm day into an angry confrontation. The police themselves recognize this. As one police official told the Study Team, "It's a victory for those just to have us on that campus."

There is no fail-safe formula for use by college and police administrators in determining when the appearance of police on campus quells or incites mobs. And while student anger at the presence of the police is predictable, college administrators have the dilemma that their institutions are peculiarly vulnerable and, against the threat of open force, they have no choice but to call the police.

APPENDIX 3

BOARD OF TRUSTEES OF THE CALIFORNIA STATE COLLEGES

5670 Wilshire Boulevard
Los Angeles, Calif. 90036

Ex Officio Members

Ronald Reagan, B.A., Governor of California
Robert H. Finch, B.A., LL.B., Lieutenant Governor of California
Max Rafferty, Jr., A.B., M.A. Ed.D., State Superintendent of Public Instruction
Jesse M. Unruh, B.A., Speaker of the Assembly
Glenn S. Dumke, A.B., M.A., Ph.D., LL.D., L.H.D., Chancellor

Appointed Members

(The terms of each trustee expires on March 1 of the year indicated in parentheses. Terms are 8 years.)

Mrs. Philip B. Conley, B.A. (1972), Fresno
Native of Sacramento; wife of Judge Philip Conley, Fourth Appellate District Court of Appeals; mother of James McClatchy, William E. McClatchy, Charles K. McClatchy, and Philip P. Conley; civic and community leader in Fresno; graduate of Vassar.

Alec L. Cory, B.A., LL.B. (1973), San Diego
President, San Diego Bar Association; appointed Deputy City Prosecutor; named Rationing Attorney for the Office of Price Administration; senior partner in law firm of Procopio, Cory, Hargreaves and Savitch; member of the Charter Review Committee of the city of San Diego; served on the education committee of San Diego's Chamber of Commerce; completed a term as president of the UC Alumni Club of San Diego County.

George D. Hart, A.B. (1975), San Francisco
President, George David Hart, Inc.; trustee, Ross School District; Director, Constantin, Ltd., of London, Liberty Mutual Insurance Co. of Boston, Liberty Mutual Fire Insurance Co., and Mutual Boiler Insurance Co.; past President, San Francisco Library Association; former member of the San Francisco Art Commission; member of the Board of Governors, San Francisco Employers Council.

Louis H. Heilbron, A.B., LL.B., LL.D. (1969), San Francisco
Attorney at law; trustee, World Affairs Council of Northern California, Newhouse Foundation, and University of California International House; past president, San Francisco Public Education Society, and State Board of Education; chairman of trustees, 1961-63.

Earle M. Jorgensen (1970), Los Angeles

President of Earl M. Jorgensen Co., steel products distributing firm; serves on the Board of Directors of Northrop Corp., Transamerica Corp., American Potash & Chemical Corp., and Hollywood Turf Club; member of board of trustees of California Institute of Technology; charter member of University of Southern California and Pomona College Associations; member of St. John's Hospital Board of Regents; past director of YMCA of Los Angeles, Junior Achievement of Los Angeles County, and California Chamber of Commerce.

Edward O. Lee, B.A. (1974), Oakland

Occupational department chairman of the East Bay Skills Center in Oakland; former Oakland High School teacher; served as business agent for the American Federation of Government Employees, Local 1533; served on Human Relations Commission and was on the Equal Opportunities Committee; past member of the Oakland Adult Minority Employment Committee; past president of Oakland Federation of Teachers, Local 771; member of the executive board of the Central Labor Council of Alameda County.

Charles I. Luckman, LL.D., A.F.D. (1974), Los Angeles

President, Luckman Associates, Architects; former president of Lever Brothers; served on Presidential Commissions on Equality of Treatment and Opportunity in the Armed Services, on Metropolitan Area Problems and Chairman of Food Commission; Director, Southern California Symphony Association; president of Los Angeles Orchestra Society; chairman of trustees, 1963-65.

Theodore Meriam, A.B. (1971), Chico

Department store manager and vice president and director of Lassen Savings and Loan Association, Chico; former mayor of Chico; past President, League of California Cities; formerly Chairman, Chico State College Advisory Board. Received honorary master's degree, Chico State College, 1959.

William A. Norris, B.A., LL.B. (1972), Los Angeles

Attorney at law; served as member and vice president of State Board of Education and board's representative on State's Coordinating Council for Higher Education; named special counsel to President Kennedy's commission on airlines in 1961; served as law clerk to Justice William O. Douglas during 1955-56 term of the U.S. Supreme Court; worked on the California-Arizona Colorado River litigation; member of American, California, and L.A. County bar associations; partner in Los Angeles law firm of Tuttle and Taylor.

Daniel H. Ridder, B.A. (1975), Long Beach

Copublisher of Long Beach *Independent-Press Telegram;* director and vice president of Twin Coast Newspapers, Inc.; Director, U.S. National Bank of San Diego; former publisher of St. Paul *Dispatch, Pioneer-Press;* past president of Western Conference of Community Chests, United Funds, and Councils; past president of Long Beach Community Chest; director, Bureau of Advertising of the American Newspaper Publishers Association; Chairman of Advisory Board of St. Mary's Hospital of Long Beach.

Albert J. Ruffo, LL.B., B.S. in E.E. (1971), San Jose

Teacher, engineer, and attorney; member of Tau Beta Pi and Woodsack Engineering and legal honor societies. Former vice president, Board of Governors, State Bar of California; member of American Bar Association and American Judicature Society; former City Councilman and mayor of San Jose; former member of faculty, University of Santa Clara; Assistant football coach, Santa Clara, Calif., and 49ers; chairman of trustees, 1965-67

Paul Spencer, B.A. (1969), San Dimas

Citrus rancher and president, Sycamore Groves, Inc., former general contractor; former building inspector for Los Angeles City School System; former project engineer for Federal Public Housing Administration; director, San Dimas Lemon Growers Association and San Dimas Orange Growers Association; director, Reliable Savings and Loan Association, West Covina; served as member and president of Bonita Union High School board of trustees; past president of Alumni Association of Occidental College; past director of Southern California Chapter of Associated General Contractors.

Dudley Swim, A.B., M.A. (1976), Carmel Valley

Chairman of Board of National Airlines; Director of Providence Washington Insurance Co.; previously appointed to Coordinating Council for Higher Education; Trustee of Rockford College, Ill., Wabash College, Ind., Cordell Hull Foundation for International Education, Free Society Association; former director of Fremont Foundation; member of advisory board of Hoover Institution on War, Revolution and Peace; a director of Stanford Research Institute; president of Monterey County Foundation for Conservation; previously served as national vice commander of American Legion.

James F. Thacher, A.B., LL.B. (1970), San Francisco

Partner in the San Francisco law firm of Thacher, Jones, Casey & Ball; Director of Actors Workshop and Neighborhood Centers of San Francisco; served on the California Toll Bridge Authority, the Commission on the Disposition of Alcatraz Island, and on the budget study committee of Northern California's United Crusade.

E. Guy Warren, B.A. (1973), Hayward

Owner, Warren Trucking Co.; member of Executive Board of California Trucking Association; member, Alameda County Fair Board of Directors, Alameda County Mental Health Advisory Board, and trustee of Hayward Union High School District; former president of California Trucking Association; past president of Western Highway Institute.

Karl L. Wente, M.S. (1976), Livermore

President of Wente Brothers Winery, Wente Farms, and Wente Land and Cattle Co.; director of Automobile Association, Livermore Valley Memorial Hospital, Livermore Water District, and the Livermore branch of Bank of America. He is a Stanford University graduate.

APPENDIX 4

A CONCEPTUAL PROPOSAL FOR A DEPARTMENT OF BLACK STUDIES

Nathan Hare
April 29, 1968

American college education is in a state of crisis. All over the country there is erupting a volcano of student alienation and resentment–doubly so in the case of black students, the group with which we are here most directly concerned.

Black students are products of experiences which robbed them of a sense of collective destiny and involvement in the educational process. This is a many-faceted problem, but the fundamentals of its solution will incorporate the stepping up of the meaningful and significant participation of black students in college life and its goals.

The black studies idea originated with the black students, the Black Student Union at San Francisco State College. It not only reflects their cries–echoed by others across the country–for relevant education; it also represents the greatest and last hope for rectifying an old wrong and halting the decay now gnawing away at American society. It is, then, more far reaching than appears on the surface, and indeed this cannot be otherwise, inasmuch as any educational system arises to care for what is felt to be a society's educational needs.

While San Francisco State College, spurred by its black students, has pioneered perhaps the first program of promise to solve the problem, there is detected about the country a growing irony: the probability that other institutions, for various reasons in the years ahead, will pass us by. In one sense, this is as it should be; in another, it is not. In any case, black studies presents a challenge, in one way or another, to San Francisco State College and its imitators.

Many persons, white and Negro, cannot understand the necessity for a black studies program. Indeed, conversations with academicians across the country on the education of Black Americana, suggest that even those persons who have accepted the basic idea of black studies do not fully understand its need. They see the goal as the mere blackening of white courses, in varying number and degree. They omit in their program the key component of community involvement and collective stimulation. Thus their program is individualistic (aimed at "rehabilitating" individual students and potential students by means of pride in culture, racial contributions generally, and regenerated dignity and self esteem); they fail to see that the springboard for all of this is an animated communalism—more about this later—aimed at a black educational renaissance.

Many well-intended efforts to rectify the situation under discussion accordingly are doomed to inevitable failure. They comprise piecemeal programs which, being imported, are based on an external perspective.

An eminent Negro professor proposed to a trouble-shooting college committee recently that the problem could be solved by increasing drastically the ratio of black (by which he meant "Negro") students and professors. The students for the most part would be admitted with the expectation that, excepting those salvaged by tutorial efforts presently in vogue, they would eventually flunk out, merrier for having acquired "at least some college." Although his proposal in principle should have been inaugurated long ago, let alone now, it is not the answer to the problem which he (and we herein) are trying to solve. As a matter of fact—and one must endorse the professor's suggestion in fact though not in theory insofar as to do otherwise would appear to condone current tokenism—there is tenable fear that such an approach may be used as a play to appease the black community while avoiding genuine solutions to the problem.

A representative from a wealthy foundation recently proposed to give full financial assistance to the "talented tenth" and to hire black persons to recruit such students and inform them of the availability of such aid. Unlike most persons, he at least realized that providing aid, while permitting persons accustomed to discriminatory treatment to remain unaware and suspicious of its existence, is only slightly better than providing no aid at all.

Be that as it may, a talented-tenth approach (in this case based frankly on "verbal facility" as the major indicator of college potential) is largely superfluous to the educational needs of the black race as a whole. Talented-tenth students, for whatever reason, have escaped the programmed educational maladjustment of the black race, just as some trees survive the flames of a forest fire. Besides, many persons with more verbal facility than the author may fail the test (in some cases) or, having passed the test, drop out of college or flunk out (often one way of dropping out) or disdain the rush to college in the first place.

Such a program, though noble on the surface, offers supertokenism at best, but neglects the important ingredient of motivation growing out of collective community involvement. It is individualistic in its orientation and only indirectly, therefore, of collective consequence.

Another fear now in the air asserts that the black studies program will comprise "a college within a college," owing to its "deplorable separatist leanings." Even if it be so that black studies would ring more separatist in tone than Latin American Studies, Oriental Studies, and the like, this is not the issue. The question of separatism is, like integrationism, in this regard essentially irrelevant. The goal is the *elevation* of a people by means of one important escalator—education. Separatism and integrationism are possible approaches to that end; they lose their effectiveness when, swayed by dogmatic absolutism, they become ends in themselves. It will be an irony of recorded history that "integration" was used in the second half of this century to hold the black race down just as segregation was so instigated in the first half. Integration, particularly in the token way in which it has been practiced up to now and the neotokenist manner now emerging, elevates individual members of a group, but paradoxically, in plucking many of the most promising members from a group while failing to alter the lot of the group as a whole, weakens the collective thrust which the group might otherwise master.

A related question frequently raised revolves around the participation of white students in the program. The anger must be ambivalent inasmuch as the program has to be aimed primarily at the black student, particularly in its motivational activities involving the black community. At the same time, it is recognized that, so long as some white graduates continue to work in the black community, they and the black community will benefit from their exposure to a least some portion of black studies. This could result in the reeducation of white society.

The danger is that white students will flood black studies courses, leaving us with a black studies program peopled predominantly by white studies. One way to draw white students off (or/and care for the surplus) is for existing departments to increase their offerings in blackness as they are doing now under the guise of "dark" (or, as sociologists say, "color-compatible") courses. This would probably result in greater benefit to the white students' needs anyway and most certainly would offset the apparent sense of threat in the minds of conventional departments. It may be necessary eventually to distinguish black education for blacks and black education for whites. There is no insurmountable incompatibility or mutual exclusiveness between black studies and ethnic group courses in other departments. Indeed they are easily reinforcing and could make a major contribution to better "race relations" or, as politicians are fond of saying now, "the effort to save the nation" in decades ahead.

Black studies represents a last-ditch, nonviolent, effort to solve a grave crisis, a particular crisis. To try to solve all problems at once is to risk weakening its impact on central crisis, although, like a stone tossed into a lake, the resulting waves might reverberate from shore to shore. Likewise, we recognize the need for a coalition, somewhere ultimately, of endeavors to improve and increase the educational participation of all ethnic groups. It is only that the assault must be both intraethnic and interethnic, for we cannot afford to lose the motivational ingredient of intraethnic espirit des corps and community involvement.

REDEFINITION OF STANDARDS

A vital issue in the quest for institutionalization of the black studies idea—particularly in its early stages—is that of "standards." Bear in mind, to begin with, what current standards evolved in large part from a need to restrict the overflow of recruits (the principle of exclusion) into existing professional riches. This gave rise to occasionally ludicrous requirements. The late social theorist, Thorstein Veblen, author of *Theory of the Leisure Class*, might hold that the liberal arts approach grew out of the leisure class mentality, where it was prestigious to be nonproductive and to waste time and effort in useless endeavor. Hence footnoting minutiae and the like. When middle class aspirants began to emulate these codes, the principle of exclusion evolved. However, now we are faced with the educational enticement of a group conditioned by way of the cake of time and custom to being excluded. How do we transform them into an included people? For example, a law school graduate with high honors might fail the "bar" exam (pun intended) because of political views, or fail the oral exam for teaching certification because of an unpopular approach to teaching. Or make mostly A's in required courses only to fail the homemade (unstandardized) "comprehensive" exam. Or pass everything required except the "lauguage" exam. It is widely known that languages studied for graduate degrees are quickly almost totally forgotten and are rarely of any use after graduation. Much of the motivation for the retention of this and even more useless requirements apparently stems from the "leisure class" origin of the "liberal arts" approach where, as Thorstein Veblen explained, prestige was attributed to "nonproductive" or wasteful useless endeavor.

In any case, the requirements for the most part were devised to serve the functions of exclusivity rather than recruitment. Not that recruitment efforts did not exist, but they have been heretofore aimed at individuals inclined to receive them. Now we are facing the necessity for collective recruitment from a group victimized as a group in the past by racist policies of exclusion from the educational escalator.

On the college level, the two most salient "qualifications" for professional rank today are the possession of a Ph.D. and a string of "scholarly" publications. While we endorse such criteria, up to a point, it is essential (particularly in light of current shortage of such credentials on the part of black candidates) to examine and stress the desirability of freedom to depart from those criteria without risking the suspicion of "lowering standards." That the Ph.D. is not necessarily synonymous with teaching effectiveness is accepted by most persons confronted with the question. Less understood is the question of publication.

Consider two candidates for a position in history, one qualified a la conventional standards, the other not. Never mind the fact that articles outside the liberal-moderate perspective have slim chances of seeing the light of day in "objective" scholarly journals. More ludicrous is the fact that the black historian, in adhering to the tradition of "footnoting," is placed in the unenviable position of having to footnote white slavemaster historians or historians published by a slaveholding society in order to document his work on the slavery era.

RECRUITING OF BLACK STUDIES FACULTY

White administrators frequently complain that they cannot find black professors (i.e., "qualified"), and this is often a legitimate complaint. A black studies program, however, would not be bound by this problem, certainly not nearly in the same degree. There is a keener interest in such a program on the part of potential professors who are black than there is making a move for a conventional professorship. Already, many have volunteered to come to San Francisco State College, but, because of our current lack of funds for the program, none has been chosen.

We speak here of black individuals with Ph.D.'s and, in some cases, creditable publications or, in many cases, high publishing potential. Remember also that the redefinition of a "qualified" professor (honoring teaching effectiveness and enthusiasm more than qualities determined by degrees held and other quantifiable "credentials") will permit dipping into the larger fund of qualified black professors without doctorates.

The question arises as to the participation of the white professor. The much-considered answer is that their participation, at least during the early, experimental stages of the program, must be cautious and minimal. However, the impracticality of recruiting sufficient number of black professors may well cause this idea to give way. Any white professors involved in the program would have to be black in spirit in order to last. The same is true for "Negro" professors. Besides, white professors are permitted–indeed urged–to increase course offerings on minority groups in regular curriculum from which white students (and interested Negroes) might benefit.

COMMUNITY INVOLVEMENT

To develop the key component of community involvement, it is necessary to inspire and sustain a sense of collective destiny as a people and a consciousness of the value of education in a technological society. A cultural base, acting as a leverage for other aspects of black ego development and academic unit, must accordingly be spawned and secured.

Students and other interested parties will be organized into Black Cultural Councils which will sponsor cultural affairs (art, dance, drama, etc.) in the black community and establish black holidays, festivities and celebrations. For example, a Black Winter Break could begin on February 21 the day they shot Malcolm X, run past George Washington's birthday and end with February 23, the birthday of the late black scholar, W. E. B. Du Bois. This could approximate the Jewish Yom Kippur.

Black information centers will be set up to increase communication, interpersonal contact, knowledge and sociopolitical awareness. In this connection, a black community press, put together by the hands of members of black current events clubs and students taking courses in black journalism or/and black communications, would seem highly beneficial. In any case, the black information center would engage in research, accumulate useful data, materials, and information to be disseminated along with advice on social problems and individual affairs such as social security benefits.

Propaganda aimed at motivating black children to acquire education–indeed to induce dropouts to return to school—could emanate in large part from this source. At the same time, campaigns (drop-back-in-school drives) would be waged, modeled on methods of voter registration, to rescue black school dropouts. Those returning to school, and others in academic trouble, will receive intensive tutorial aid from qualified black college students.

For the direction of this and other educational efforts, a Bureau of Black Education could be established to provide black scholars mutual aid and stimulation, and to organize black textbook and syllabi writing corps. Much teaching, however, especially on the college level, would disdain current racist textbooks in an effort to escape the confines of perfunctory learning and utilize the laboratory of life.

There is a need for professors relevant to the needs of black students, professors with whom they can identify and take as models of emulation, professors who have the capacity to inspire students to search for knowledge and social mobility. A teacher needs three–must have at least three–qualifica-

355-234 O - 69 - 12

tions: 1) an effective relationship to learners; 2) relationship to the content of the school's program; 3) and depth in understanding how learning takes place and of the art-science of instruction.[2]

Much of this—and more—could be stimulated in part by faculty unity. Along with conventional departmental meetings, faculty unity and cross-fertilization will be developed by means of: 1) a program of exchange lecturing, where one professor lectures to the class of another; 2) chain-teaching, sometimes interdisciplinary, where several professors assigned to a course rotate at respective stages in the course; and 3) the central lecture with subsidiary discussion sessions particularly for interdisciplinary courses.

Central lectures might be held in church auditoriums so that individuals in the community could partake of them. Persons known to be making a significant impact on American society in the areas under study could be recruited as guest lecturers, or salaried part-time lecturers, in an intensive effort to utilize the resources of the black community while simultaneously increasing the community's sense of involvement in the educational process. In the latter connection, it will be useful to establish some kind of off-campus college extension, ultimately, with special emphasis on adult education and where mothers and others might receive correspondence courses. The courses would be geared, in the case of mothers, to improve their ability to exploit the educational potential of their special relationships with their children, preparing some of them to people a program of associate-teaching in the elementary and preschool levels. Such preparations could be rounded off by on-the-job-training. Most of the foregoing is in no way new.

Finally, to wed and cement community and curriculum practicums and apprenticeships in connection with course work would seem invaluable. This would tend to increase the commitment of black students to the community while simultaneously permitting them to "learn to do by doing" and comprising a flow of volunteer assistance to cooperating functionaries in the community—i.e., businessmen, politicians, leaders, social workers, community organizers, teachers, preachers, educators, and the like.

THE BLACK STUDIES CURRICULUM—A FIVE YEAR PLAN

To insure the measurement of significant results, the black studies program must comprise at least a five-year plan. The initiation of the program is to be accomplished in two stages: (1) Phase I, involving the pulling together of some of the currently experimental courses into a new department by September 1968; and (2) Phase II, the inauguration of a major consisting of an integrated body of black courses revolving around core courses such as black history, black psychology, black arts, and the social sciences. Such a curriculum has been constructed, but certain rough edges are still being ironed out, and, because it is not essential to this conceptual proposal, it is not being presented here. Phase II could follow by September 1969. The administration at Yale University, for example, recently approved such a major (African and Afro-American Studies).

However, Yale's program omits the key components of student field work, as a part of the course requirements, in the black community. This is an old idea on the surface, but as here conceived, it further involves an effort to transform the community while educating and training the student. For example, students in black history might be required to put on panel discussions for younger children in church basements, elementary and junior high school classes, and so forth. A class project might be the formation of a black history club. A class in community organization could form civic clubs, while individual students served apprenticeships under community organizers. Students in black journalism, black economics (business), education courses (teachers), black politics or what not, could do the same. Thus education is made relevant to the student and his community while the community is, so to speak, made relevant to education.

In this direction (bearing in mind the anticipated growth of the college population generally) we propose the admission of 300 additional black students in the school year 1969-70, 500 in 1970-71, 1,000 by 1971-72, 1,500 more by 1972-73, and 2,000 by 1974-75. These numbers should be adjusted, of course, to suit the developing needs for educational and socioeconomic parity on the part of the black race.

STUDENT SCREENING

Criteria complementary to, or/and exclusive of, currently standard tests will be used to determine college potential of black students. These are to be developed, using available consultants, by the admissions wing of the black studies program.

Remedial and tutorial work will be necessary as well. However, special care will be taken to safeguard against the situation, such as recently became apparent at a predominantly Negro college in Washington, D.C., in which many students were failing remedial courses while passing courses in the regular program for which remedial courses supposedly were preparing them.[3] Also, in spite of a high flunkout rate arising largely from an open-admission policy and a desire to "raise standards" (using proportion flunked as the major index), more students with a "C" average or above failed to return to school each year than in the case of those with less than a "C" average.

Professors and staff also must be added at appropriate rates, beginning with three professors by September 1969, and accelerating to a full departmental staff with each succeeding year.

The specific content of the curriculum follows herewith. Although it is much of it expressive (geared to ego-identity building, etc.), the utilitarian function has by no means been omitted; it can be expanded as knowledge of its implementation accumulates. The black race woefully needs concrete skills, in a technological society, both for individual mobility and community development.

While the black studies program—as our model indicates—would not preclude electives outside the black curriculum, even for majors, it would seek to care for a wide range of academic training in the humanities, the social and behavioral sciences. Though most persons enrolled in black studies courses would not be majors, those graduating as such could become probation officers, preparation for careers as lawyers, social workers, teachers, scholars, professors, research scientists, businessmen, administrators, and so on. They would, other things being equal—we feel certain—quickly emerge and predominate in the upper echelons of the black community.

Aside from the matter of intensified motivation (and increased commitment) to the struggle to build the black community) students who have mustered even a smattering of black studies courses would be advantaged in their postcollege work in the black community. They would be armed with early involvement and experience in the community superior to that of students not so trained. Like their Chinese, Greek, Jewish, and other pluralistic counterparts, those employed outside the black community would possess a keener sense of security as individuals and would be better equipped to present the black perspective. This would benefit the black community indirectly and perhaps assist those members of the white community who, like the black studies program, seek, in a roundabout way, a better society for all of its members.

Tentative Black Studies Major For Fall, 1969

Course	*Units*
Core courses:	
Black History	4
Black Psychology	4
Survey of Sciences: Method and History	4
Black Arts and Humanities	4
	16
Black arts concentration:	
The Literature of Blackness	4
Black Writers Workshop	4
Black Intellectuals	4
Black Fiction	4
Black Poetry	4
Black Drama	4
The Painting of Blackness	4
The Music of Blackness	4
Sculpture of Blackness	4
	36
Behavioral and social sciences concentration:	
Black Politics	4
Sociology	4
Economics of the Black Community	4
The Geography of Blackness	4
Social Organization of Blackness	4
Development of Black Leadership	4
Demography of Blackness	4
Black Counseling	4
Black Consciousness and the International Community	4
	32

References

1. The Outstanding Young Teacher, for Washington, D.C., in 1966, as chosen by the Junior Chamber of Commerce, the World Book Encyclopedia, and American University's Department of Education, moved recently to another city, armed with a master's degree plus 30 additional hours accumulated in meeting the requirements

of other school systems in the past, only to be told that she must pass the National Teachers' Exam in her field. She informed the personnel officer that she had passed the test in her field plus one other. Then she was told that she would have to take five additional courses in order to "qualify" for teaching credentials.

2. Robert H. Anderson, *Teaching in a World of Change* (New York: Harcourt, Brace & World, 1966).
3. There is no documentation for this. It was privately shown me in the registrar's office by a former employee of the registrar's office. However, it was publicly bemoaned at a faculty meeting on the problem that many students were passing regular courses while flunking remedial courses.

APPENDIX 5

San Francisco Examiner & Chronicle Accounts of Student Strike Settlement, March 21-23, 1969

[*S. F. Examiner,* Friday, Mar. 21, 1969]

HAYAKAWA REPORTS ON STRIKE PACT

By Phil Garlington, Jr.

Acting President S. I. Hayakawa will make public today the bones and muscle of his pact with striking students that has brought the contentious four month strike at San Francisco State College to an official but anticlimatic finish.

Both sides announced yesterday that the strike was over, but some administrators gave the impression they were unhappy with the settlement worked out by Hayakawa's Select Committee.

The committee, composed of six administrators and faculty, was empowered by Hayakawa to resolve the issues contained in the 15 demands of the Black Students Union and the Third World Liberation Front.

Amnesty Row

Although the two sides had reached a basic accord on most issues nearly a week ago, the question of amnesty not only prevented an earlier settlement but also threatens to become a problem once again.

According to Frank Brann, attorney for the striking students, the amnesty agreement with the administration is as follows:

There will be no expulsions. Students found guilty of violence–meaning an attack on another person–will be suspended for two semesters, while students guilty of disrupting classrooms will be suspended for the remainder of the semester.

Those charged with lesser offenses, amounting to approximately 95 percent of the cases, will be given a written reprimand.

Also, Bishop Mark J. Hurley, chairman of the Mayor's Citizens Committee on S.F. State, is expected to exert his influence to lessen the penalties meted out to students in the civil courts.

Charges Stick

The mayor, however, repeated yesterday that the City would not drop charges against those accused of violent acts although he said he would favor amnesty for students charged with minor violations.

Although Hayakawa gave the Select Committee power to negotiate with the strikers and reach a settlement, it appeared yesterday afternoon that he and his top staffers were dissatisfied with at least the part of the agreement dealing with amnesty.

Hayakawa, who has earned much of his reputation as a college president for a hard line against disruption, reportedly was upset with the rather sweeping provisions for amnesty conceded by this committee.

Under other provisions of the pact, a panel of minority community leaders is to take "a leading role" in implementing the demand for a School of Ethnic Studies, in which would be the Black Studies Department.

This panel would decide on such things as who would be chairman and who would teach in the school and departments.

Rehiring

Brann implied that this panel would be free to rehire Nathan Hare, who was fired as chairman of the Black Studies Department by Hayakawa, and George Murray, the Black Panther and ex-English teacher who is now serving six months in jail as a parole violator.

The rehiring of the two were included in the demands.

Although it is not certain either Hare or Murray would return to State even should they be offered a job, it does not seem likely that the administration would consider their return acceptable.

The problem underscores what one administrator termed "the crucial fault" with the settlement: that it does not set out who has the ultimate authority in hiring faculty for the new minority curriculums, a subject over which disputes are bound to arise.

Admission

Another demand of the strikers, that Helen Bedesem, head of the financial aids, be replaced, was resolved by the placement two months ago of a black administrator in that office to handle the cases of minority students.

In regard to the demand for unlimited admission of minority students, Brann said the agreement stipulated that "virtually all" those minority students who wished would be admitted.

The signing of the agreement late yesterday provided one of the few moments of public drama during a week in which most of the action took place behind closed doors.

Contingents of students representing the various groups within the TWLF streamed up to a conference room on the third floor of the Humanities Building where they were met by two members of the Select Committee for the signing ceremony.

First Step

Afterwards, the TWLF and BSU met newsmen briefly to say the ending of the strike was merely a first step in the fight against institutionalized racism and that "the struggle will now intensify."

Benny Stewart, a member of the BSU central committee, said the strike and the settlement would serve as a "model" for high schools, colleges and universities to follow.

* * *

[*S. F. Examiner,* Saturday, Mar. 22, 1969]

S.F. STATE PACT TERMS A MONTH OLD

By Phil Garlington, Jr.

The settlement between the San Francisco State College Select Committee and the student strikers contains basically the same provisions as were offered by the administration over a month ago.

Released by the committee late yesterday, the text of the agreement differs from the administration's position of last month only on the question of amnesty.

Acting President S. I. Hayakawa said yesterday, however, that he did not feel the recommendations on disciplinary procedures were binding on him, even though it was Hayakawa himself who empowered the Select Committee "to resolve the issues of the strike."

In fact, Hayakawa yesterday claimed that there had been no strike, since "cutting classes, individually or collectively is not a strike, in the labor sense."

He'll Wait

The famed semanticist said, however, that he had made an agreement with the strikers to wait until April 11 before making any final decision on disciplinary penalties.

And he accepted the main conclusions of the agreement as administration policy.

Although there was a place on the agreement for Hayakawa's signature, the president said he did not feel it was necessary for him personally to sign the document.

On amnesty, the agreement stated that the committee and the strikers joined "in recommending to the President" that penalties against all students–except those convicted of violence–be reduced to written reprimands.

After Hayakawa made public his reservations about mitigating penalties, the Select Committee, composed of six faculty and administrators, went into an immediate meeting.

Distraught

Reportedly, the members were distraught over Hayakawa's apparent rebuke of their amnesty recommendation. But when the committee released the text of the agreement yesterday afternoon, it was accompanied only by a mildly worded letter asking him to "reconsider" his position on the amnesty recommendation.

The TWLF and the BSU, meanwhile, had no official comment on Hayakawa's stand.

Hayakawa said the settlement did not signal "defeat or victory" for any side, but in Los Angeles Governor Reagan said the settlement was a "victory for the people of California."

Reagan said, "Hayakawa is not recommending amnesty. Each individual case will be treated as an individual case."

"On the surface there would certainly seem to be room for optimism," the Governor said.

After the settlement was announced, signs such as "Reagan has won," and "No amnesty for campus criminals" appeared on walls around a construction site in the college quadrangle.

In other action on the State campus, several dozen professors belonging to the American Federation of Teachers picketed the business building to protest the failure of the School of Business to reinstate Morgan Pinney, an associate professor of accounting.

Pinney, an AFT teacher who took part in the teacher's strike, was not reinstated because he did not return to class by the deadline set by the Council of Academic Deans, the administration says.

The AFT, however, claims it was a violation of the agreement settlement.

* * *

[*S. F. Sunday Examiner & Chronicle,* Mar. 23, 1969]

GAINS AND LOSSES IN S.F. STATE PACT

By Phil Garlington, Jr.

The strike settlement at San Francisco State College represents—in the main—a liberal response to the demands of militant minority students.

The broad, long range demands—for a minority curriculum and for the admission of more minority students—were granted.

The narrower demands, however, for such things as the retention of certain people and the replacement of others, were either compromised or lost.

As it turned out, the 15 demands were "non-negotiable" only so long as an active and at times violent strike crippled the campus. When that petered out, the Black Students Union and the Third

World Liberation Front quickly became as pragmatic about talks with the management as any labor union.

When the bitter rhetoric finally dies away, it will become clear that the college has taken several strides toward bringing that much heralded relevant education within reach of larger numbers of non-white students.

Indorsed in its main conclusions by acting President S. I. Hayakawa, the settlement is mild, liberal and reasonable, in the recognized academic tradition.

Most of the provisions were drawn up by a select committee of six members, faculty and administration, and presented to the BSU and TWLF.

These provisions were pretty much accepted by the BSU and TWLF, but they insisted on mitigation of penalties for those arrested in disturbances.

Hayakawa, however, who declined to sign the agreement, has not committed himself as yet to the so-called "amnesty" recommendations.

He said he will wait until April 11 to make any final decision regarding penalties, in accordance with an agreement with the BSU on March 11 that there would be a cooling off period.

The agreement states that police will be withdrawn immediately on the restoration of peace, and that the state of emergency will be rescinded immediately upon settlement of the strike, together with the emergency regulations restricting assemblies, rallies, etc.

By not signing the agreement and by making public his reservations about the amnesty recommendations, Hayakawa retains the integrity of his original hardline position against student unrest.

Getting a healthy minority curriculum started quickly has become mandatory because of one far reaching provision of the agreement—and one which Hayakawa did seem to agree to.

This centers on BSU demand number five: "That all black students wishing to do so, be admitted in Fall, 1969."

For openers, the administration agreed to try to get the law changed so that the college can waive the usual admission requirements for 10 percent of the yearly applicants rather than the present four percent.

That could mean as many as 1,800 nonwhite students unqualified under the present rules—could attend the college yearly.

More immediately, the college pledged to "actively recruit" non-white students. This fall, 1000 of the expected 4670 new students will be non-white, meaning there will be 4750 non-white students out of a total enrollment of 17,700—26 percent.

In agreeing to set up a School of Ethnic Studies (part of which will be the Black Studies Department) the administration approved a community board to oversee development, but did not specify what form this board will take.

Appointments on this board must be agreeable to the college, to the Third World faculty, "involved" Third World students and the Third World communities.

Hayakawa, however, will retain final authority over hiring.

On personnel matters the situation is still obscure.

Hayakawa says his decision to fire Nathan Hare as chairman of the Black Studies Department still stands. Likewise for George Murray, Black Panther–ex-English teacher serving six months for parole violation.

Hare, however, says he thinks he will be chairman "because the black community" wants him.

Other agreements in the pact include:

Staffing and admission policies on the School of Ethnic Studies shall be nondiscriminatory, meaning that whites can be teachers and students in the school.

Differences in interpretation are to be worked out by a three man panel, one member chosen by the president, one by the Dean of the School of Ethnic Studies, and the third by the first two.